the
good food book
for families

With over 150 recipes to please kids of all ages, inspired by the new Canada's Food Guide

Brenda Bradshaw & Cheryl Mutch, M.D.

the
good food book
for families

random house canada

© 2008 Brenda Bradshaw and Cheryl Mutch

All rights reserved under International and Pan-American Copyright Conventions. No part of this book may be reproduced in any form or by any electronic or mechanical means, including information storage and retrieval systems, without permission in writing from the publisher, except by a reviewer, who may quote brief passages in a review. Published in 2008 by Random House Canada, a division of Random House of Canada Limited. Distributed in Canada by Random House of Canada Limited.

www.randomhouse.ca

Random House Canada and colophon are trademarks

LIBRARY AND ARCHIVES CANADA CATALOGUING IN PUBLICATION

Bradshaw, Brenda (Brenda E.)
The good food book for families / Brenda Bradshaw and
Cheryl Mutch.

Includes bibliographical references and index.

ISBN 978-0-307-35670-3

1. Cookery. 2. Nutrition. I. Mutch, Cheryl II. Title.

RA784.B682 2008   641.5'63   C2007-906839-1

Cover and text design by Leah Springate

Front cover photographs (clockwise from top left): Stockbyte, Photodisc, Stockbyte, Gulfimages, Digital Vision, Foodcollection (all Getty Images)

Author photograph: Jeff Petter

This book is printed on paper that is ancient-forest friendly
(100% post-consumer recycled) and chlorine-free.

Printed and bound in Canada

10 9 8 7 6 5 4 3 2 1 ·

To our children, Charlie, Chelsea, Ashley and Elliotte,

and to our husbands, Dan and Jeff

contents

foreword

There are still a few people around who are convinced that any food or recipe reputed to be "good for you" will, by definition, be categorized somewhere on a taste scale that runs from "bland" to "ugh." For example, many years ago, *The New Yorker* featured a now classic cartoon, depicting a well-to-do mother sitting with her very young son at a large dining room table. "Eat it, dear, it's broccoli," she urges him. "I say it's spinach, and I say the hell with it," the boy replies.

This book puts such myths about healthy eating permanently to rest. In fact, simply reading the recipes in this excellent book will induce a good deal of salivation, since most of them should appeal to anyone who has ever been a child. There is plenty of variety, and the authors have given as much attention to eye and taste appeal as they have to nutritional value.

But there is another subtle but compelling reason to explain why translating these recipes into meals could pay major family dividends. To understand this requires some historical perspective. There was a time—it now seems so very long ago—when the kitchen was the epicentre of family life. Typically, it occupied considerably more space than its modern counterpart. The room's focal point in those early days was a large table, with enough chairs to accommodate the whole family. At that very same table, children regularly did their homework and played games. This was also where the entire family sat down to meals together, and where friends, neighbours and relatives would gather to drink coffee or tea, and to chat. There were no frozen foods, no microwaves, no pre-packaged "nuke and serve" meals.

Of course, many factors have combined to make that nostalgic picture a relic of the past. These include geographic dispersal of the extended family, both parents working outside the home (and on different schedules), single-parent families, and the pandemic of electronic distractions that serve as conversation stoppers (radio, TV, video games and cellphones, to name but a few). In far too many households, these factors, collectively, have conspired to reduce communication between family members to a dangerously low level. This despite the fact that it is well documented that warm, open and frequent communication is a key element in determining emotional health in families, particularly in children. The more often families eat together, the more emotionally healthy the children are likely to be.

The other evolutionary change that has altered the eating habits of folks of all ages is the extraordinary diversity of choices available in the supermarkets of so-called developed countries. Frozen foods, precooked meals and processed foods occupy an increasing amount of shelf space. Small wonder that so many confused consumers seek professional guidance from nutritionists and/or doctors who have a special interest in the nutrition of infants, children and adolescents. This explains why Brenda Bradshaw and Dr. Cheryl Mutch have performed such a valuable service by writing this highly reader- and eater-friendly book. Putting their recipes and recommendations into practice offers one way to make families simultaneously healthier and happier.

Richard B. Goldbloom O.C., M.D., F.R.C.P.(C.)
Professor of Pediatrics, Dalhousie University,
Halifax, N.S., Canada

introduction

Like most parents, you want to do what is best for your family. You try to balance your schedule with the kids' after-school activities and homework, while trying to get a meal on the table. You know good nutrition is critical to the health and well-being of children, but your kids seem to be constantly exposed to high-calorie processed foods. New fast food restaurants seem to pop up on every corner, and your children always seem to have another birthday party to attend. At the end of the day, you are exhausted and packaged food is all too convenient.

Take heart—this is no time to throw in the towel. Feeding your family nutritious meals is easier than you may think. *The Good Food Book for Families* contains over 150 nutritious, simple-to-make recipes for the entire family—recipes that stress the importance of whole foods and fresh ingredients.

As working parents, we too face the many challenges of feeding our kids. Brenda, the co-author of *The Baby's Table*, loves cooking and eating good food. Cheryl, a busy pediatrician, has become increasingly concerned about the nutrition-related illnesses facing our children. Most important, we bring to this book our own experience feeding finicky eaters, big eaters, constant grazers and fickle preschoolers.

The days of making separate meals for your picky eater are over. With some of the recipes, we suggest modifications to ensure they appeal to the entire family. Many of the recipes can be made in bulk and frozen to facilitate easy serving for evenings when you are just too busy or too tired to cook. All recipes are kid tested, pediatrician reviewed and parent approved!

The Good Food Book for Families covers the finicky toddler to the ravenous teen and all stages in between. Alongside the recipes, we have added sidebars addressing the myriad of feeding issues parents of children ages 2 to 18 may face. Topics covered include the best foods for brain development, vegetarian diets, coping with small appetites, omega-3 fatty acids, food additives, childhood obesity, food allergies and what to do when your teen wants to go on a diet.

This book is based on the guidelines from "Eating Well with Canada's Food Guide," published in 2007. The first Canadian Food Guide came out in 1942, and it has been revised many times since. Though the names, messages and format have changed, it has always stayed true to its original goal: promoting health by guiding the food choices of Canadians.

Based on the latest scientific evidence, the new Guide advocates a pattern of eating that will help your family get the nutrients needed to achieve overall health, while lessening the possibility of developing nutrition-related diseases. It does so by recommending amounts and types of food.[1]

The specific needs of children and adults are addressed more thoroughly in the new Guide. Children are categorized by age and sex, with specific recommendations for each group.

Though this may sound complicated, it's not. *The Good Food Book for Families* contains everything you need to understand and use Canada's new Food Guide to its fullest. The Food Guide (page 12), along with the meal planners (page 255), nutritional sidebars and easy-to-follow recipes, will help you ensure your children are getting what they need to thrive.

With the rise in childhood obesity, type 2 diabetes and eating disorders in children of all ages, this information has never been more timely. *The Good Food Book for Families* provides the recipes and information you need to raise children to be lifelong healthy eaters. Congratulations—your family is on the road to a healthier, happier future!

For the rest of this book, "Eating Well with Canada's Food Guide: A Resource for Educators and Communicators" will be referred to as Canada's Food Guide.

**raising
a healthy
eater**

Most children come into the world interested in and willing to try new foods. For their lucky parents, it is as simple as understanding the basics of good nutrition, offering healthy choices and being good role models. But if that doesn't sound like your child, don't worry. There are many ways to positively influence your child's eating habits. Healthy eaters are often created, not born. It takes perseverance and dedication. But the rewards will offer lifelong advantages for your child's health.

Ellyn Satter, a well-known dietitian and author, advocates what she calls "the division of responsibility in feeding." She says: "Parents are responsible for what is presented to eat and the manner in which it is presented. Children are responsible for how much and even whether they eat."[1]

This "division of responsibility in feeding," may seem like a novel and scary concept to many parents. However, it can relieve mealtime anxiety. Parents will no longer feel the need to get their children to finish everything on their plates and children will come to the table happily, knowing their choices will be respected.

This concept however, assumes that parents have an understanding of nutrition and can offer appropriate, healthy options in an environment where the children feel supported in their food choices. Those who feel supported are more likely to try different foods.

As adults, we tend to avoid foods we do not like and children will naturally do the same. Kids control very little in their lives; what they put in their mouths is one of the few exceptions. Children who feel pressured to eat tend to eat less. If forced, they will likely remember the experience and be reluctant to try new foods again. Children who are allowed to decide what to eat will be more willing to try new foods in the future. It is best to avoid getting into battles over food; force feeding almost always backfires.

Young children tend to be fickle when it comes to food. Don't conclude your child dislikes a food because it has been rejected, even a few times. Many parents say their children do not like fish, but it is a dietary staple in some cultures. Most Inuit children eat fish because they are repeatedly served it from an early age. If you want your child to like a certain food, keep offering it in a relaxed environment. As many as 10 to 20 exposures may be required before a new food is accepted. Be reassured that with each exposure, the chance of acceptance will increase.

Be careful not to impose your food preferences or expectations on your child. Just because you do not like tomatoes does not mean your child will dislike them. In North America, we often assume children will not like spicy foods; however, in India and Thailand children eat spicy foods from an early age. Expose your child to a wide variety of healthy foods and flavours, then step aside to see what choices they make. You might be pleasantly surprised!

Though it is important for children to learn what healthy eating is, it is equally vital for them to learn to regulate their food consumption. A healthy baby comes into the world instinctively knowing when to turn his head away, indicating he has had enough. As children grow, many will ignore the sensation of feeling full and, as a result, they overeat. Allowing your child the freedom to choose how much he eats will help him learn to stop eating when full.

Alternatively, children whose food intake is restricted tend to become preoccupied with food and are more likely to overeat when given the chance. Therefore, we don't advocate dieting for children unless under the care of a pediatric specialist. Instead of limiting the quantity of the food your child eats, improve the quality. Stress the importance of whole foods and fresh ingredients, and limit "junky" processed foods, which are high in salt, sugar and fats, as well as undesirable additives.

We live in a world of convenient abundance, and where childhood obesity is on the rise. As a result, teaching children how to listen to their bodies and eat what is needed for energy, growth and maintenance of a healthy weight has never been more crucial. Many of the messages we inadvertently give children are counterproductive. Is it better to eat everything on your plate or to learn to stop eating when you feel full? Having the opportunity to "pig out" can also be a valuable experience. Feeling uncomfortably stuffed after overeating may be a more powerful lesson than having someone constantly monitor what goes into your mouth. Avoid using food for comfort or as a reward. These are not patterns you want to establish, as they can lay the foundation for problems such as eating disorders in the future.

Equally important is to lead by example. Children learn from what we do, not what we say. Now is the time to evaluate your own relationship with food. Eat regular meals together as a family, and make healthy choices yourself. Those who have healthy eating habits are more likely to inspire them in their children.

Understanding the "division of responsibility in feeding" is one thing, but implementing it is quite another. Most parents of healthy eaters will probably find they are already applying this approach. When preparing a meal, this means creating a number of nutritious dishes and allowing the children to help themselves. Obviously, it is important that there are some choices you know your children will like. For example, a meal might consist of a portion of meat, three vegetables and a glass of milk. If you are concerned that there won't be enough for your child to eat, serve the meal with whole grain bread—it's filling, and most children like it. If your child is still hungry, offer fruit and/or yogurt for dessert. Since children tend to like fruit, always have a variety of fresh fruits on hand.

Implementing the "division of responsibility in feeding" does not mean becoming a short-order cook. Try not to offer substitutes, such as a grilled cheese sandwich instead of grilled chicken. This can be a slippery slope that leaves you making several different meals each night. Children need to understand that mealtimes are for eating. If they choose not to eat, the next meal or scheduled snack will not be too far away. Raising a healthy eater takes perseverance and dedication, but the dividends will last a lifetime.

what is healthy eating?

Healthy eating is essential for the proper development of growing children, providing the fuel they need to reach their intellectual and physical potential. Healthy eating is the sum of all food choices made over time. It will provide your child with the energy needed to fight infections and will lessen the possibility of developing nutrition-related problems throughout their lifespan. Such problems include obesity, certain types of cancer, cardiovascular disease, anemia, osteo-porosis, dental disease and type 2 diabetes. Instilling a lifelong commitment to healthy eating will help your child maintain an appropriate weight and an overall sense of well-being.

Canada's new Food Guide defines the food groups as follows:
• Vegetables and Fruit
• Grain Products
• Milk and Alternatives
• Meat and Alternatives

Eating a variety of foods is recommended because each of the 4 food groups provides a different set of key nutrients. The nutrient value of foods within each group also varies. For example, beef and chicken, while part of the same food group, contain different amounts of iron, beef possessing significantly more. By offering variety, you encourage your child to enjoy foods with different colours, textures and flavours, as well as foods from diverse cultures. A varied diet promotes sufficient intake of vitamins, minerals and other nutrients.

Generally low in calories and fat, fruits and vegetables are excellent sources of vitamins, minerals, carbohydrates, antioxidants and fibre. A diet rich in fruits and vegetables is thought to reduce the risk of heart disease and certain cancers. Health Canada's Food Guide recommends daily consumption of at least one dark green vegetable. These vegetables are an excellent source of folate, which is a vitamin needed for the healthy division of rapidly dividing cells. Examples of dark green vegetables include green peas, spinach, kale, beet greens, romaine lettuce, Brussels sprouts, arugula, asparagus, broccoli and fresh parsley.

Children should also be encouraged to eat at least one orange vegetable per day. They are an excellent source of carotenoids, which the body converts into vitamin A. Vitamin A is crucial for maintaining healthy cells, boosting immune function and helping the body fight infection. Examples of vegetables that are good sources of carotenoids include carrots, squash, sweet potatoes and pumpkin. Some orange fruits, such as apricots, mango, papaya and cantaloupe, also contain carotenoids. Although oranges provide vitamin C and folate, they are not considered good sources of carotenoids.[2]

Grain Products provide your child with carbohydrates, fibre, vitamins and minerals. When choosing grain products, pick those low in salt, sugar and fat. Make sure at least half the grain products you serve are whole grain, which are higher in fibre. High-fibre foods help regulate bowel function, prevent constipation, and keep you feeling full longer. A diet rich in whole grains is thought to reduce the risk of cardiovascular disease.[2]

Meat and Alternatives provide your child with protein, fat, vitamins and important minerals including iron, zinc and magnesium. Canada's Food Guide recommends regularly serving alternatives to meat, such as lentils, beans and tofu. Seeds and nuts are also found in this group. Although comparatively high in calories, they contain heart-healthy polyunsaturated fats. When serving meats, select leaner cuts, such as skinless poultry, flank steak, pork tenderloin, ground poultry and extra-lean ground beef. Always remove the skin, cut off visible fat and cook meats with little or no excess fat. Instead of frying your meats, try baking, roasting, broiling, grilling or poaching.[2]

Your children should also be encouraged to eat at least 2 Food Guide servings of fish per week (2½ oz or 75 g/serving). According to Canada's Food Guide, all fish contains at least some omega-3 fatty acids called EPA (eicosapentaenoic acid) and DHA (docosahexaenoic acid). Omega-3 fatty acids are considered essential nutrients. This means they must come from our diet because our bodies cannot make them in sufficient quantity to meet our physiological needs. Omega-3 fatty acids are important for the healthy development of growing brains and good vision. They also reduce the risk of cardiovascular disease. The best sources of omega-3 fatty acids include herring, char, mackerel, rainbow trout, sardines and salmon.[2]

Milk and Alternatives provide your child with protein, fat, vitamins (most notably vitamin D) and minerals (such as calcium and magnesium). Sources of Milk and Alternatives include milk, fortified soy beverage, cheese, yogurt and powdered milk. Calcium, magnesium and vitamin D are essential for the growth and maintenance of healthy bones and teeth. Since dairy is one of the few dietary sources of vitamin D, children should drink at least 2 cups of milk (or alternatively a fortified soy beverage) a day. Children with healthy bones are less likely to develop osteoporosis later in life.[2]

Young children should eat a diet that is higher in fat than recommended for adults because fats provide a dense source of energy needed during periods of rapid growth and development. Fats also constitute a major part of the developing nervous system. For this reason, children under 2 should be served full-fat dairy products (whole milk, 3.25% MF). After the age of 2, lower-fat products gradually become more appropriate, and by later childhood (ages 9 to 12), most children should be drinking skim, 1% or 2% milk (or lower-fat milk alternatives) and choosing other low-fat dairy products when possible.

One of the best ways to ensure your family is eating a healthy diet is to stress the importance of whole foods, that is, foods that are in their natural state and have not been processed. Frozen fruits and vegetables and some whole grain breakfast cereals are examples of nutritious processed foods. However, processing often relies on the use of chemicals to make the food look better, last longer and taste better. Foods that are highly processed tend to be high in salts, sugars, fats and chemical additives with minimal nutritional value. Examples include packaged cookies, cakes, pastries, chips, candies, doughnuts, chicken nuggets and soft drinks.

Highly processed foods should not be a part of your child's daily diet. Instead of serving a dinner of packaged chicken nuggets and fries, try a grilled chicken breast, brown rice, vegetable sticks and a glass of milk. Preparing whole foods may take a little longer, but the results will have lifelong benefits for your family's health.

Healthy eating is all about moderation and balance. Make a concerted effort to serve nutritious whole foods on a daily basis, but don't worry about the occasional birthday party. Eating candy and cake is a wonderful part of childhood and, in moderation, can be part of a healthy diet. The nutritional choices of one day or meal can be balanced by choices made at other times. Be reassured that what you serve on a daily or even weekly basis will have a greater impact on your child's future food choices and long-term health than any single meal. The goal is to raise children who not only understand healthy eating but also are likely to sustain these habits throughout their lifetime.

how do i use the food guide?

Many countries have food guides designed to promote health. Canada's new guide came out in 2007. Based on scientific evidence, it was developed to help Canadians establish a pattern of eating that meets nutritional needs while reducing the risk of developing chronic diseases. It recommends both the amounts and types of food Canadians should be eating. The guide is designed as a rainbow, with each of the 4 food groups represented by a band of colour. The differing sizes of the colour bands indicate the proportion of food Canadians should consume from each of the food groups. For example, green and yellow are the largest bands, indicating Canadians should eat more servings of Vegetables and Fruit, as well as Grain Products.

In addition to the 4 food groups, there is a separate category for Oils and Fats. That section is designed to ensure people consume adequate amounts of essential fatty acids (omega-3 and omega-6) while limiting their intake of trans and saturated fats. Canada's Food Guide recommends Canadians consume 2 to 3 tbsp of unsaturated fats per day to ensure they meet their fatty acid requirements. This amount includes oils used for cooking (canola, olive and soybean oil), mayonnaise, salad dressing and soft, non-hydrogenated margarine. People are also encouraged to limit consumption of butter, hard margarine, shortening and lard.

Canada's new food guide

Source: "Eating Well with Canada's Food Guide, (2007), Health Canada. Reproduced with the permission of the Minister of Public Works and Government Services Canada, 2007.

Recommended Number of Food Guide Servings per Day

	Children			Teens		Adults			
Age in Years	2-3	4-8	9-13	14-18		19-50		51+	
Sex	Girls and Boys			Females	Males	Females	Males	Females	Males
Vegetables and Fruit	4	5	6	7	8	7-8	8-10	7	7
Grain Products	3	4	6	6	7	6-7	8	6	7
Milk and Alternatives	2	2	3-4	3-4	3-4	2	2	3	3
Meat and Alternatives	1	1	1-2	2	3	2	3	2	3

The chart above shows how many Food Guide Servings you need from each of the four food groups every day.

Having the amount and type of food recommended and following the tips in *Canada's Food Guide* will help:

- Meet your needs for vitamins, minerals and other nutrients.
- Reduce your risk of obesity, type 2 diabetes, heart disease, certain types of cancer and osteoporosis.
- Contribute to your overall health and vitality.

What is One Food Guide Serving?
Look at the examples below.

Fresh, frozen or canned vegetables
125 mL (½ cup)

Leafy vegetables
Cooked: 125 mL (½ cup)
Raw: 250 mL (1 cup)

Fresh, frozen or canned fruits
1 fruit or 125 mL (½ cup)

100% Juice
125 mL (½ cup)

Bread
1 slice (35 g)

Bagel
½ bagel (45 g)

Flat breads
½ pita or ½ tortilla (35 g)

Cooked rice, bulgur or quinoa
125 mL (½ cup)

Cereal
Cold: 30 g
Hot: 175 mL (¾ cup)

Cooked pasta or couscous
125 mL (½ cup)

Milk or powdered milk (reconstituted)
250 mL (1 cup)

Canned milk (evaporated)
125 mL (½ cup)

Fortified soy beverage
250 mL (1 cup)

Yogurt
175 g
(¾ cup)

Kefir
175 g
(¾ cup)

Cheese
50 g (1 ½ oz.)

Cooked fish, shellfish, poultry, lean meat
75 g (2 ½ oz.)/125 mL (½ cup)

Cooked legumes
175 mL (¾ cup)

Tofu
150 g or
175 mL (¾ cup)

Eggs
2 eggs

Peanut or nut butters
30 mL (2 Tbsp)

Shelled nuts and seeds
60 mL (¼ cup)

Oils and Fats
- Include a small amount – 30 to 45 mL (2 to 3 Tbsp) – of unsaturated fat each day. This includes oil used for cooking, salad dressings, margarine and mayonnaise.
- Use vegetable oils such as canola, olive and soybean.
- Choose soft margarines that are low in saturated and trans fats.
- Limit butter, hard margarine, lard and shortening.

Make each Food Guide Serving count…
wherever you are – at home, at school, at work or when eating out!

▶ **Eat at least one dark green and one orange vegetable each day.**
  · Go for dark green vegetables such as broccoli, romaine lettuce and spinach.
  · Go for orange vegetables such as carrots, sweet potatoes and winter squash.

▶ **Choose vegetables and fruit prepared with little or no added fat, sugar or salt.**
  · Enjoy vegetables steamed, baked or stir-fried instead of deep-fried.

▶ **Have vegetables and fruit more often than juice.**

▶ **Make at least half of your grain products whole grain each day.**
  Eat a variety of whole grains such as barley, brown rice, oats, quinoa and wild rice.
  Enjoy whole grain breads, oatmeal or whole wheat pasta.

▶ **Choose grain products that are lower in fat, sugar or salt.**
  Compare the Nutrition Facts table on labels to make wise choices.
  Enjoy the true taste of grain products. When adding sauces or spreads, use small amounts.

▶ **Drink skim, 1%, or 2% milk each day.**
  · Have 500 mL (2 cups) of milk every day for adequate vitamin D.
  · Drink fortified soy beverages if you do not drink milk.

▶ **Select lower fat milk alternatives.**
  · Compare the Nutrition Facts table on yogurts or cheeses to make wise choices.

▶ **Have meat alternatives such as beans, lentils and tofu often.**

▶ **Eat at least two Food Guide Servings of fish each week.***
  · Choose fish such as char, herring, mackerel, salmon, sardines and trout.

▶ **Select lean meat and alternatives prepared with little or no added fat or salt.**
  · Trim the visible fat from meats. Remove the skin on poultry.
  · Use cooking methods such as roasting, baking or poaching that require little or no added fat.
  · If you eat luncheon meats, sausages or prepackaged meats, choose those lower in salt (sodium) and fat.

Enjoy a variety of foods from the four food groups.

Satisfy your thirst with water!

Drink water regularly. It's a calorie-free way to quench your thirst. Drink more water in hot weather or when you are very active.

* Health Canada provides advice for limiting exposure to mercury from certain types of fish. Refer to www.healthcanada.gc.ca for the latest information.

how do the food guide servings work?

You will likely find that most meals consist of several servings of food from different food groups. For young children and those with smaller appetites, one serving from a food group can be broken into smaller amounts and served throughout the day. For example, 1 egg served for breakfast and 1 tbsp of peanut butter served as part of an afternoon snack add up to 1 serving of Meat and Alternatives. For children under the age of 8, this fulfills their daily requirement of Meat and Alternatives. Alternatively, ½ cup of milk in your child's morning cereal and ½ cup of milk for lunch would be one serving of Milk and Alternatives.

Older children and those with larger appetites may eat several servings of food from one food group at a single sitting. For example, a typical sandwich made with 2 slices of bread is equivalent to 2 servings of Grain Products. A typical restaurant portion of meat may be as many as 2 to 3 servings of Meat and Alternatives—restaurant portions tend to be on the large side. Children of a healthy weight who need to eat more, such as those who are going through growth spurts and/or are very active, should be encouraged to eat additional servings from the 4 food groups. The daily meal planners in Appendix I (page 255) will help you use the new Food Guide to plan your children's meals.

the importance of macronutrients

Most of what we eat is a combination of 3 macronutrients: carbohydrates, protein and fat. These macronutrients provide children with the energy and materials needed to sustain healthy growth and development.

protein power During digestion, the body breaks protein into amino acids, which are the essential building blocks for muscle development. They are also required in the building and repairing of body tissue. There are 9 essential amino acids. Foods containing all of them are considered high-quality proteins. These include plant-based soy protein, as well as foods derived from animals, such as fish, poultry, meat, cheese, eggs, yogurt and milk. Most plant-based proteins (grains, nuts, seeds and legumes) are lacking in one or more of the essential amino acids. Therefore, combining 2 or more plant-based proteins at a meal makes sense.

Amino acids play an important role in growth. Infants and young children have a higher need for high-quality protein than older children or adults do. While the typical North American meets this requirement, children on strict vegetarian diets might not get adequate protein. These children may benefit from consultation with a pediatric nutritionist. See page 159 for more information on vegetarian diets.

formula for success

Raw food? Low fat? High protein or low carb? It's hard to keep up with the latest trends in adult diets. Despite the claims made by the proponents of these diets, the exclusion of one macronutrient is unhealthy and possibly dangerous for children. Young children need sufficient calories for growth and development. It is difficult to obtain enough on reduced-fat diets. Do not restrict nutritious foods because of their fat content. A balanced diet for children will have a mixture of foods that provide all the macronutrients in the rough ratios cited on the next page.

crucial carbohydrates Carbohydrates are our primary source of fuel. Carbohydrates are broken down into glucose for immediate energy and into glycogen for stored energy. Every cell in the body depends on glucose for energy; the brain depends almost entirely on glucose for proper functioning. Carbohydrates are found in highly nutritious foods such as fruits, vegetables, whole grains and legumes, as well as in foods with little nutritional value other than their high caloric content. The latter—chips, soda pop, candies, pastries, cakes and doughnuts—tend to be high in sugar, fat and salt. Parents should limit "junk carbs" and make an effort to serve healthy carbohydrates more often. In addition to providing fibre, vitamins and minerals, foods containing healthy carbohydrates generally take longer to break down. Therefore, they provide a steady stream of energy while keeping children satisfied longer. They will then be less likely to overeat!

acceptable macronutrient distribution ranges

age group	percentage of total calories from		
	carbohydrate	protein	fat
1–3 years	45 to 65 %	5 to 20 %	30 to 40 %
4–18 years	45 to 65 %	10 to 30 %	25 to 35 %
19 years +	45 to 65 %	10 to 35 %	20 to 35 %

Source: "Eating Well with Canada's Food Guide, (2007), Health Canada.
Reproduced with the permission of the Minister of Public Works and Government Services Canada, 2007.

the skinny on fats Despite its negative press, dietary fat is essential for the healthy growth and development of children. Negative health consequences stem from the consumption of too much *or* too little fat. In addition to flavouring food, fat provides a dense source of calories for energy, insulates against cold, helps maintain cell membranes, allows our guts to absorb fat-soluble vitamins (A, D, E and K), and constitutes a major part of the developing brain. Because early childhood (1 to 3 years of age) is a period of rapid brain growth, healthy foods should not be restricted because of their fat content. As children grow, lower-fat choices gradually become appropriate.

While eating the right amount of fat is important, so is consuming the right kinds. There are 4 main types of fats: saturated fats, trans fats, monounsaturated fats and polyunsaturated fats. Saturated fats are solid at room temperature and come from meat, dairy products and tropical oils (palm and coconut oil). Consumption of saturated fats is linked to heightened cholesterol levels and increased risk of cardiovascular disease. People living in countries that have the highest amount of saturated fats in their diet also have the highest rate of heart disease. Saturated fats are known to raise LDL (low-density lipoprotein) cholesterol. LDL cholesterol is often called the "bad" cholesterol, and is linked to an increased risk of heart attacks. In contrast, HDL (high-density lipoprotein) cholesterol seems to protect against heart disease.

So what does this have to do with children? More and more children are developing elevated cholesterol levels, putting them at risk for lifelong problems with cholesterol. Therefore, it is important that children get off to a heart-healthy start by eating the right types of fats from an early age.

Trans fats are found naturally in small amounts in certain foods (such as dairy products, beef and lamb). However, the vast majority of the trans fats in our diet are manmade. They are formed by a chemical process called "partial hydrogenation," which turns a liquid fat into a solid. These fats are added to prolong the shelf life of processed products, such as fast foods, commercial cookies, doughnuts, crackers, cakes, hard margarine, pastries, microwave popcorn, white bread, chips, french fries and chicken nuggets, among others. They have no meaningful nutritional value and are, in fact, harmful. They have been linked to increased risk of heart disease and have been proven to lower the good HDL levels and raise the bad LDL levels. The presence of trans fats in commercially prepared foods is just another reason to serve whole foods, limit processed foods and avoid trips to fast food restaurants.

The unsaturated fats—monounsaturated and polyunsaturated—are the heroes. They are liquid at room temperature. When it comes to heart disease, these fats are thought to have a protective effect. Monounsaturated fats lower bad LDL levels and, at the same time, raise the good HDL levels. Many plant oils contain a mixture of monounsaturated and polyunsaturated fats. Sources of monounsaturated fats include olive oil, canola oil, avocados and some nuts (peanuts, almonds). The high consumption of olive oil in Mediterranean countries is thought to contribute to the lower rate of heart disease in the region.

trans fat facts

Concern about the direct link between trans fats and coronary heart disease arose in the early 1990s. Despite these concerns, the prevalence and consumption of trans fats in our food supply has continued to rise. By the mid-1990s, research suggested that Canadians had one of the highest intakes of trans fats worldwide. In 2003, the World Health Organization recommended that trans fat intake be limited to less than 1% of a person's overall energy intake. In 2005, Canada was the first country to regulate mandatory labelling of trans fats in foods. In 2006, the United States followed suit by instituting "mandatory declaration of trans fats in foods containing more than 0.5 grams per serving."[3]

The combination of mandatory labelling and consumer awareness has prompted many manufacturers to reduce and even eliminate trans fats from their products. Despite this good news, trans fats continue to make up as much as 45% of the fat in foods like french fries, fast foods, snack foods, pastries and so on. The best way to reduce your child's intake of these fats is to start reading nutrition labels and ingredient lists. Avoid products that list shortening, and hydrogenated and partially hydrogenated vegetable oils, in their ingredient list.

Polyunsaturated fats provide our bodies with the essential fatty acids: omega-3 and omega-6. These fats are essential because our bodies cannot make them and so they must come from the diet. Sources of omega-6 fats include nuts, seeds, and vegetable oils like corn oil, sunflower oil and soybean oil. Sources of omega-3 include canola oil, soybean oil, flaxseed, omega-3 eggs, walnuts and fish. In addition to reducing the development of heart disease, omega-3 fatty acids are thought to improve vision and cognitive function. To obtain the right balance between omega-3 and omega-6 fatty acids, most people need to eat more fish and less meat.

what are the healthiest fats to use for cooking?

Compared with other common cooking oils, canola oil has the least amount of saturated fat. It is also a good source of omega-3 fatty acids, is mild in flavour and has a high smoke point, which means it won't break down and burn at higher temperatures. It is therefore an excellent choice for sautéing, grilling, frying and baking. Cold first-pressed (which means it has been through less processing) olive oil has a delicious flavour but breaks down at higher temperatures. It is therefore a good choice for cooking at lower temperatures, as well as for use in dips and salad dressings. For that reason, most of the recipes in this book call for canola oil for cooking and olive oil for salad dressings. Instead of tossing cooked vegetables in butter, do as the Italians do and toss them in olive oil. Instead of buttering your bread, dip it in olive oil swirled with a drizzle of balsamic vinegar. And when buying margarine, choose a soft non-hydrogenated one.

Although heart disease usually does not declare itself until adulthood, the disease is often the result of a lifelong pattern of poor eating habits. The best way to ensure your child has a heart-healthy future is to eliminate manufactured trans fats and to decrease her intake of saturated fats.

Foods particularly high in saturated fats include hot dogs, sausages, bacon, cold cuts, salami, red meat, cream cheese, cream, ice cream and butter. You can lower your child's intake of both saturated and trans fats by serving more fruits, vegetables, whole grains, seafood, peas, beans, lentils, seeds and nuts. When you do eat meat, opt for leaner cuts and try substituting ground turkey or chicken for ground beef. Choose heart-healthy vegetable oils such as olive, canola and soybean oil, and go veggie more often!

childhood obesity

Obesity is the most common nutrition-related health issue affecting our children. The percentage of overweight and obese children has increased dramatically over the past 20 years. The prevalence of obesity in Canadian children tripled between 1981 and 1996. Almost 25% of American youth are considered obese.[4] Complications of obesity include high cholesterol and triglycerides, as well as high insulin levels or type 2 diabetes. Obese children are also at risk for hypertension (high blood pressure), and respiratory, orthopedic and psychological problems.

Obesity is the result of a chronically positive energy balance—in other words, too many calories ingested compared to the number of calories burned. The problem exists on both sides of the equation. Our children eat too many foods high in calories and fat while not getting enough exercise to burn off those excess calories. We know that obese parents are more likely to have obese children. And while genetics does play a role, the rapid increase in obesity in the past 25 years demonstrates the potent effect of environment on the condi-

body mass index

A person's body mass index (BMI) measures weight as it relates to height. It is a reliable indicator of body fat for most children, teens and adults. The BMI is defined as the weight (in kilograms) divided by the height (in centimetres) squared and multiplied by 10,000. Once calculated, the BMI number is plotted on a BMI growth chart to obtain a percentile ranking. The percentile indicates the relative position of the child's BMI number among children of the same sex and age. If a child's BMI is below the fifth percentile, she is considered underweight, and if it is over the 85th percentile, she is considered overweight.

You can calculate your child's BMI by going to http://apps.nccd.cdc.gov/dnpabmi/Calculator.aspx.

tion. The dietary and exercise habits of parents strongly influence the habits of their children.

We know that 7 out of 10 children aged 4 to 8 do not eat the recommended number of daily servings of Vegetables and Fruit.[5] Their diets contain more than the recommended amount of fat. Many children eat regularly at fast food restaurants, where portion sizes are inappropriately large. They are physically inactive, spending a significant amount of time engaged in sedentary activities such as watching television, playing video games and sitting at the computer.

just do it!

Talk to your children about the importance of regular physical activity and get the whole family involved. Set regular goals and stay positive by being an active role model.

- Set and stick to limits for watching TV, playing video games, instant messaging and surfing the Net.
- If it's less than a mile, walk it.
- Take the stairs instead of elevators and escalators.
- Do chores together as a family: rake the leaves, weed the garden, shovel the snow and walk the dog.
- Encourage your children to become involved in both school and community sports.
- Take your children hiking, biking, swimming, skating and skiing.
- Encourage your children to play outside, and take them to the park.
- Have a snowball fight or build a snow fort.
- Teach your children the skills they need to enjoy an active lifestyle, such as swimming, riding a bike, throwing and hitting a ball, dancing, kicking a ball, jumping rope, and so on.
- Put on music and dance!

Forty per cent of obese 7-year-olds and 70% of obese adolescents become obese adults.[4] Because it is more difficult to lose weight as an adult, preventing children from becoming obese is of critical, long-term importance to their health. If you suspect that your child has a weight problem, consult your doctor.

Lack of physical activity is a major contributor to weight gain and obesity. According to Health Canada, over half of Canada's children are not active enough for optimal growth and development. Children tend to become less active as they get older. School-age children should be doing at least 90 minutes of physical activity a day. This can be achieved through a combination of moderate and vigorous activities. Moderate activities include playing outdoors, brisk walking, skating, swimming and biking. Running and soccer are examples of more vigorous activities. If your child is not getting the recommended minimum amount of exercise, increase the time spent on physical activity by a total of at least 30 minutes per day. Then reduce the time spent on "non-active" activities such as playing video games, watching TV and surfing the Net by 30 minutes per day. To ease into this goal, activity can be increased by accumulating short periods (5 to 10 minutes) every day. Once this is achieved, slowly increase your child's total daily physical activity by 15 minutes every month until he is doing at least 90 minutes of physical activity per day.[6]

Although it is hard work, this is your opportunity to establish healthy habits that can last a lifetime. Lead by example and involve the whole family. Go for a walk or a bike ride after dinner. Use community parks and recreation centres. If your child is reluctant, consult the physical activity counsellor at your local community centre, your child's PE teacher and/or your doctor about ways to get the family moving.

breakfast

Children who eat a good breakfast do better in school. Those who go to school hungry tire easily, have more trouble solving problems and have shorter attention spans. We know that 31% of elementary school students and 62% of high school students do not eat a nutritious breakfast before heading to school.[1] Make sure your children do not become part of this statistic. Starting the day with a good breakfast is a great way to help your child succeed.

For breakfast, children should be encouraged to eat foods from at least 3 of the 4 food groups. For example, a healthy breakfast for a school-aged child could include a piece of whole grain toast, scrambled eggs, orange juice and seasonal fresh fruit. Alternatively, children might enjoy whole grain cereal with milk, a piece of fresh fruit and a yogurt smoothie.

Seventy per cent of Canadian children do not eat enough fruits and vegetables.[2] Breakfast is the perfect opportunity to promote fruit. It is quick to prepare and can be eaten on the go. Aim to include 2 servings of fruit as part of your child's daily breakfast. This may seem like a lot, but remember that ½ cup of orange juice and a banana count as 2 servings, as do an apple and a frozen fruit smoothie.

Healthy eating means eating a variety of foods, so make an effort to serve an assortment of different fruit, including tree fruits, melons, tropical fruits, citrus fruits and berries. When choosing canned fruits, opt for those packed in juice rather than sugary syrup.

weekday breakfasts

The following breakfast recipes can be made in less than 10 minutes and are ideal for rushed weekday mornings.

banana nutmeg porridge

This recipe calls for honey, although its use is optional. Try it first without, as it's always better to limit your child's sugar intake. Do not serve honey to children less than one year of age as it may contain botulism spores. After age one, your child's immune system is more than strong enough to handle it.

1½ cups water
Pinch salt
⅔ cup quick oats
1 rounded tbsp raisins
¼ tsp ground nutmeg
Dash cinnamon
1 banana, diced
½ tbsp liquid honey
   (optional)
½ cup milk

- In a small saucepan, bring water and salt to a boil.
- Slowly stir in oats, raisins, nutmeg and cinnamon and cook for 3 minutes over medium heat, stirring occasionally.
- Remove from heat. Add banana, honey (if using) and milk.
- Stir and serve.

Yield: Serves 2 to 3

Serving Suggestion: Serve with ½ cup orange juice.

nutritious breakfasts to go!

Just because mornings are rushed does not mean that your child cannot reap the benefits of a healthy breakfast. The following ideas are quick and easy. Choose 1 food from at least 3 of the following 4 food groups, and you are set for the day!

meat and alternatives:

eggs Although often relegated to weekends, eggs are easy to cook and quick to prepare any time. They are an excellent source of protein, which will keep your child satisfied all morning long. Scrambled, poached and soft-boiled eggs can be prepared in minutes. Hard-boiled eggs can be cooked the night before, refrigerated and eaten on the go.

nut butters Peanut butter and other nut butters, such as cashew butter and almond butter, are high in heart-healthy unsaturated fats and are a good source of protein. Avoid peanut butter with added sugar and fat.

dairy products Yogurt, milk and cheese can all be a part of a healthy breakfast. Buy a plain yogurt and mix it with fresh fruit or a homemade fruit sauce (page 246–47).

grain products Whole grain muffins, toast and cereal are all quick to prepare and can be part of a healthy breakfast. When buying grain products, read labels carefully and use the Nutrition Facts table (page 51) to compare cereals. Choose one that is low in sugar and high in fibre. Old-fashioned porridge oats are always a healthy option.

fruit Fruit (served fresh or blended into a smoothie) should be part of your child's morning breakfast. When buying canned fruit, choose a brand that is packed in unsweetened juice instead of syrup.

daf's homemade granola

Obviously, homemade granola takes more than 10 minutes to make. However, this nutritious breakfast is definitely worth the effort. It is designed to be made in bulk; once made, it can be served in seconds! Extra granola should be stored in airtight containers.

6 cups rolled oats
1 cup sunflower seeds
1 cup sesame seeds
1 cup wheat bran
1 cup wheat germ
1 cup ground flaxseed
1 cup slivered almonds
1 cup unsweetened
  shredded coconut

1¼ cups dried
  cranberries
1¼ cups raisins
1 cup skim milk powder
¾ cup canola oil
1¼ cups liquid honey

- Preheat oven to 250°F.
- In a large bowl, thoroughly mix together dry ingredients.
- In a saucepan over medium heat, thoroughly mix together oil and honey until honey is dissolved. This can also be done in the microwave (approximately 1 minute).
- Add honey mixture to dry ingredients and mix thoroughly.
- Evenly spread granola onto three large baking pans and bake for 60 to 70 minutes or until golden brown and lightly toasted. Stir every 15 minutes. If you use a cookie sheet, you will have to watch the granola carefully as it will likely cook a little faster.
- When done, remove from oven and allow to cool.

Yield: Approximately 16 ½ cups

Serving Suggestion: Serve with a fruit smoothie.

fabulous fibre

Fibre is an important part of your child's diet. Fibre refers to carbohydrates that cannot be fully digested and absorbed. Fibre is found in all edible plants, including fruits, vegetables, nuts, seeds, legumes and whole grains. Eating adequate fibre helps regulate bowel function and prevent constipation, and it's also associated with reducing the risk of diabetes and heart disease by helping to lower blood glucose and cholesterol levels. Because fibre is filling, it aids in weight maintenance and can help prevent childhood obesity.

Adults should aim to eat 25 to 30 grams of fibre per day, while children (over the age of 2) should have an amount equal to their age in years plus 5 grams. To ensure your child's diet is high in fibre, serve a variety of whole grains, fruits, vegetables, seeds and legumes. When choosing a whole grain cereal, read labels carefully and choose one that is high in fibre and lists the whole grain first. Adding some berries to the morning cereal will boost your child's daily total fibre intake. For a list of high-fibre foods see Fibre Facts (page 33).

granola yogurt cups

Granola Yogurt Cups are easy to make and can be assembled ahead of time. Brenda often serves these when having a family brunch. Layering the granola with yogurt and fruit in a martini glass is aesthetically appealing, but when serving to young children, a cup or bowl is more appropriate. Instead of a nectarine and blueberries, you can substitute whatever seasonal fruit is freshest. For younger children (over age 1), you can mix a teaspoon of honey with the yogurt, but try it without first.

½ cup Balkan-style plain
  yogurt (above 3% MF)
½ cup Daf's Homemade
  Granola (page 31)
½ nectarine, peeled and
  thinly sliced
½ cup fresh blueberries
1 mint leaf (optional)

- Spoon ¼ cup of the yogurt into the bottom of a martini or other glass.
- Top with ¼ cup of the granola and then layer with half of the fruit.
- Repeat layers and top with mint leaf (if using).

Yield: Serves 1

fibre facts

fibre, total dietary (g) content of selected foods per common measure

food	common measure	content per measure
Lentils	1 cup	15.642
Canned baked beans	1 cup	12.7
Canned chickpeas	1 cup	10.56
Green frozen peas, cooked and drained	1 cup	8.8
Bulgur, cooked	1 cup	8.19
Raisins, seedless	1 cup	5.365
Broccoli, cooked and drained	1 cup	5.148
Sweet potato, baked in skin	1 potato	4.818
Potato, baked in skin	1 potato	4.444
Brown long-grain rice, cooked	1 cup	3.510
Blueberries, raw	1 cup	3.48
Apple with skin, raw	1 apple	3.312

Carrots, raw	1 cup	3.3
Banana, raw	1 banana	3.068
Instant oats	1 packet	2.832
Whole wheat bread, commercially prepared	1 slice	1.932
White bread, commercially prepared	1 slice	1.080
White long-grain rice, cooked	1 cup	0.990
Peanut butter, smooth style	1 tbsp	0.944

Adapted from USDA National Nutrient Database

homemade muesli

Making your own muesli is a great way to eliminate excess sugar and unnecessary additives found in many commercial cereals. To serve, mix with cold milk.

2 cups bran flakes
2 cups corn flakes
½ cup dried apricots, diced
¼ cup raisins
¼ cup dried cranberries
½ cup sunflower seeds
½ cup sliced almonds
⅓ cup unsweetened shredded coconut

• Mix together all of the ingredients.
• Extra muesli can be stored in airtight containers.

Yield: 6 cups

Serving Suggestion: Serve with a fruit smoothie and a nectarine.

what should a toddler or preschooler eat?

Young children (ages 2 to 5) need enough calories to sustain healthy growth and development. Small children have smaller appetites and tend to fill up quickly—therefore, they benefit from eating 3 small snacks and 3 small meals per day. Snacks and meals should be scheduled so as not to interfere with the next meal. Whenever possible, meals should be enjoyed as a family.

Be wary of choking hazards, such as popcorn, hard candies, chewing gum, nuts, olives, raisins and cough drops. Cut wieners, carrots and grapes lengthwise. When eating, young children should be supervised and sitting upright at a table or in a high chair.

Young children have an innate preference for sweet foods. When given the choice, they will usually choose juice over water, raisins over grapes and fruit leathers and candies over fresh fruit and vegetables. Over-consumption of these foods can lead to tooth decay, add excess calories and result in a lifelong preference for sweeter foods. To avoid this, offer unprocessed, whole foods and help your child establish a preference for healthy foods from day one.

Higher-fat, nutrient-dense foods, such as nut butters and cheese, should not be restricted because of their fat content. A low-fat diet is not appropriate for young children.

At this stage of their lives, appetites vary day to day and even meal to meal, depending on growth, activity level, social setting, frustration, fatigue and illness. When excited or overly tired, children may lose interest in food, and when hungry they will concentrate on eating. This could mean they skip or pick at the occasional meal. Instead of worrying about one missed meal, evaluate your child's nutritional intake over several days or weeks. In most cases, the variations in the amount eaten will average out, providing your child with all the nutrients needed. This is especially true in the case of children who are provided nutritious foods and allowed to stop eating when they are full. This teaches them to listen to their bodies. Encouraging this habit for life is more important than teaching children to finish everything on their plate.

eggs

soft-boiled eggs with whole wheat toast soldiers

This traditional English breakfast can be served any time of the day. Children love to dip toast soldiers into egg yolks.

1 egg
1 slice whole wheat toast, cut into strips

• Fill a small saucepan with water and bring to a simmer. Little bubbles should be coming off the bottom of the pan.
• With a slotted spoon, gently lower the egg into the water. The egg should be completely submerged. Allow the egg to simmer with lid on for 1 minute. Remove the saucepan from the heat and allow the egg to sit for 7 to 8 minutes, covered. A 7-minute egg will produce a runny centre

and a white that is just set. An 8-minute egg should produce a creamier centre with a set white.
• With the slotted spoon, remove the egg and place in an egg cup.
• With a knife, gently cut off the top of the egg and serve with the whole wheat toast strips.

Yield: Serves 1

Serving Suggestion: Serve with milk and whatever fruit you have on hand.

dilly delicious scramble

Taking just minutes to prepare, scrambled eggs are easy weekday fare. For a change, shred a little Cheddar cheese and add it to the eggs along with some diced tomatoes.

The following recipe calls for fresh dill. Do not substitute dried dill, as the flavour is not comparable.

6 eggs

2 tbsp milk

1 tsp soft non-hydro-
genated margarine

½ tsp chopped fresh dill
(optional)

• In a small bowl, thoroughly whisk together eggs and milk.

• Melt margarine in a frying pan over medium-low heat.

• Pour egg mixture into frying pan and scramble until desired degree of doneness, 5 to 7 minutes.

• Remove from heat, add dill (if using) and stir until combined.

Yield: Serves 3

Serving Suggestion: Serve with orange juice, whole wheat toast and Homemade Salsa (page 111)

eggs and cholesterol

Despite the bad reputation eggs have for being high in cholesterol, they remain a healthy choice for the vast majority of children. We now know that it is the saturated and trans fats, more so than the dietary cholesterol, that have the biggest impact on blood cholesterol levels. Unless your child or family members have been diagnosed with high cholesterol or have an egg allergy, there is no need to limit eggs.

danny's scrambled wrap

If your children don't have time to sit down for breakfast, they can eat the following on the run. If eating at home, serve with salsa and either plain yogurt or light sour cream.

2 eggs, scrambled
1 large soft whole wheat flour tortilla (approximately 10 inches)
2 tbsp shredded Cheddar cheese (approximately 1 oz)
1 rounded tbsp diced tomato (optional)

• Place scrambled eggs in the centre of the tortilla.

• Top with cheese, and tomatoes (if using).

• Fold opposite ends (1½-inch piece) of the tortilla inward, then roll up tightly to enclose filling.

• Place tortilla in microwave and heat until cheese melts and is warmed through (approximately 20 seconds).

• Wrap in a napkin and you're ready to go.

Yield: Serves 1

Serving Suggestion: Serve with Jeff's Blueberry Blitz (page 47).

egg-tastic

Low in calories and high in nutrients, eggs pack a powerful punch. They are versatile, quick to cook and contain all 9 essential amino acids, making them a complete protein. Two eggs count as 1 serving of Meat and Alternatives. They are also a good source of vitamin A and iron, and are one of the few dietary sources of vitamin D. Serve them frequently so they become a familiar favourite. Scrambled eggs and toast make an easy last-minute dinner, and a hard-boiled egg is a nutritious addition to any packed lunch.

toad in a hole

Using a cookie cutter to make the shapes can turn this traditional breakfast into a fun meal that your little ones are sure to gobble up!

1 slice whole wheat bread
½ tsp soft non-hydro-
    genated margarine
1 egg

• With a small cookie cutter, cut a shape out of the centre of the bread and discard the cut-out piece.
• In frying pan, melt margarine over medium heat.
• Place bread in frying pan and crack the egg into the centre of the bread.
• Cook for 4 minutes, then turn the bread over and cook for another 2 to 3 minutes or until egg is cooked.

Yield: Serves 1

breakfast sandwiches

Quick to prepare, these sandwiches can be eaten on the go when time is tight.

½ tsp mayonnaise
1 whole wheat English
    muffin, toasted
1 leaf romaine lettuce,
    shredded
1 egg, fried or poached
1 slice Cheddar cheese
1 slice tomato
1 slice good-quality
    cooked ham (optional)

• Lightly spread mayonnaise over English muffin.
• On one half of English muffin, layer lettuce, egg, cheese, tomato, and ham (if using).
• Top with other half of English muffin and serve.

Yield: Serves 1

Serving Suggestion: Serve with a glass of milk and a peach.

should my child take a multivitamin?

It was in the early 1900s that researchers first recognized there are substances in food that are "vital to life." While all the recommended vitamins can be provided by eating an adequate diet, there are times when diet alone will not meet an individual's needs. Subtle nutrient deficiencies can occur in extremely finicky eaters and dieting teens, or in those who bleed excessively during menstruation. Likewise, pregnant women and women of childbearing age require folate, while breastfeeding infants require vitamin D. Some vegetarians may also require supplementation. Multivitamins are taken by many people in the hope of making up for what may be an inadequate diet. It is important to realize that nutrient imbalances or toxicities can occur when a supplement is taken to the extreme. Because of their smaller size, children are more susceptible to the potentially toxic effects of supplements. Furthermore, a multivitamin is not an insurance policy against letting your child eat a poorly balanced diet. Most children will benefit more from eating a well-balanced diet than from taking a vitamin.

muffins

Whole grain muffins served with orange juice, fresh fruit and yogurt are a healthy breakfast. Alternatively, muffins can be added to packed lunches or offered as yummy after-school snacks. To cut down on saturated fat, the following muffins are made with heart-healthy canola oil instead of butter. Because muffins freeze well, doubling the following recipes and freezing extra in airtight containers is a good way to ensure you always have homemade muffins on hand. To serve, simply defrost and enjoy.

mixed berry oatmeal muffins

These muffins are made with fresh berries, but you can substitute frozen blueberries. Frozen raspberries aren't recommended, however, because they might make the muffins soggy.

1 cup rolled oats
1 cup low-fat buttermilk
  (1.5% MF)
1 large egg, beaten
½ cup packed brown
  sugar
½ cup canola oil
⅓ cup ground flaxseed
  or wheat germ
½ cup all-purpose flour
2 tsp baking powder
½ tsp baking soda
½ cup whole wheat
  flour
½ cup blueberries (plus 1
  tbsp to sprinkle on top
  of muffins)
½ cup fresh raspberries
  (plus 1 tbsp to sprinkle
  on top of muffins)

• If making with frozen blueberries, remove from freezer so they have time to thaw.

• Preheat oven to 400°F and line 12 muffin tins with paper liners.

• In a large bowl, combine oats and buttermilk and let stand for 5 minutes.

• Add egg, sugar, oil and ground flaxseed (or wheat germ) to oat mixture and stir until all ingredients are incorporated.

• In another bowl, sift together all-purpose flour, baking powder and baking soda.

• Add whole wheat flour and mix.

• Add berries and gently mix until just coated.

• Fold wet ingredients into flour mixture and mix until just incorporated.

- Divide batter evenly into muffin tins. Sprinkle extra berries on top of muffins and bake for approximately 20 minutes or until golden brown and a toothpick inserted into an area of muffin without a berry comes out clean.

- Remove from oven and cool in pan on wire rack for 5 minutes. Turn muffins out of pan and let cool on rack for 20 minutes.

 Yield: 12 muffins

banana pecan muffins

Even if your children don't like nuts, don't shy away from making these healthy muffins. The pecan flavour is fairly mild. Brenda's son, who dislikes nuts, devours these muffins. If allergies are the issue, substitute ground flaxseed for the pecans. Always choose overripe bananas, as their flavour is more intense. If the skins of your bananas are still yellow, throw them in the oven for 15 minutes at 350°F before peeling and using in the recipe. This will bring out the intensity of the banana flavour.

1 cup all-purpose flour
2 tsp baking powder
½ tsp baking soda
½ tsp ground nutmeg
½ cup whole wheat flour
1 large egg, beaten
1¼ cups mashed ripe
  bananas
½ cup packed brown
  sugar
½ cup canola oil

½ cup finely ground
  pecans, toasted

TIP: Toast nuts in microwave for 1 minute, remove from microwave, stir, and toast for another minute.

¼ cup low-fat buttermilk
  (1.5% MF)
⅓ cup wheat germ
12 thin banana slices

- Preheat oven to 400°F and line 12 muffin tins with paper liners.
- In a large bowl, sift together all-purpose flour, baking powder, baking soda and nutmeg.
- Add whole wheat flour and mix.
- In another bowl, combine egg, mashed bananas, sugar, canola oil, pecans, buttermilk and wheat germ.
- Fold wet ingredients into dry and mix until just incorporated.
- Evenly divide batter into muffin tins and place 1 slice of banana on each.
- Bake for 20 minutes or until muffins are golden brown and a toothpick inserted into the middle of a muffin comes out clean.
- Remove from oven and cool in pan on wire rack for 5 minutes. Turn muffins out of pan and let cool on rack for 20 minutes.

 Yield: 12 muffins

blueberry bran muffins

1 cup low-fat buttermilk
(1.5% MF)
½ cup packed brown sugar
¼ cup canola oil
¼ cup molasses
2 eggs
1 cup all-purpose flour

1½ tsp baking powder
½ tsp baking soda
½ tsp salt
1½ cups wheat bran
1 cup fresh or frozen
blueberries

The following recipe calls for blueberries. You can use either fresh or frozen. If you would prefer a more traditional bran muffin, substitute ½ cup raisins for the berries.

- Preheat oven to 400°F and line 12 muffin tins with paper liners.
- In a large bowl, combine buttermilk, sugar, canola oil, molasses and eggs. Set aside.
- In another bowl, sift together flour, baking powder, baking soda and salt.

43

- Add bran and mix thoroughly.
- Add berries to dry ingredients and gently mix until just coated.
- Combine wet ingredients with dry and mix until just incorporated.
- Evenly divide batter into muffin tins.
- Bake for approximately 20 minutes or until muffins are golden brown and a toothpick inserted into the middle of a muffin comes out clean.
- Remove from oven and cool in pan on wire rack for 5 minutes. Turn muffins out of pan and let cool on rack for 20 minutes.

Yield: 12 muffins

the whole truth about whole grains

Consumption of whole grains has been linked to a reduced risk of cardiovascular disease, obesity, diabetes and cancer.[3] Whole grains or foods made from them should retain all three components of the original grain kernel: the bran, germ and endosperm. In the refining process, the bran and germ are removed, resulting in the loss of dietary fibre, B vitamins, minerals and antioxidants.

The labelling of grain products can be deceiving, so read labels carefully. Just because bread is brown does not mean that it is whole grain. For example, added molasses can turn white bread brown. Grain products labelled "multi-grain," "wheat flour," "stone ground," "100% wheat," "seven grain" and "cracked wheat" are usually not whole grain products. Wheat flour is what is used to make most white breads, and multi-grain just means a variety of grains are used. When choosing whole grains, look for the word "whole"—it should appear before the grain ingredient's name. For example, the first ingredient in a whole grain cereal might be whole oat flour, and a good-quality brown bread should be made with 100% whole wheat flour.

Introduce whole grains early so that your children will develop a preference for them. If you have been serving white bread, it's never too late to switch.

carrot zucchini breakfast muffins

Grating vegetables into baked goods is a good way to entice finicky eaters to eat their veggies.

2 eggs, beaten
½ cup packed brown sugar
½ cup canola oil
1 cup zucchini, grated
1 cup carrot, peeled, grated
1 cup mashed ripe bananas
1 cup unsweetened shredded coconut
1 cup all-purpose flour
1 tsp baking powder
½ tsp baking soda
½ tsp cinnamon
½ tsp ground nutmeg

• Preheat oven to 400°F and line a 12-muffin tin with paper liners.

• In a large bowl, mix together eggs, brown sugar and oil.

• Add zucchini, carrot, mashed banana and coconut flakes and mix until combined.

• Sift together flour, baking powder, baking soda, cinnamon and nutmeg. Add to bowl.

• Mix until ingredients are just incorporated.

• Evenly divide batter into muffin tins.

• Bake for 20 to 25 minutes or until muffins are golden brown and a toothpick inserted into the middle of a muffin comes out clean.

• Remove from oven and cool in the pan for 5 minutes.

• Turn muffins out of pan and let cool on rack for 25 minutes.

 Yield: 12 muffins

whole grain examples

To boost your consumption of whole grains, look for foods that list one of the following first in the ingredient list: **graham flour, quinoa, whole rye, bulgur, pot barley, buckwheat, oatmeal, popcorn,* 100% whole wheat, brown rice, whole oats, 100% whole wheat flour, wild rice, whole oat flour, whole grain corn.**

* When purchasing microwave popcorn, read labels carefully; many varieties contain trans fats. Instead of serving popcorn with butter, try it tossed with olive oil and a little freshly grated Parmesan cheese.

smoothies

Many kids love smoothies made with fruit and yogurt. And they're not just for breakfast—they make nutritious after-school snacks, too. The following smoothies are made with frozen fruit because they give the shake a yummy, frosty texture. Frozen fruit, which has the advantage of being available all year long, offers the same nutritional benefits as fresh fruit. Whenever possible, choose plain yogurt as it is the best way to eliminate added sugars, sweeteners and additives often found in flavoured varieties. If your child is unable to eat dairy products, fortified soy beverage can be substituted for milk, and soy yogurt can be substituted for regular yogurt.

strawberry mango smoothie

1 cup milk
½ cup plain yogurt
½ mango, pit and skin removed
12 frozen strawberries

• Combine all of the ingredients in a blender and mix until smooth.

Yield: Serves 2 to 3

raspberry banana smoothie

If your kids find this smoothie too seedy, substitute the raspberries with strawberries or blueberries.

1 cup milk
½ cup plain yogurt
1 banana
1 cup frozen raspberries

• Combine all of the ingredients in a blender and mix until smooth.

Yield: Serves 2 to 3

what is an antioxidant?

Antioxidants help protect cells from damage caused by free radicals. Free radicals are a natural by-product of metabolism and are implicated in a variety of life-threatening diseases, including cancer and cardiovascular disease. The best way to ensure your child reaps the benefits of disease-fighting antioxidants is to serve a diet rich in plant-based foods. Such foods include whole grains, legumes, vegetables and fruits.

jeff's blueberry blitz

1 cup frozen blueberries
½ cup plain yogurt
1 cup orange juice

• Combine all of the ingredients in a blender and mix until smooth.

Yield: Serves 2 to 3

blueberries

Blueberries are a nutritional powerhouse. They are high in vitamin C and fibre, and are packed full of disease-fighting antioxidants, most notably anthocyanins. Anthocyanins give blueberries and foods like red cabbage, red grapes and other berries their blue-red colour. Anthocyanins help to neutralize free-radical damage, which is associated with reduced risk of certain cancers and heart disease. In animal studies, blueberries have been proven to improve memory and brain function.[4] Whether this extends to children is unclear.

As an antioxidant, berries rank higher than most fruits and vegetables.[4] Serve them frequently so that your kids will learn to love them. Sprinkle them on yogurt, ice cream and cereal. Frozen berries can be mixed into muffins (page 40) and added to a morning smoothie. Try Jeff's Blueberry Blitz (page 47).

mixed fruit smoothie

This smoothie can be made with any combination of frozen fruit. Try a mixed bag of frozen peaches, strawberries and blueberries.

1 cup mixed frozen fruit
1 banana
½ cup plain yogurt
1 cup milk

• Combine all of the ingredients in a blender and mix until smooth.

Yield: Serves 2 to 3

morning glory smoothie

Adding tofu to your morning smoothie is a great way to give your child a protein boost!

1½ cups orange juice
⅓ cup soft tofu
1½ cups mixed frozen berries

• Combine all of the ingredients in a blender and mix until smooth.

Yield: Serves 3 to 4

weekend breakfasts

The following recipes take a little longer to prepare and are therefore more suitable for weekends or other days when your schedule is a little more relaxed.

ham and cheese breakfast frittata

If you have leftover potatoes from last night's dinner, substitute them for the parboiled ones to save a step.

2 russet or baking potatoes, peeled and cut into 1-inch cubes
1 tbsp canola oil
1 cup packed shredded old Cheddar cheese (approximately ½ lb)
8 slices good-quality Black Forest ham, diced
10 eggs, beaten

• Preheat oven to 350°F.
• In a saucepan, parboil potatoes in boiling water until just tender but not cooked through.
• Drain potatoes.

- In a frying pan, sauté potatoes in oil over medium heat for 10 minutes.
- In a large bowl, combine potatoes, cheese, ham and eggs, and mix thoroughly.
- Pour mixture into greased 8" x 8" baking dish and bake for 35 to 45 minutes or until frittata is cooked through, golden brown around the edge and just firm to touch. If in doubt, insert a knife into the middle of the frittata. It should come out clean.

Yield: Serves 6

Serving Suggestion: Serve with whole wheat bread, Fruit Salad (page 65) and orange juice.

spinach, tomato, mushroom and feta frittata

½ lb mushrooms, sliced
2 tbsp canola oil
1 cup fresh baby spinach, stems removed
1 cup crumbled feta cheese
1 tomato, diced
⅓ cup chopped fresh basil
10 eggs, beaten
¼ tsp salt
¼ tsp freshly ground pepper

- Preheat oven to 350°F.
- In a large frying pan, sauté mushrooms in oil for 10 minutes over medium heat and set aside.
- Using the same pan, wilt spinach until cooked (approximately 3 minutes). Once cool, squeeze spinach to drain excess liquid, then dice.
- In a large bowl, combine mushrooms, spinach, cheese, tomatoes, basil, eggs, salt and pepper. Mix thoroughly.

• Pour into a greased 8" x 8" baking dish and cook for 35 to 45 minutes or until frittata is cooked through, golden brown around the edges and just firm to touch. If in doubt, insert a knife into the middle of the frittata. It should come out clean.

Yield: Serves 6

Serving Suggestion: Serve with whole wheat toast and a fruit smoothie.

nutrition facts table

Nutrition labelling is now mandatory on most packaged foods.[5] Canada's Food Guide recommends Canadians read and compare Nutrition Facts tables to choose products that contain less fat, saturated fat, trans fats, sugar and sodium.[6] Bear in mind that the nutrients and calories shown are for the serving size listed at the top of the Nutrition Facts table.

standard format makes information easier to find and use

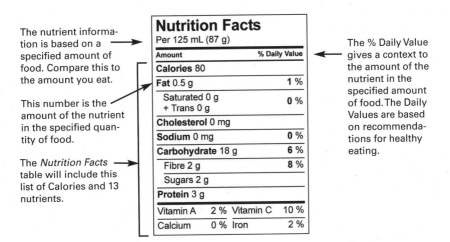

The nutrient information is based on a specified amount of food. Compare this to the amount you eat.

This number is the amount of the nutrient in the specified quantity of food.

The *Nutrition Facts* table will include this list of Calories and 13 nutrients.

The % Daily Value gives a context to the amount of the nutrient in the specified amount of food. The Daily Values are based on recommendations for healthy eating.

Nutrition Facts
Per 125 mL (87 g)

Amount	% Daily Value
Calories 80	
Fat 0.5 g	1 %
Saturated 0 g + Trans 0 g	0 %
Cholesterol 0 mg	
Sodium 0 mg	0 %
Carbohydrate 18 g	6 %
Fibre 2 g	8 %
Sugars 2 g	
Protein 3 g	

Vitamin A	2 %	Vitamin C	10 %
Calcium	0 %	Iron	2 %

Source: Nutrition Facts Table, Health Canada, January 2003. Adapted and reproduced with the permission of the Minister of Public Works and Government Services Canada, 2007.

steel cut oats with caramelized green apples

Steel cut oats have a slightly nuttier and chewier texture than other types of oats. They have also been through less processing than regular rolled oats, and as a result take longer to cook. Although all oats have the same nutritional value, steel cut oats have a lower glycemic index (GI). This means they are digested more slowly. As a result, they provide a steady stream of energy which may keep you feeling full longer. To enjoy the benefits of steel cut oats on weekday mornings, consider cooking them the night before. Refrigerate and reheat in the morning.

2 cups water
½ cup steel cut oats
2 green apples, peeled and diced
2 tbsp brown sugar
Dash cinnamon
1 tbsp non-hydrogenated margarine
½ cup milk
3 slices green apple for garnish

• Bring water to a brisk boil.
• Add oats and stir.
• When oatmeal begins to thicken, reduce heat and simmer uncovered for 30 minutes, stirring occasionally.

• While oats are cooking, place diced apples in a small mixing bowl and sprinkle with sugar and cinnamon. Mix until coated.
• In saucepan, melt margarine over medium heat; add apples and sauté until they begin to caramelize (approximately 10 minutes). Set aside.
• Once oatmeal is cooked, add apples and milk. Mix to combine.
• Ladle porridge into bowls and garnish with a slice of green apple.

Yield: Serves 3

Serving Suggestion: Accompany with a glass of orange juice.

breakfast

just the facts: kids and constipation

Constipation means having infrequent and hard, often painful bowel movements—and it's very common in childhood. Young children require a diet high in fat, which places them at risk for the problem. Constipation often begins when an infant is introduced to solid foods, such as baby cereals. It can worsen when an infant transitions from breast milk (which is easily digested) to infant formula or cow's milk.

Foods that are common culprits in the constipation cycle include hard cheeses and other full-fat dairy products, white rice, white pasta, white bread, potatoes and bananas. While no one food alone is the cause of constipation, an excessive intake of these foods in a susceptible child can bring it on.

To prevent constipation, offer plenty of water, particularly during warmer months. You might also need to limit dairy products. (See page 14 for the recommended number of servings of Milk and Alternatives per day.) Offer high-fibre foods, such as whole grains, legumes, fruits and vegetables. See Fibre Facts for a list of high-fibre foods (page 33).

Exercise also plays an important role in preventing constipation by prompting contraction of the muscles of the abdominal wall and the muscles of the digestive tract.

If a higher-fibre diet, increased water intake and increased exercise don't result in alleviation of constipation, see your child's doctor.

Water should not be offered to a baby under the age of 6 months, that is, before he is taking solid food, because it may decrease his appetite for breast milk or formula. Formula-fed babies over 6 months taking solid food do not need more than 32 ounces of formula per day. By the age of 2 years, toddlers should transition to the cup and only drink 2 cups (16 oz) of milk or fortified soy beverage per day.

breakfast cups

For toddlers, you may want to simplify this recipe by omitting the basil, tomatoes and even the cheese. Alternatively, you could substitute 4 thin slices of green onion for the basil in each breakfast cup.

4 slices Black Forest ham
4 eggs
¼ cup shredded
   Cheddar cheese
1 tomato, seeded and
   diced
1 tsp chopped fresh basil

• Preheat oven to 350°F.
• Using standard-size muffin tin, grease 4 muffin cups.
• Line muffin cups with ham.
• Crack 1 egg into small bowl and whisk with ¼ tsp basil and 1 tbsp diced tomato.

• Pour egg into ham cup and top with 1 tbsp cheese.
• Repeat with the other 3 eggs.
• Place pan in oven and bake for 15 minutes. Remove from oven and cool on rack for 5 minutes.
• Remove breakfast cups from muffin tins and serve.

Yield: Serves 4

Serving Suggestion: Serve with whole wheat toast and a Raspberry Banana Smoothie (page 47)

coping with small appetites

Many healthy young children have small appetites and generally eat fewer and smaller servings of food. This can be stressful for parents.

When dealing with small appetites, it is important to respect your child's individuality. Avoid pressuring your child to eat, which often backfires and can cause her to be turned off food. Instead, offer small portions and allow for seconds. Serve nutritious snacks between meals and remember that 1 serving from a food group can be broken into smaller amounts and served throughout the day. For example, ½ cup milk served with your child's breakfast cereal and another ½ cup served with lunch is 1 serving of Milk and Alternatives.

Children with smaller appetites can become iron deficient, so parents should make an effort to serve nutrient-rich foods that are high in iron. Such foods include enriched grain products, red meat, peas, beans and lentils. Because these children are eating smaller amounts of food, constipation can also be an issue. To prevent this, offer water, as well as high-fibre foods such as fruits, vegetables and whole grains. These children also benefit from eating energy-dense foods, such as nut butters, cheese, higher-fat yogurts and whole milk. If you are still worried, see your doctor, who will likely reassure you that there is no cause for alarm.

raspberry claflouti

Claflouti is a traditional French dish that can be enjoyed either as a dessert or for a special weekend breakfast.

½ lb fresh raspberries
1 tbsp unsalted butter
¼ cup granulated sugar (divided)
Zest of half a lemon (optional)
3 large eggs
1 cup milk
1 tsp vanilla extract
Pinch salt
½ cup all-purpose flour

- Preheat oven to 425°F.
- Sauté raspberries in butter with 2 tbsp of the sugar and lemon zest (if using) until berries are just soft and exude a little juice, about 2 minutes.
- In a separate bowl or blender, beat eggs, remaining sugar, milk, vanilla and salt.
- Slowly add flour and mix until lumps disappear.
- Evenly spread fruit and juice in greased 8" x 8" pan or gratin dish and top with batter.
- Bake for 20 to 30 minutes or until edges are puffed and golden.

Yield: Serves 4 to 5

kids and cholesterol

Cholesterol is a fat-like waxy substance that comes from our diet and is also made in the liver. Cholesterol serves many useful purposes, including insulating nerves, as well as playing a crucial role in the production of vitamin D and other hormones.

Unfortunately, high levels of cholesterol are linked with heart disease. Traditionally considered an adult condition, elevated cholesterol levels in children are increasing. These early elevations seem to put the child at risk for elevated cholesterol levels in adulthood, which, in turn, increase the risk of coronary artery disease.

Risk factors for elevated cholesterol include eating a diet high in saturated and trans fats, and having a family history of high cholesterol levels. Others who may benefit from screening are those who are overweight, who smoke, who have high blood pressure or diabetes, or who are inactive.

It is recommended that adults eat a diet containing no more than 35% total fat with no more than 10% saturated fat (i.e., from animal sources). Children under the age of 2 years require a higher-fat intake (approximately 50%) in order to sustain adequate growth and development. But children over the age of 2 years still require adequate calories for growth and nutrition, which is difficult to attain on a low-fat diet. A diet containing a variety of choices, including complex carbohydrates and lower-fat foods, is appropriate.

During early adolescence, fat intake can be gradually decreased toward that of adult recommended levels.

pancakes

Pancakes cooked from scratch are delicious! Extra batter can be stored in the fridge for up to 24 hours, so if you make the batter on Sunday, you can easily cook pancakes for Monday's breakfast.

whole wheat double berry pancakes

Make the following recipe with any of your child's favourite fruit combinations. Instead of blueberries and raspberries, try adding sliced strawberries, grated apple or diced banana. If you don't have fresh fruit, use frozen instead. When using frozen fruit that's bigger than blueberries, dice it so you don't get chunks of cold fruit in your pancakes. To boost the antioxidant power of your pancakes, serve them with Homemade Blueberry Sauce (page 247) instead of maple syrup.

1 cup all-purpose flour
1 tsp baking powder
½ tsp baking soda
½ cup whole wheat flour
2 tbsp granulated sugar
2 large eggs
2½ cups low-fat butter-
　milk (1.5% MF)

1 tbsp melted non-
　hydrogenated
　margarine
2 tsp vanilla extract
¾ cup fresh or frozen
　blueberries
¾ cup fresh or frozen
　raspberries

- If using frozen berries, defrost them.
- In a large bowl, sift together all-purpose flour, baking powder and baking soda.
- Add whole wheat flour and sugar and mix to blend.
- In another bowl, with a fork, mix together eggs, buttermilk, margarine and vanilla.
- With same fork, mix together wet and dry ingredients until just incorporated and lumpy batter forms.

- Pancakes should be cooked either on a hot griddle or in a large frying pan. If you are not cooking the pancakes on a non-stick surface, a thin coating of canola oil or vegetable spray should be spread across pan prior to cooking.
- Heat frying pan over medium heat until drops of water sizzle on the pan. Pour ⅓ cup of the batter onto the pan.
- Sprinkle with berries and cook pancakes over medium heat. The pancake is ready to turn when the surface is covered with gently breaking bubbles, the edges are dull and other side is golden brown, 3 to 4 minutes. If you are unsure if your pancake is ready, lift the edges to check for colour.
- Turn and cook until underside is lightly browned, approximately 3 minutes.
- Once cooked, pancakes can be kept warm in an oven preheated to 140°F.

Yield: 12 pancakes (serves 4 to 6)

Serving Suggestion: Serve with a Raspberry Banana Smoothie (page 47).

buckwheat banana pancakes

Buckwheat is a good source of both protein and fibre. Although often considered a whole grain, it's actually the seed of a plant that's related to rhubarb.

1 cup all-purpose flour
1 tsp baking powder
½ tsp baking soda
½ cup buckwheat flour
2 tbsp granulated sugar
1 tsp cinnamon
1 tsp ground nutmeg

2½ cups low-fat buttermilk (1.5% MF)
2 eggs
1 tbsp melted non-hydrogenated margarine
1 tsp vanilla extract
2 or 3 bananas, sliced

- In a large bowl, sift together flour, baking powder and baking soda.
- Add buckwheat flour, sugar, cinnamon and nutmeg and mix until blended.
- In another bowl, with a fork, mix together buttermilk, eggs, margarine and vanilla.
- Combine dry ingredients and wet ingredients until incorporated and lumpy batter forms.
- Pancakes should be cooked either on a hot griddle or in a large frying pan. If you are not cooking your pancakes on a non-stick surface, a thin coating of oil or vegetable spray should be spread across pan prior to cooking.
- Heat frying pan over medium heat until drops of water sizzle on the pan. Pour ⅓ cup batter onto the pan. Place 4 or 5 slices of banana on each pancake.
- Cook pancakes over medium heat. The pancake is ready to turn when the surface has a few popped bubbles, the edges are dull and the underside is lightly browned, approximately 4 minutes.
- Turn pancake and cook until done, approximately 3 to 4 minutes.
- Once cooked, pancakes can be kept warm in an oven preheated to 140°F.

Yield: 12 pancakes (serves 4 to 6)

Serving Suggestion: Serve with orange juice and Fruit Salad (page 65).

the abuse of juice

Fruit juice can be a part of a balanced diet, and 100% fruit juices are a good way to get a serving of fruit. Juices contain vitamin C and some minerals but usually lack the fibre found in the whole fruit. Half a cup of fruit juice can count as a serving of fruit. The problem with drinking juice is that it is very easy to overdo it.

Young children usually have a preference for sweet things and will often take juice over water if given a choice. Children who drink too much fruit juice may not feel as hungry, so they miss out on important nutrients that other foods provide. The acidity and fructose content of fruit juice can be damaging to tooth enamel and can feed plaque-forming bacteria, leading to cavities. As a child gets older, this preference for sweet drinks will likely move from fruit juices to soda pop.

How much juice to offer, if any? According to Canada's Food Guide, 1 serving is equivalent to ½ cup. Diluting is not recommended. With diluting comes the tendency to drink more, continually bathing the teeth in plaque-forming bacteria. It is best to stick to 1 serving or less per day.

german apple pancake

Our children love these pancakes so much we often serve them as dessert. Fuji apples are a good choice for cooking. They are sweet in flavour and tend to be available all year long.

3 tbsp non-hydrogenated
  margarine
2 apples (approximately
  1 lb), peeled, cored and
  sliced into ¼-inch
  segments
¼ tsp cinnamon
¼ cup granulated sugar
  (divided)
1 tbsp orange zest
3 large eggs
½ cup milk
1 tsp vanilla extract
½ cup all-purpose flour,
  sifted

• Preheat oven to 425°F.
• In a large frying pan, melt margarine over medium heat.
• Remove 1 tbsp of the melted margarine and set aside in a mixing bowl.
• To the frying pan add apple slices, cinnamon, 2 tbsp of the sugar and orange zest and sauté until apples can be pierced easily with a fork but are not mushy, approximately 12 minutes.
• In a separate bowl or blender, beat together eggs, remaining sugar, reserved melted margarine, milk and vanilla.
• Slowly add flour to wet ingredients and mix until just incorporated.
• Evenly pour apples and their syrup into greased ovenproof 8" x 8" pan or gratin dish and top with batter.
• Bake for 20 minutes or until puffed and golden.

Yield: Serves 4

Serving Suggestion: Serve with orange juice and a fruit salad.

french toast banana sandwiches

This is a fun alternative to traditional French toast. These sandwiches are fairly large, so young children will probably eat only half a sandwich. If making this for the whole family, the recipe can easily be doubled. Again, serving this with a yummy fruit sauce instead of maple syrup will boost its nutritional value. For a special treat, press a few chocolate chips into the banana mixture.

2 eggs

1 cup milk

½ tsp vanilla extract

½ tsp ground nutmeg (optional)

¼ tsp cinnamon

4 slices whole wheat bread

1 tbsp non-hydrogenated margarine

1 large banana, mashed

1 tbsp chocolate chips (optional)

- Preheat oven to 350°F.
- In a bowl, whisk together eggs, milk, vanilla, nutmeg (if using) and cinnamon.
- Soak 2 slices of bread in mixture until saturated.
- In a frying pan, melt margarine over medium heat.
- Place both bread slices in pan and sauté until golden brown and almost crisp, 8 to 10 minutes. Turn bread and sauté for another minute.
- Spread half of the mashed banana onto the crisp side of one of the bread slices. If using chocolate chips, press a few into banana mixture. Then place the other piece of the bread, crisp side down, on top of the banana to make a sandwich.
- Continue to sauté until both sides are golden brown and crispy, 3 to 4 minutes per side.

- Place sandwich in oven for 5 to 7 minutes to make sure banana is warmed through.
- Repeat above steps to make the second sandwich.

Yield: Serves 2

Serving Suggestion: Serve with Strawberry Mango Smoothie (page 46)

helping your child develop a positive body image

Children who feel comfortable with their bodies are more confident. Developing a positive body image is becoming increasingly difficult as our children are bombarded with unrealistic body images. Many of these images come from the media. Just like adults, children come in a variety of shapes and sizes, and these differences are determined largely by genetics. Children gain height and weight at different rates, and it is not uncommon for them to gain weight prior to growth spurts. This can make even the most confident child feel chubby.

To help your children develop a positive body image, focus on them, not their weight. Overweight children know they have a problem. They need love, acceptance and support, not criticism or ridicule. Lead by example. Children who see their parents eating a healthy diet and maintaining an active lifestyle are more likely to do so themselves. For tips to help your family maintain a healthy weight, see Just Do It! (page 24) and Weight Maintenance (page 195).

fruit

fruit kebabs with minty yogurt dip

Served with a Minty Yogurt Dip, these kebabs make a delicious breakfast, dessert or after-school snack.

½ pineapple, peeled and
   cored
½ cantaloupe, peeled and
   seeded
2 kiwi fruit, peeled
20 strawberries, hulled
14 wooden skewers
Minty Yogurt Dip (recipe
   follows)

• Cut fruit into 1-inch cubes.
• Thread 5 pieces of fruit onto each skewer. Serve with Minty Yogurt Dip.

Yield: 12 to 14 skewers

minty yogurt dip

1½ cups Balkan-style plain
   yogurt (above 3% MF)
1½ tbsp liquid honey
1 rounded tbsp finely
   chopped fresh mint

• Combine above ingredients and mix thoroughly.

Yield: 1½ cups

breakfast

fruit salad

1 mango, peeled and cut into cubes

12 strawberries, hulled and sliced

2 kiwi fruit, peeled, cut in half and sliced

1 cup fresh raspberries or blueberries

1 banana, sliced

1 tbsp freshly squeezed lemon juice

½ tsp finely chopped fresh mint

½ tsp granulated sugar

• In a bowl, combine all of the ingredients and mix thoroughly. Serve immediately to prevent fruit from turning brown.

lunch

Packing school lunches is the bane of many parents' existence. Too many children take the same old sandwich to school every day. With a little forethought and creativity, nutritious lunches can be prepared in no time at all.

The first step is to get your children involved. They are more likely to eat a lunch they have helped make. Teach them about Canada's Food Guide and ask them to choose one food from each of the 4 groups.

It is important that your child's lunch contain a source of complex carbohydrates. These take longer for the body to break down and therefore provide a sustained source of energy to keep your child going. Sources of complex carbohydrates include bread, rice, legumes and pasta. In addition, try to pack at least 2 servings of Vegetables and Fruit. For example, a healthy lunch may contain a sandwich or a Thermos of warm food, a drink and 2 to 3 additional snacks: one snack should be a vegetable, one a fruit and the third could be a granola bar or yogurt. For nutritious snack ideas, see Snacks to Pack (page 97).

Whether packing a wrap, pita pocket or traditional sandwich, always choose whole grain breads and read labels carefully. That way you are sure to avoid those pesky trans fats found in many baked goods. Lightly toast the bread before making the sandwich. This helps prevent sandwiches from going soggy. Lunches containing mayonnaise, eggs, dairy products and meats should always be packed with an ice pack. If you do not have an ice pack, you can freeze water or juice in a reusable container. This will keep your child's lunch fresh and the drink will be thawed by lunchtime. For more sandwich ideas, see Sandwiches to Go! (page 69).

When it comes to packing drinks, choose water, milk or good-quality fruit and vegetable juices. Milk can be kept cold in a Thermos or by packing it in a reusable container next to an ice pack. Again, be sure to read labels carefully, as many drinks marketed for children are full of unwanted sugars and additives. Be wary of so-called "fruit drinks." They are often high in sugar, contain unnecessary additives and have very little real fruit juice. Instead, choose 100% real fruit or vegetable juice without any added sugar. As well, children should be encouraged to drink water throughout the day to alleviate thirst, especially after physical activity.

Packed in a Thermos, homemade soups, beans, pastas and leftovers make delicious alternatives to sandwiches. Your child's favourite pasta sauce can be frozen in ice cube trays to facilitate easy last-minute school lunches. The night before, place cubes of sauce in the fridge to defrost. In the morning, cook the pasta and toss with sauce over medium heat

lunch

sandwiches to go!

- Tuna salad
- Veggie Wrap (page 77)
- Salmon salad
- Mexican Wrap (page 79)
- Egg salad
- Veggie Pita Pockets (page 82)
- Cheddar cheese and cucumber
- Mighty Tuna Pita Pockets (page 74)
- Cheese and veggies
- Cottage cheese, avocado and cucumber
- Ham, veggies and cheese
- Shredded cheese, sliced apple and sliced pear
- Jam* and cream cheese‡
- Peanut butter and grated apple
- Pickles and cheese
- Chicken, cheese and salad
- Tuna salad mixed with canned corn
- Cream cheese,‡ cucumber and grated carrot
- Any nut butter and jam*
- Hummus and sliced cucumber
- Turkey, cheese and veggies
- Cream cheese mixed with finely diced dried fruit
- Chicken Salad Sandwich (page 70)
- Veggie Hummus Pita Pocket (page 75)
- Chopped hard-boiled eggs mixed with canned tuna or salmon

* Choose low-sugar jams that are high in fruit.

‡ For the older child and adult, choose low-fat cream cheese.

until warmed through (3 to 4 minutes). See the pasta section (page 184) for additional pasta ideas. Also see the Beans and Grains (page 157) section, as beans also pack well. If you do not have time to make baked beans from scratch, canned brown beans are a good substitute.

Throughout the book, look for the lunch box icon following many of the recipes. It indicates which recipes pack well, making nutritious additions to your child's lunch.

packable lunches

The following recipes travel well, making healthy additions to packed lunches.

chicken salad sandwich

An easy way to increase your child's consumption of vegetables is to add them to sandwiches. Remember to choose folate-rich dark-coloured greens such as arugula, romaine lettuce and spinach.

1 skinless, boneless chicken breast, cooked
1 green onion, sliced
½ stalk celery, diced
2 tbsp mayonnaise
Salt and freshly ground pepper
4 slices whole wheat bread
4 leaves romaine lettuce, shredded
6 slices cucumber

• Dice chicken breast into small bite-sized pieces.
• Mix chicken with onion, celery and mayonnaise.
• Add salt and pepper to taste.
• If the sandwich is for a lunch box, lightly toast bread to prevent it from getting soggy.
• Evenly spread chicken salad on 2 of the bread slices.
• Top each with romaine lettuce, cucumbers and the remaining bread.

lunch

- Cut in half to serve.

 *Yield: Serves 2*

Serving Suggestion: Serve with cantaloupe cubes and a glass of milk.

pickle roll-up

1 tbsp low-fat cream
  cheese
1 slice whole wheat
  bread, crusts removed
1 tbsp shredded Cheddar
  cheese
¼ dill pickle, cut
lengthwise

- Spread cream cheese over bread.

- Evenly scatter with Cheddar cheese.
- Place pickle on one side of the bread and roll up.
- Cut crosswise into 4 pieces to serve.

 *Yield: Serves 1*

calcium for growing bones

Calcium is required for blood clotting, muscle contraction and relaxation, nerve impulse transmission, and the calcification and strengthening of bones and teeth. Adequate calcium intake is necessary to maximize peak bone mass and to minimize the risk of fractures in adolescence and the risk of developing osteoporosis in adulthood. Peak bone mass is achieved by the second decade of life. Insufficient calcium intake during the growing years cannot be made up for later in life. Therefore, it is important your children get enough calcium now.

Important dietary sources of calcium include dairy products, tofu, broccoli, leafy greens, chickpeas, baked beans, nuts, canned salmon (with bones), vitamin D–fortified soy beverage, as well as breast milk and formula for infants.

lunch

what should i do if my child won't—or can't—drink milk?

Canada's Food Guide recommends children consume 2 cups of milk or fortified soy beverage per day. Drinking milk is an easy way to ensure your child gets enough calcium and vitamin D, which are essential for building healthy bones and teeth.

However, some children do not like milk or, because of a milk intolerance or allergy, cannot drink it. For those children, fortified soy beverage is a good substitute. When buying soy beverage, read the label to make sure it is fortified with both vitamin D and calcium. Although some rice beverages, as well as orange juices, are also fortified with calcium and vitamin D, they do not contain the same amount of protein as milk and therefore are not comparable.

We know that more than one-third of children aged 4 to 9 do not get the recommended 2 servings of Milk and Alternatives per day.[1] To ensure that this doesn't happen to your child, offer milk or fortified soy beverage with meals, yogurt for dessert and cheese in salads or sandwiches. As it can be difficult to get enough vitamin D and/or calcium without eating dairy products, you might benefit from consultation with either your doctor or a registered dietitian to see whether calcium and/or vitamin D supplementation is advisable.

fiona's veggie sandwich

Named after an old friend, Fiona's sandwiches were the envy of Brenda's school lunchroom. Fiona's trick was to pack the tomato separately to prevent the sandwich from getting soggy.

1 tsp mayonnaise
2 slices whole wheat bread, toasted
¼ avocado, sliced
Freshly squeezed lemon juice
3 slices Cheddar cheese
2 leaves butter lettuce
1 pickle, thinly sliced
1 thin slice red onion
4 slices tomato
Pinch salt
Freshly ground pepper

mother knows best

Milk is an important source of calcium throughout life. During adolescence, milk intake tends to decline, partly due to an increase in soft drink consumption. A recent study indicates that mothers who drank more milk had daughters who drank more milk and fewer soft drinks.[2] Therefore, it is essential parents set a good example by choosing milk whenever possible.

- Evenly spread mayonnaise on both pieces of toast.
- Top with avocado and squeeze with lemon to prevent avocado from turning brown.
- Top with cheese, lettuce, pickle, onion, tomato (if eating right away), salt and pepper to taste.
- If packing for a school lunch, place the tomato in a separate container to prevent the sandwich from going soggy.

 Yield: Serves 1

mighty tuna pita pockets

Watercress is high in calcium, but its peppery taste may not appeal to young children. If that is the case with your child, use shredded romaine lettuce instead.

1 can (170 g) light tuna, drained

1 rounded tbsp mayonnaise

1 squeeze fresh lemon juice (optional)

1 tbsp red onion, finely diced

½ stalk celery, finely diced

1 whole wheat pita

8 slices cucumber

1 rounded cup watercress, stalks removed and roughly chopped

> TIP: If you're having a tough time opening your pita bread, warm it in microwave for 30 seconds. When warmed, pita bread opens with ease.

- Mix together tuna, mayonnaise, lemon juice (if using), onion and celery.
- Cut pita in half and open up pockets.
- Spread half of the tuna mixture inside each pita pocket on one side only.
- Place 4 cucumber slices on top of each.
- Divide watercress in half and stuff into pita pockets.

 Yield: Serves 1 adult or 2 small children

lunch

veggie hummus pita pockets

If packing this for lunch, leave out the tomato or pack it separately to avoid making the sandwich soggy.

1 whole wheat pita

4 tbsp Middle Eastern Hummus (page 113) or store-bought equivalent

1 carrot, grated

8 slices cucumber

4 slices tomato (optional)

2 leaves romaine lettuce, shredded

1 thin slice onion, halved (optional)

• Cut pita in half and open up pockets.

• Spread half of the hummus inside each pita pocket on one side only.

• Stuff desired veggies into each pocket.

 Yield: Serves 1 adult or 2 small children

coping with food jags

Food jags occur when children insist on eating the same food or foods repeatedly. Food jags are one of the ways children assert their independence. This is a normal part of development, and the less you make of it the better. If your child insists on eating a peanut butter and jam sandwich for lunch every day, try broadening her horizons by making the sandwich with different types of nut butters, different fruit spreads and different whole grain breads (for example, pita bread, wraps). You can even try to sneak a few slices of banana into the sandwich. Add more variety by serving the sandwich with different fruits, vegetables and beverages. But whatever you do, don't get into a battle over food.

what is the difference between food allergies and food intolerances?

Food intolerance is an umbrella term encompassing all adverse reactions to foods. This can include an allergy, an enzyme deficiency, reactions to food additives and food sensitivities. For instance, people with lactose intolerance cannot tolerate dairy products with lactose (the sugar found in milk). They are not allergic to the food. Those who are sensitive to MSG may develop flushing and headaches if they consume large quantities of it. Young children will sometimes develop behavioural reactions after eating large amounts of chocolate. Usually such reactions are caused by the caffeine and caffeine-like substances in the chocolate and not the sugar, as most parents wrongly assume.

In general, food intolerances not due to allergies are not life-threatening, whereas food allergies may well be. An allergic reaction to food occurs when the body's immune system over-reacts to a food protein or additive. The symptoms of an allergy range from itchy eyes, runny nose, skin rashes, nasal congestion, cramps, nausea, vomiting and diarrhea to life-threatening anaphylaxis. Anaphylaxis is a rare condition characterized by mouth or throat swelling, difficulty breathing and/or collapse and shock.

The majority of food allergies in children are caused by one of the following foods: milk, peanuts, soy, fish (including crustaceans and shellfish), eggs, wheat, tree nuts, sesame seeds and sulphites. It is estimated that over 600,000 Canadians (2% of the population) could be affected by a life-threatening allergy, and the numbers are increasing, especially among children.[3] If you suspect your child has an allergy or intolerance, see your doctor immediately. For more information on anaphylaxis, see page 89.

veggie wrap

1½ tbsp light cream
cheese

1 large soft whole wheat
flour tortilla (approxi-
mately 10 inches)

1 tsp mayonnaise

1 leaf romaine lettuce,
shredded

5 thin slices sweet red
pepper

5 thin slices sweet green
pepper

½ carrot, grated

5 thin slices cucumber,
diced

1 tsp red onion, diced
(optional)

1 dill pickle, quartered
lengthwise

- Evenly spread cream cheese over tortilla.
- Spread mayonnaise on top.
- Evenly scatter lettuce, peppers, carrot, cucumbers, and red onion (if using) on top of tortilla.
- Place pickles end to end at the edge of the wrap.
- Fold opposite ends of tortilla inward 1½ inches from edge. Roll up tightly to enclose filling.
- If making for a packed lunch, immediately wrap tortilla in plastic wrap or foil so that it stays rolled up.

 Yield: Serves 1

Serving Suggestion: Serve with a glass of milk and a piece of fruit.

managing lactose intolerance

Lactose intolerance, unlike true milk allergy (which involves the immune system), occurs when there is insufficient lactase, which is the enzyme needed to digest lactose, the sugar found in milk. Lactase activity is the highest after birth. Because of this, lactose intolerance is extremely rare in infancy. However, lactase activity declines dramatically throughout childhood and adolescence, and some children develop lactose intolerance. If this is the case, your child may suffer from cramps, bloating, gas and diarrhea after drinking milk. It is also not uncommon to become temporarily lactose intolerant after an illness. Anyone can develop lactose intolerance; however, those of Asian, First Nations and African American descent are most susceptible.

People's ability to tolerate lactose varies widely, and in most instances, being lactose intolerant does not mean that dairy products need to be totally eliminated. In fact, excluding all dairy products can lead to nutrient deficiencies, as dairy products are a major source of calcium and vitamin D. Many people with lactose intolerance are able to eat yogurt because the live bacterial cultures in it partially digest the lactose. Many can also eat hard cheeses and cottage cheese because most of the lactose is removed while the cheese is processed. Lactose-free milk is available at most grocery stores. Alternatively, taking a lactase supplement before consuming dairy products provides the enzyme needed to safely digest them. If you suspect lactose intolerance, see your doctor.

lunch

mexican wrap

The following is delicious either warm or cold. When serving as part of a lunch to go, pack the salsa on the side to prevent the wrap from going soggy.

2 tbsp canned refried beans

1 large whole wheat soft flour tortilla (approximately 10 inches)

1 leaf romaine lettuce, shredded

¼ cup shredded Cheddar cheese

5 thin slices sweet green pepper, diced

3 tbsp canned black beans, rinsed and drained

¼ avocado, sliced into thirds

1 squeeze fresh lemon juice

¼ cup mild salsa, drained to remove excess liquid

1½ tbsp sour cream (optional)

• Evenly spread refried beans over tortilla.

• Evenly scatter lettuce, cheese, green pepper and black beans over tortilla.

• Place the 3 avocado slices end to end in the centre of the wrap and sprinkle with lemon juice to prevent them from going brown.

• Drizzle with salsa, and sour cream (if using).

• Fold opposite ends of tortilla inward 1½ inches from edge. Roll up tightly to enclose filling.

• If making for a packed lunch, immediately wrap tortilla in plastic wrap or foil so that it stays rolled up.

• To serve warm, heat in microwave until warmed through, approximately 30 seconds.

 Yield: Serves 1

Serving Suggestion: Serve with a glass of milk and veggie sticks.

picky eaters

Young children between the ages of 2 and 5 are notoriously finicky. Although frustrating for parents, this is a very normal part of childhood. How quickly a child moves through this stage often depends on how it is handled. Remember, it is the parents' responsibility to choose and prepare the food, and it is up to the child to decide what and how much to eat. This approach to feeding will eliminate dinnertime battles.

Children who are anxious about eating may develop feeding problems and even eating disorders. It doesn't matter if your children choose not to eat carrots, as long as they are eating other orange fruits and vegetables. Instead of focusing on a single meal, keep your eye on the real goal: to raise a healthy eater. Be reassured that most finicky eaters become food-loving adults! For ideas on how to handle picky eaters, see Hints for Handling Picky Eaters (page 86).

west coast salmon pita pockets

1 can (213 g) salmon, drained

1 rounded tbsp mayonnaise

½ stalk celery, finely diced

1 green onion, thinly sliced

1 tsp chopped fresh dill (optional)

1 generous squeeze fresh lemon juice

2 whole wheat pitas

8 slices cucumber

2 leaves romaine lettuce, shredded

• Mix together salmon, mayonnaise, celery, onion, dill (if using) and lemon juice.

• Cut pita pockets in half and open up pockets.

lunch

- Spread approximately 2 tbsp of the salmon mixture inside each pita pocket on one side only.
- Place 2 cucumber slices on top of salmon.
- Fill each pocket with shredded romaine lettuce.

 Yield: Serves 4 small children or 2 adults

Serving Suggestion: Serve with Fruit Kebabs (page 64) and a glass of milk.

lunch box safety

School lunches tend to sit at room temperature all morning long. This increases the risk of bacterial overgrowth and contamination. The following tips will help keep your child's lunch safe.

1) Choose a thermally insulated lunch kit.
2) Keep hot foods hot by packing them in an insulated Thermos. Preheat the Thermos with boiling water prior to putting hot food in.
3) Keep cold foods cold by packing them with an ice pack. If you don't have an ice pack, water or juice can be frozen in a reusable container.
4) Anything you take out of your refrigerator must be kept cold. Such items include meats, eggs, dairy products and any sandwiches mixed with mayonnaise. Be sure to pack these foods together and next to an ice pack.
5) Wash lunch boxes daily with hot soapy water.

veggie pita pockets

If you are lucky enough to have a child who's a veggie lover, serve these sandwiches as often as possible. If sending to school, omit both the Herb Dip (if using) and the tomato or pack the tomato separately. A couple of slices of Cheddar cheese can be added, if desired.

1 whole wheat pita

1 squeeze fresh lemon
   juice

4 slices avocado

1 tbsp light cream cheese

4 slices tomato

4 slices cucumber

4 slices sweet red pepper

1 tbsp finely diced red
   onion (optional)

2 tbsp Fresh Herb Dip
   (see page 110) or 1 tsp
   mayonnaise

2 leaves romaine lettuce,
   shredded

• Cut pita in half and open up pockets.

• Squeeze lemon over avocado.

• Evenly spread cream cheese inside each pocket.

• Divide vegetables in half and stuff into each pocket.

• Drizzle 1 tbsp Fresh Herb Dip (if using) over each pita pocket to serve. If using mayonnaise, evenly spread onto each pita pocket.

Yield: Serves 2 small children or 1 adult

weekend lunches

The following recipes do not travel well and are therefore best enjoyed at home.

jeff's meatball sandwich

Served with veggie sticks, this meal makes a nutritious lunch or dinner. The number of meatballs per sandwich will depend on appetites. For small children, 2 mashed meatballs on half a bagel are probably sufficient. Those with larger appetites may prefer 3 to 4 meatballs.

1 whole wheat bagel
4 to 8 meatballs in Tuscan
   Tomato Sauce (page 187)
$2/3$ cup shredded mozzarella cheese

• Cut bagel in half and toast lightly. This prevents the bagel from going soggy when topped with tomato sauce.
• Meanwhile, heat meatballs until warmed through.
• Top each half bagel with meatballs, breaking them up for younger children.

• Evenly sprinkle cheese overtop and broil in oven until cheese begins to bubble, 2 to 3 minutes.

Yield: Serves 2 small children or 1 adult

Serving Suggestion: Serve with veggies and dip and a glass of milk.

what about beverages?

In addition to drinking 2 cups of milk or fortified soy beverage per day, children should be encouraged to drink water frequently. Every day our bodies lose water that must be replaced in order to avoid the risk of dehydration.

Children and the elderly are the most susceptible to dehydration. Symptoms include fatigue, weakness, headache, dizziness and impaired physical performance. Children need more water when it's hot and when they are physically active. Unless your child is a triathlete there is little reason for children to drink sport or energy drinks. In addition to being high in sugar, many of these drinks contain unwanted caffeine and sodium. Drinking water is the best way to hydrate the body. It quenches thirst and contains no calories.

almond butter banana sushi

For those who are stuck in a PB & J rut, almond butter is a nutritious alternative. Almonds are a good source of fibre, protein, vitamin E and heart-healthy monounsaturated fats.

3 tbsp almond butter
1 large whole wheat soft flour tortilla (approximately
   10 inches)
1 banana

- Evenly spread almond butter over tortilla.
- Place banana on one side of the tortilla and roll tortilla around banana.
- Slice roll into 1-inch segments.

Yield: Serves 1

cheese quesadilla

This is a favourite quick-and-easy lunch or dinner at Cheryl's house.

2 large whole wheat soft flour tortillas (approximately 10
inches each)
¼ cup shredded Cheddar cheese (approximately 2 oz)
¼ cup shredded Monterey Jack cheese (approximately 2 oz)
1 tsp finely chopped green onion (optional)
Homemade Salsa (page 111) and/or Guacamole (page 112)

• Place 1 tortilla in large frying pan. Scatter with cheese, and green onion (if using).
• Cover with second tortilla and cook over medium heat for 3 to 4 minutes on each side or until cheese is thoroughly melted and tortilla is beginning to brown.
• Using scissors or a knife, cut quesadilla into triangles and serve with Homemade Salsa and/or homemade Guacamole.

Yield: Serves 2 children or 1 adult

is bottled water better?

Not necessarily. The reality is that city water is much more highly regulated and monitored for quality, whereas bottled water is not. It can legally contain many things that would not be tolerated in municipal drinking water.[4] As well, consider the environmental impact of all those plastic bottles, many of which end up in landfills, not to mention the fuel necessary to ship bottled water around the world.

lunch

hints for handling picky eaters

- Mealtimes should be enjoyable for everyone. Focus on your child and not on what he is eating.
- Don't force or pressure children to eat what they do not like or when they are not hungry. Such tactics can backfire, causing them to be turned off food.
- Make sure both parents and caregivers are in agreement as to how feeding problems should be resolved so you can avoid sending mixed messages.
- Don't use food as a reward. Withholding dessert until the main course is eaten may lead to a preference for dessert and an aversion to vegetables.
- When preparing food for young children, make sure it is cut in manageable bite-sized pieces.
- Limit eating to scheduled meal and snack times. This helps to ensure children have an appetite at mealtimes. Eating should be limited to the high chair or table.
- Even if your child is extremely picky, resist the temptation to offer substitutions such as a jam sandwich instead of fish. Instead, make sure there is a side dish he can fill up on.
- Ensure your child gets plenty of exercise. This is the best way to build up an appetite.
- If your child is still not hungry, look at her milk, juice or soda consumption. Water is the best drink to alleviate thirst and it doesn't affect appetite.

lunch

chicken and cheese quesadilla

This easy-to-prepare last-minute lunch or dinner dish is a yummy way to use up leftover chicken.

2 large whole wheat soft
   flour tortillas (approximately 10 inches each)
½ cup shredded
   Cheddar cheese
   (approximately 4 oz)
4 oz cooked chicken,
   shredded
1 tsp finely chopped
   green onion (optional)
Homemade Salsa (page
   111) and/or Homemade
   Guacamole (page 112)

• Place 1 tortilla in large frying pan. Scatter with cheese, chicken, and green onion (if using).

• Cover with second tortilla and cook over medium heat for 3 to 4 minutes on each side or until cheese is thoroughly melted and tortilla is beginning to brown.
• Using scissors or a knife, cut quesadilla into 8 triangles and serve with Homemade Salsa and/or homemade Guacamole.

Yield: Serves 2 small children or 1 adult

Serving Suggestion: Serve with veggies and dip and a glass of milk.

introducing new foods

- Serve fresh foods and present them in an appealing way.
- Lead by example. Children are more inclined to try new foods if they see you enjoying them.
- Take advantage of peer pressure. Children are more likely to try new foods when they see their friends eating them.
- Play the "colour game" with young children: offer a variety of naturally coloured foods and encourage them to see how many different colours they can eat.
- Reward success with praise and stay positive when foods are rejected.
- Be patient and respect your child's individuality. Just like us, children have different likes and dislikes.
- Start early—new flavours are most readily accepted when introduced before 2 years of age.
- Consider implementing the "one-bite policy": encourage your children to try at least one bite of everything offered at each meal.
- Involve your children in the shopping, preparing and growing of food. This will help familiarize them with different foods. In time, familiarity will lead to acceptance.
- Above all, be persistent. If your child rejects a new food, don't give up. Children are fickle, and with each exposure the chances increase that your child will eventually accept the food.

black bean quesadilla

1 sweet red pepper, seeded and diced

1 tbsp canola oil

2 large soft whole wheat flour tortillas (approximately 10 inches each)

lunch

⅓ cup shredded Cheddar cheese (approximately 4 oz)
2 tbsp black beans, rinsed and drained
Homemade Salsa (page 111) and/or Guacamole (page 112)

• Sauté red peppers in oil over medium heat until peppers are cooked through, 10 to 12 minutes. Set aside.

• Place 1 tortilla in large frying pan. Scatter with cheese and top with black beans and red peppers.

• Place second tortilla on top and cook over medium heat for 3 to 4 minutes per side or until cheese is thoroughly melted and tortilla is beginning to brown.

• Using scissors or a knife, cut quesadilla into triangles and serve with Homemade Salsa and/or homemade Guacamole.

Yield: Serves 2 small children or 1 adult

peanut allergy

Peanut allergies are becoming increasingly common. Allergic reactions to peanuts are often life-threatening or anaphylactic. Symptoms can include hives, nausea, vomiting, wheezing, shortness of breath and shock. If your child has a peanut allergy, strict avoidance of all peanut-containing foods is the rule. Even foods labelled "may contain traces of peanut" must be excluded from the diet. Your child should always carry an adrenalin injector, and caregivers must be trained to use it. If you suspect a child in your care is having a reaction to peanuts, administer the adrenalin, then call 911 immediately.

Occasionally, foods are recalled if they have been contaminated—for instance, with peanuts. Canada's Food Inspection Agency has a free e-mail service that you can sign up for so you will automatically be advised of food recall warnings (www.inspection.gc.ca).

fruit-filled almond butter pita pockets

The following is another alternative to PB & J. When choosing jam, select one that's low in sugar and high in fruit.

1 whole wheat pita
1 rounded tbsp almond
   butter
1 tbsp raspberry jam

10 banana slices
8 fresh raspberries or
   other fruit

- Cut pita in half and open up pockets.
- Spread one side of each pocket with almond butter.
- Spread the other side with jam.
- Stuff half of the banana slices into each pocket. Sprinkle with raspberries or whatever other fruit your child most enjoys.

Yield: Serves 1

peanut butter pizza

Children enjoy decorating their peanut butter pizzas. Lay out the fruit and let them decorate as desired. Any combination of fruit can be used; try blueberries and blackberries for a change.

Partially hydrogenated oil or trans fat is added to some peanut butters to stop them from separating. When buying peanut butter, read ingredient lists carefully and avoid those containing any added fat or sugar. The only ingredient in your peanut butter should be peanuts.

1 whole wheat pita
2 tbsp peanut butter
1 tbsp raspberry jam
½ banana, sliced
6 fresh raspberries

lunch

- Insert a knife into the edge of the pita and carefully separate into halves.
- Evenly spread peanut butter on one side of the pita.
- Sandwich the 2 sides together with the peanut butter in the middle.
- Spread jam on top and decorate with fruit.
- With scissors, cut pizza into triangular slices.

Yield: Serves 1

Serving Suggestion: Serve with veggies and dip.

sprout alert!

Sprouts (including mung beans and alfalfa sprouts) are the germinating form of seeds and beans. Worldwide, at least 37 outbreaks of foodborne illness between 1973 and 2005 have been linked to sprouts. The largest outbreak took place in Japan; 6,000 people got sick and 17 died. In most cases, the illnesses were caused either by E. coli or salmonella.

Raw sprouts contaminated with salmonella have been linked to a number of outbreaks in Canada.[5] Scientists believe that the conditions needed for growing sprouts are ideal for rapid growth of bacteria. Anyone who eats sprouts is at risk. As a result, Health Canada advises that young children, senior citizens and people with weak immune systems avoid sprouts. When eating in restaurants and cafés, check for sprouts in sandwiches and salads. Healthy adults can reduce their risk by buying fresh sprouts, refrigerating them as soon as possible, respecting the "best before date" and eating them cooked.

shrimp pita pockets

Many people wrongly assume children won't like seafood. The reality is that many children love fish, especially those who have been exposed to it at a young age. However, if you have waited to introduce your child to fish, don't be discouraged. Start slowly. Make this yummy pita pocket for yourself and offer your child a small bite. You may be surprised to find your lunch being devoured!

1 whole wheat pita

1 tbsp light cream cheese

½ cup cooked and peeled shrimp

4 slices avocado

4 slices cucumber

1 leaf romaine lettuce, shredded

2 tbsp Fresh Herb Dip (see page 110) or 1 tbsp mayonnaise

- Cut pita in half and open up pockets.
- Spread half of the cream cheese on the inside of each pita pocket.
- Stuff each with half of the shrimp.
- Divide vegetables in half and layer on top of shrimp.
- Drizzle each pocket with half of the Fresh Herb Dip (if using) to serve. If using mayonnaise, evenly spread onto each pita pocket.

Yield: Serves 2 small children or 1 adult

variety is the spice of life

Try not to fall into the trap of sending your children to school with the same lunch every day. A healthy diet is varied. This means eating foods from each of the 4 food groups on a daily basis. It also means varying the foods within each group because different foods have different nutrient values. For example, oranges are rich in vitamin C, apricots in vitamin A. Furthermore, the excessive consumption of a single food can be dangerous because some foods may contain trace elements of a single contaminant. A tuna sandwich is a healthy choice, but eating one every day may increase the risk of mercury toxicity.

When eaten in moderation, most foods are unlikely to cause harm. Explain the importance of a varied diet to your children, and brainstorm together to create a list of 5 different lunches and snacks your children most enjoy. Put the list on the fridge and work your way through it each week. Each term, try to add a few more choices to the list. Use this as an opportunity to teach your children about the importance of healthy eating.

snacks

Most children are unable to eat enough at a single sitting to keep going until their next meal. As a result, snacks constitute an important part of your child's nutritional intake. This is especially true of young children and those going through growth spurts.

Evaluate your child's nutritional intake over several days and use snacks as an opportunity to fill the gaps. Try to create snacks that contain foods from at least 2 of the 4 food groups. For example, if your child has not been eating a lot of fruits and vegetables, offer veggies and dip served with a glass of milk, or consider a fruit smoothie with a whole grain muffin. For additional snack ideas, see Snacks to Pack (pages 97).

For younger children, snacks should be offered at planned times and be evenly spaced between meals to ensure they have an appetite for the next meal. For toddlers and preschoolers, 3 small meals and 3 snacks a day is appropriate. If they choose to skip or pick at a meal, you shouldn't be concerned because the next scheduled snack is not too far away. Older children will need 3 meals plus 1 to 3 additional snacks. For those at school, snacks will likely be consumed during recess and after school. If your child is going directly to an after-school activity, make sure you pack an extra snack to be eaten then.

As children approach the middle school and teenage years, they will begin to make their own snacks. At this point, your job is to ensure that a variety of healthy choices are available. When stocking your kitchen, try to represent each of the 4 food groups. Stock your fridge with a variety of low-fat cheeses, yogurt and milk. In your fridge, you should also have vegetable sticks sitting in cold water, ready to go. This, along with a tempting dip, will encourage your children to eat more veggies. Always ensure there are good-quality fruit and vegetable juices in the fridge and that there is a bowl of prewashed fruit on the counter. Nut butters, trail mix, hummus, nuts and hard-boiled eggs are all convenient snacks and are excellent sources of protein. Stock your pantry with a variety of whole grain breads, muffins and cereals. When purchasing munchies, choose baked over fried and offer air-popped popcorn. When buying baked goods, always read labels carefully, as many contain unwanted trans fats.

Homemade baked goods are an excellent way to eliminate trans fats and other unwanted additives found in many commercially prepared goods. Making your own baked goods is also a good way to demonstrate appropriate portion size. Chances are your homemade cookies are smaller than store-bought ones.

When it comes to snack foods, moderation is the key. If all goodies are eliminated, children are more likely to overindulge when the opportunity arises. Your job is not to control but to provide guidance. As children grow, they are constantly bombarded with less than ideal food choices, so they need to learn how to make healthy decisions themselves. You do not want to raise an adult who is incapable of stopping after one cookie. Do not create an environment in which the "forbidden fruit" becomes appealing. Try making your own granola bars, muffins and cookies. Take comfort in knowing that a snack such as 2 oatmeal raisin cookies served with a glass of milk is approximately 1 serving of Grain Products and 1 serving of Milk and Alternatives.

snacks to pack

Packing snacks for school is as important as packing lunches. In addition to the main course, which might consist of a sandwich or a Thermos of warm food, you should also pack 2 to 3 snacks. Use snack foods as the opportunity to fill the nutritional gaps in your child's diet.

grain products

- Whole grain cereals packed in reusable containers
- Muffins (page 40)
- Toasted Whole Wheat Pita Chips (page 106)
- Whole wheat bread, wraps, bagels, etc.
- Homemade Granola Bars (page 104)
- Homemade cookies (pages 98–103)
- Banana Bread (page 115)
- Whole grain crackers
- Popcorn
- Whole grain rice crackers
- Ross's Pumpkin Bread (page 117)

vegetables and fruit
- Fresh fruit
- Canned fruit packed in juice, not syrup
- Veggies served with dip*
- Frozen fruit smoothies

meat and alternatives
- Hard-boiled eggs
- Middle Eastern Hummus (page 113)
- Roasted Garlic and White Bean Hummus (page 114)
- Nuts and seeds
- Peanut Butter Hummus (page 115)
- Trail Mix (page 108)

milk and alternatives
- Yogurt
- Cheese slices, served with veggies or whole grain crackers
- Chocolate pudding (on occasion)

* Remember, Canada's Food Guide recommends at least 1 dark green vegetable and 1 orange vegetable per day.

sarah bell's homemade chocolate chip cookies

Sometimes there is nothing better after school than homemade chocolate chip cookies with a glass of milk. Nobody makes better cookies than Brenda's friend Sarah Bell. According to Sarah, the key to making good cookies is to thoroughly cream the butter with the sugar prior to adding flour. If possible, use either an electric mixer or an egg beater.

1 cup unsalted butter, softened
¾ cup granulated sugar
1 cup packed light brown sugar

snacks

2 large eggs

2 tsp vanilla extract

2½ cups all-purpose flour

1 tsp baking soda

½ tsp salt

1 bag (300 g) mini chocolate chips

- Preheat oven to 350°F.
- In a large bowl, use an electric mixer to cream butter until colour lightens and texture is fluffy.
- Add sugar and mix until well blended, scraping down bowl periodically with a rubber spatula to ensure all ingredients are incorporated.
- Add eggs and vanilla and continue beating until colour lightens.
- Sift dry ingredients into the bowl and mix until just incorporated.
- Stir in the chocolate chips with a spoon.
- Place dough on cookie sheet by the tablespoonful, spacing cookies a few inches apart.
- Bake for 10 to 13 minutes or until cookies are pale in colour and just beginning to brown around the edges. If you prefer chewy cookies, take them out after 10 minutes. If you prefer crisper cookies, let them bake a little longer.
- Allow cookies to cool on cookie sheet for 2 to 3 minutes, then place on racks to cool.
- Extra cookies can be placed in airtight containers and stored in the freezer.

 Yield: 4¼ dozen

high fructose corn syrup

High fructose corn syrup (HFCS) is a commercially prepared sweetener. It contains fructose and glucose in roughly equal parts. The consumption of HFCS increased 1,000% between 1970 and 1990, far exceeding the changes in intake of any other food or food group.[1] This increase in consumption mirrors the rapid rise in childhood obesity.

Unlike glucose, fructose does not stimulate insulin secretion or enhance leptin production, both of which help us to regulate our food intake. Therefore, it is thought that because fructose does not trigger a sense of being full the way other sugars do, we are eating more.

Regardless of whether or not HFCS is the reason we are eating more, it adds excess empty calories to the diet. It is found in an abundance of processed foods, including soda pop, fruit drinks, candy, ketchup, yogurt, salad dressings and a variety of baked goods. The best way to avoid HFCS is to stress a diet of whole foods and read ingredient labels carefully.

oatmeal and raisin cookies

The following recipe can be made with either raisins or chocolate chips. If your kids don't like raisins, substitute 1 cup of chocolate chips for the raisins. With the oats, they become a slightly healthier chocolate chip cookie.

1 cup softened unsalted butter
1 cup packed light brown sugar
¾ cup granulated sugar
2 large eggs
1 tsp vanilla extract

1 cup all-purpose flour
1 tsp baking soda
½ tsp salt
2 cups rolled oats
1 cup raisins

snacks

- Preheat oven to 350°F.
- In a large bowl, use an electric mixer to cream butter until colour lightens and texture is fluffy.
- Add brown and granulated sugars and mix until well blended, scraping down bowl periodically with a rubber spatula to ensure all ingredients are incorporated.
- Add eggs and vanilla, mixing thoroughly until mixture lightens.
- Sift together flour, baking soda and salt and combine with wet ingredients.
- Stir in the oats and raisins and mix until incorporated.
- Place dough on cookie sheet by the tablespoonful, spacing cookies a few inches apart.
- Cook cookies for 10 to 13 minutes or until pale in colour and golden around the edges. If you prefer chewy cookies, take them out after 10 minutes. If you prefer crisper cookies, let them bake a little longer.
- Allow cookies to cool on cookie sheet for 2 to 3 minutes, then place on racks to cool.
- Extra cookies can be placed in airtight containers and stored in the freezer.

 Yield: 5½ dozen

snacking is good for the brain!

Glucose fuels the brain—in fact, the brain consumes about 3 times as much glucose as the rest of the body. Compared with an adult brain, a child's brain is larger in proportion to his body size, while his liver is smaller. A child therefore needs to eat more frequently to keep his brain fuelled and his blood glucose level stable. This explains why school performance and behaviour can be affected when meals are skipped. Young children need 3 small meals and 3 small snacks a day. Older children need 3 meals and 1 to 3 snacks, depending on activity level and growth.

cranberry flaxseed cookies

1 cup unsalted butter, softened

¾ cup granulated sugar

1 cup packed brown sugar

2 large eggs

1 tsp vanilla extract

1 cup all-purpose flour

1 tsp baking soda

½ tsp salt

1¼ cups rolled oats

¾ cup ground flaxseed

½ cup dried cranberries

½ cup mini chocolate chips

• Preheat oven to 350°F.

• In a large bowl, use an electric mixer to cream butter until colour lightens and texture is fluffy.

• Add sugar and mix until well blended, scraping down bowl periodically with a rubber spatula to ensure all ingredients are incorporated.

• Add eggs and vanilla, mixing thoroughly until colour lightens.

• Sift together flour, baking soda and salt and combine with wet ingredients.

• Stir in oats, flaxseed, dried cranberries and chocolate chips and mix until just incorporated.

• Place dough on cookie sheet by the tablespoonful, spacing cookies a few inches apart.

• Bake cookies for 10 to 13 minutes or until cookies are golden brown in colour. If you prefer chewy cookies, take them out after 10 minutes. If you prefer crisper cookies, let them bake a little longer.

• Allow cookies to cool on cookie sheet for 2 to 3 minutes, then place on racks to cool.

• Extra cookies can be placed in airtight containers and stored in the freezer.

 Yield: 5½ dozen

lorraine's birdseed cookies

Seeds are high in protein and a good source of healthy monounsaturated fats. These amazing cookies hail from Newfoundland and contain pumpkin seeds which, packed with magnesium, zinc and iron, are one of the healthiest seeds around.

1 cup all-purpose flour

2 tsp baking powder

2 tsp baking soda

1 cup whole wheat flour

1½ cups rolled oats

½ cup unsweetened shredded coconut

1 cup dried cranberries

1½ cups sunflower seeds, unsalted

½ cup sesame seeds

½ cup pumpkin seeds

1 cup ground flaxseed

1½ cups chocolate chips

1 cup packed brown sugar

1 cup softened butter, unsalted

2 eggs

1 tsp vanilla

- Preheat oven to 350°F.
- In a large bowl, sift together flour, baking powder and baking soda.
- Add whole wheat flour and mix until combined.
- Add oats, coconut, cranberries, seeds and chocolate chips.
- In a separate large bowl, cream sugar, butter, eggs and vanilla with electric mixer.
- Stir dry ingredients into wet about 1 cup at a time.
- Drop by heaping tablespoon onto cookie sheet and bake for 10 to 12 minutes, or until slightly browned.

 Yield: 3½ dozen cookies

what's the deal with flaxseed?

In addition to being a good source of fibre and brain-boosting omega-3 fatty acids, flaxseed is an excellent source of lignans. Lignans act as phytosterols, which block estrogen activity in the body. This may reduce the risk of certain types of cancers, including breast, ovarian, colon and prostate cancer.[2] To increase your children's consumption of lignans, sprinkle ground flaxseed on their morning cereal, mix it into porridge, pancakes, breads and muffins, and try Cranberry Flaxseed Cookies (page 102). Once opened, flaxseed should be stored in the freezer or refrigerator.

homemade granola bars

Making granola bars from scratch is a great way to eliminate the unwanted additives and trans fats found in many commercial bars. This recipe calls for chocolate chips; although their use is optional, they go a long way to encourage little ones to gobble up this nutritious snack!

3½ cups rolled oats
1 cup sliced almonds
½ cup ground flaxseed
½ cup sunflower seeds
½ cup raisins
½ cup dried cranberries
½ cup diced dried apricots
½ cup unsweetened
   shredded coconut

½ cup plus 2 tbsp canola
   oil
½ cup plus 2 tbsp liquid
   honey
2 large eggs, beaten
½ tsp vanilla extract
½ tsp salt
¼ cup chocolate chips
   (optional)

snacks

- Preheat oven to 350°F.
- In a large bowl, combine oats, almonds, flaxseed and sunflower seeds and toast on a cookie sheet for 8 minutes.
- Remove from oven and stir. Return to oven and toast for another 8 minutes.
- Remove from oven and return to large bowl.
- Add dried fruit and coconut to toasted oat mixture and mix thoroughly.
- In a saucepan, combine oil and honey over medium heat and stir until mixed thoroughly and honey dissolves, 5 to 10 minutes. (Alternatively you can microwave the oil and honey for approximately 1 minute.)
- Add honey to oat mixture and mix thoroughly.
- In a small bowl, mix together eggs, vanilla and salt and add to oat mixture. Mix thoroughly.
- Grease 9" x 13" baking dish and evenly spread granola mixture in pan.
- Press with the back of a spoon so that granola fills the pan.
- Sprinkle with chocolate chips (if using) and press into granola.
- Bake at 350°F for 20 to 25 minutes or until granola is golden brown in colour.
- Allow to cool for 25 minutes.
- Cut granola into bars and allow to set in the refrigerator, approximately 30 minutes. Extra bars should be stored in the refrigerator.

 Yield: 18 bars

toasted whole wheat pita chips

Whole wheat pita chips are a healthy alternative to potato chips or store-bought crackers, which often contain unwanted trans fats. Pita chips served with cheese or any of the dips in this book make a healthy snack. This recipe makes a fairly large quantity. Extra chips can be stored in airtight containers for up to 10 days.

4 whole wheat pitas

¼ cup olive oil

1 clove garlic, crushed

½ tsp salt

¼ tsp freshly ground pepper

- Preheat oven to 425°F.
- Heat pita in microwave for 30 seconds.
- Slit top of pita pocket in half with a knife and separate the 2 sides of the pita. Repeat with other pitas.
- Cut each half of the pita into quarters and place on a cookie sheet.
- In a small bowl, mix together olive oil, garlic, salt and pepper.
- With a pastry brush, brush oil mixture onto each pita triangle.

- Bake in oven until chips are golden and beginning to brown around the edges.

 *Yield: 32 chips*

Serving Suggestion: Serve with Middle Eastern Hummus (page 113), Roasted Garlic and White Bean Hummus (page 114) or Tzatziki (page 109).

snacks

salt

Sodium is an essential nutrient that plays an important role in metabolism and maintenance of blood pressure. Sodium occurs naturally in most foods. Salt is added to foods to enhance flavour. It imparts its own tangy taste while suppressing bitter flavours.

The nutrition recommendations for Canadians state that the sodium, or salt, content of our diets should be reduced.[3] Diets rarely lack sodium, and even when intakes are low, the body adapts by reducing sodium loss through urine and sweat. Limiting sodium intake may reduce blood pressure in those who are susceptible, which may, in turn, reduce the incidence of heart attacks and strokes.

In general, processed foods have the most sodium, whereas whole foods, such as fresh fruits, vegetables, milk and meats, have the least. As a matter of fact, about 75% of dietary sodium comes from processed foods, 15% from salt added in cooking and at the table, and only about 10% from the natural content in foods.

Follow these tips to cut your family's salt consumption:

- Avoid offering processed foods to children, so they don't develop a taste for salt.
- Cut down on sodium in cooking; use spices, lemon juice or vinegar instead.
- Always taste foods before adding salt.
- Avoid pickled foods, salty or smoked meats and fish, prepared snack foods like potato chips and popcorn, prepared sauces and condiments, processed cheeses, canned and instant soups.
- Put the salt shaker in the cupboard. Watch your own salt intake and set a healthy example.
- Eating foods with less salt may seem unappealing at first, but the palate will gradually adjust.

how much salt is too much?

* 1 tsp salt contributes about 2,000 mg sodium to the diet.

age (yr)	adequate intake (mg/day)	tolerable upper intake level (mg/day)
Infant (0–0.5)	120	Source should be from breast milk or formula only.
Infant (0.5–1)	370	Not determinable.
Children 1–3	1,000	1,500
Children 4–8	1,200	1,900
Adolescent 9–13	1,500	2,200
Adolescent 14+	1,500	2,300

Source: Dietary Reference Intakes, Health Canada 2005-08-04. Adapted and Reproduced with the Permission of the Minister of Public Works and Government Services Canada, 2007.

trail mix

Trail mix, full of nuts, is an excellent source of protein and heart-healthy fats. Most of the ingredients can be found in the bulk bin section of your local grocery store. The use of chocolate chips is optional, however they do serve to enhance the appeal of this healthy snack. If you have a nut lover on hand, add an extra ⅓ cup whole almonds and skip the chocolate chips.

1 cup peanuts
½ cup sunflower seeds
½ cup sliced almonds
½ cup raisins

⅓ cup diced apricots
⅓ cup banana chips
⅓ cup chocolate chips (optional)

snacks

- In a bowl, combine peanuts, sunflower seeds, almonds, raisins, apricots, banana chips, and chocolate chips (if using). Stir.
- Store in an airtight container.

 Yield: 3 cups

dips

Children of all ages are expert "little dippers." Dips make wonderful snacks—they can be served with an assortment of freshly cut vegetable sticks, whole grain crackers or Toasted Whole Wheat Pita Chips (page 106). When choosing crackers, opt for the whole grain varieties and read labels carefully—many are high in salt and may contain unwanted trans fats.

The following recipes are delicious. Healthy homemade dips are a good alternative to the store-bought varieties that tend to be high in fat, sugar, salt and unnecessary additives. Packed in small reusable containers, veggies and dip make a nutritious addition to any lunch.

· tzatziki

½ English cucumber, grated (approximately ½ lb)
1 cup Balkan-style plain yogurt (above 3% MF)
1 or 2 cloves garlic, crushed
Salt and freshly ground pepper

- With clean hands, squeeze cucumber to remove excess liquid.
- In a bowl, combine yogurt, cucumber and 1 clove garlic to taste and mix thoroughly. (1 cup of yogurt usually requires 1½ cloves of garlic.) You want to be able to taste the garlic, but it should not be too overpowering.

- Add salt and pepper to taste.
- Let stand for 30 minutes.

 Yield: 2½ cups

Serving Suggestion: Serve with Toasted Whole Wheat Pita Chips (page 106) or veggie sticks.

nitrites

Nitrites are antimicrobial agents added to foods to enhance their flavour and colour (for example, the pink hue in hot dogs and other cured meats), to prevent rancidity and to protect against bacterial overgrowth. In the human body, nitrites can be converted into nitrosamines. Nitrosamine formation from nitrites has been found to cause cancer in animals. However, to cause cancer in humans, nitrite levels would have to be a lot higher than those used in the food industry. Nitrosamine exposure from cigarette smoking or from new car interiors and cosmetics is much higher than that from foods. However, many of the foods high in nitrites are also high in saturated fats, so moderation is the key.

 ## fresh herb dip

1 cup Balkan-style plain
   yogurt (above 3% MF)
Juice of half a lemon
1 small clove garlic,
   crushed
⅓ cup light sour cream
2 tbsp finely chopped
   fresh dill
2 tbsp finely chopped
   cilantro

2 tbsp finely chopped
   fresh basil
Salt and freshly ground
   pepper to taste

- Combine all of the ingredients in a bowl and mix thoroughly.

 Yield: 2 cups

snacks

soda pop is liquid candy

Over the past 40 years, consumption of carbonated and non-carbonated soft drinks (including fruit drinks, iced teas and ades) has exploded. Between the late 1970s and 2001 the percentage of calories coming from soft drinks consumed by children 2 to 18 has more than doubled. The average teenager gets 13% of his daily calories from these drinks. A 12-ounce can of soda pop contains approximately 10 teaspoons of refined sugar.[4] Needless to say, these drinks are highly caloric, and it is no coincidence that the rise in consumption of soft drinks parallels the rise in childhood obesity.

Soft drinks are problematic for what they contain as well as what they push out of the diet. As our children's soft drink consumption has increased, their milk intake has declined. Heavy soft drink consumption is associated with lower intake of vitamins, minerals and dietary fibre. It is also associated with increased risk of obesity, diabetes, tooth decay and osteoporosis, especially for those who drink soft drinks instead of milk. Furthermore, caffeine, a common ingredient in many popular sodas, is a mildly addictive stimulant. It also increases the excretion of calcium, possibly increasing the risk of developing osteoporosis later in life.

homemade salsa

No store-bought variety can beat homemade salsa. It's delicious on grilled fish or served with scrambled eggs. This salsa recipe is very mild, but if you prefer a spicier version, add a finely diced jalapeño pepper.

5 tomatoes, cored and seeded (approximately 1¾ lb)
⅓ cup finely chopped cilantro
¼ cup finely diced red onion
Squeeze of lime juice (optional)
½ tsp salt

- Dice tomatoes.
- In a small bowl, mix together tomatoes, cilantro, onion, lime juice (if using) and salt.
- Refrigerate for 30 minutes before serving.

Yield: Approximately 3 cups

guacamole

Avocados are one of the few fruits that contain heart-healthy monounsaturated fats. They are also a good source of vitamin E, folate, fibre, potassium and magnesium. Serve them often so they become a familiar favourite. Avocados can be enjoyed in salads and sandwiches or sliced and served with whole grain crackers.

2 avocados, halved and pitted
¼ cup finely chopped red onion
¼ tsp salt
1 to 3 tbsp freshly squeezed lemon juice
1 tbsp chopped cilantro (optional)

- In a small bowl, mash avocados with a fork, keeping a nice lumpy texture.
- Mix in onion and salt.
- Slowly add lemon juice to desired taste.
- Sprinkle with cilantro (if using) and serve.

Yield: Approximately 1½ cups

Serving Suggestion: Serve with Homemade Salsa (page 111) and Toasted Whole Wheat Pita Chips (page 106).

snacks

middle eastern hummus

3 cups canned chickpeas,
   rinsed and drained
½ cup plus 2 tbsp chick-
   pea liquid (from can)
6 to 8 tbsp freshly
   squeezed lemon juice
3 cloves garlic, roughly
   chopped
1½ tsp ground cumin
½ cup tahini
1 tbsp olive oil
Sprig parsley (optional)

• Place chickpeas, chickpea liquid, 6 tbsp of the lemon juice, garlic, cumin and tahini in a food processor and blend until very smooth. Add extra lemon juice as needed. Refrigerate 1 hour prior to serving.

• To serve, drizzle olive oil over hummus and top with sprig of parsley (if using).

 Yield: 2½ cups

Serving Suggestion: Serve with raw veggies, warm pita bread or Toasted Whole Wheat Pita Chips (page 106)

put on your poker face!

Even if your child is an extremely finicky eater and you sometimes wonder how she is surviving at all, resist the temptation to bribe, threaten, cajole or give in to demands for high-calorie processed foods. You don't want to teach your child that if she holds out long enough, something else will be served. This is a slippery slope and only reinforces the behaviour.

There are many reasons children reject food. Sometimes they do it to get attention, exert control and/or simply because they do not like or are not familiar with what is being served. As frustrating as this may be, it is a normal part of childhood. After the meal is over, bite your tongue and try to smile.

roasted garlic and white bean hummus

If you cannot find Italian flat-leaf parsley, curly parsley can be substituted.

> 1 small head garlic (or ½ large head)
> Drizzle olive oil
> 1 can (19 oz) white kidney beans, rinsed and drained
> Juice of half a lemon
> 1 tbsp olive oil
> ¼ cup chopped fresh flat-leaf Italian parsley
> Salt and pepper

- Preheat oven to 375°F.
- Cut top off garlic head. Drizzle with olive oil, wrap in foil and roast in oven for 45 minutes.
- Remove from oven and allow to cool.
- Place kidney beans in food processor.
- Squeeze garlic onto beans, add lemon juice and olive oil, and purée until smooth.
- Place hummus in bowl. Add parsley and mix with a spoon.
- Add salt and pepper to taste.
- Refrigerate for 30 minutes before serving.

 Yield: 2 cups

Serving Suggestion: Serve with veggie sticks or warmed whole wheat pita bread.

peanut butter hummus

This recipe is inspired by one in *More Easy Beans* by Trish Ross and Jacquie Trafford. It is loved by kids and adults alike.

1 can (19 oz) chickpeas, drained and rinsed
2 tbsp water
¼ cup freshly squeezed lemon juice
¼ cup olive oil
½ cup peanut butter
3 cloves garlic, crushed
3 tbsp chopped fresh parsley

• Blend together chickpeas, water, lemon juice, olive oil, peanut butter and garlic in a food processor until smooth.
• Transfer to a bowl, add parsley and mix.

 Yield: 2½ cups

Serving Suggestion: Serve with warm pita triangles or raw vegetables.

banana bread

Because the following is made with canola oil instead of butter, it is a little lighter in taste and a healthier alternative to traditional banana bread. The key to good banana bread is using well-ripened bananas. Their skins should be almost black. If still yellow, throw them in the oven for 15 minutes at 350°F. Doing so will bring out the banana flavour.

1½ cups all-purpose flour
2¼ tsp baking powder
¼ tsp salt
⅓ cup wheat germ
2 eggs

1 cup mashed very ripe banana
⅔ cup granulated sugar
⅓ cup canola oil
1 tsp lemon zest

- Preheat oven to 350°F.
- Grease and flour a loaf pan and set aside.
- In a large bowl, sift together flour, baking powder and salt.
- Add wheat germ and mix with a fork.
- In another bowl, lightly beat eggs. Mix in banana, sugar, oil and lemon rind.
- Combine wet and dry ingredients and pour into loaf pan.
- Bake for 1 hour or until a toothpick inserted into the centre of the loaf comes out clean.
- Cool on wire rack for 10 minutes. Turn loaf out of pan and let cool completely on rack.

 Yield: 1 loaf

sleep and appetite

Both children and adults get less sleep than they did 40 years ago, an average of 2 hours less per night. That loss comes at a cost to our health. Sleep is a major regulator in the production of the hormones leptin (which suppresses appetite) and ghrelin (which promotes hunger). With less sleep, our stomachs secrete more ghrelin while our fat cells produce less leptin, making us more likely to overeat. Getting your kids to bed on time is a fantastic way to cut their cravings.

snacks

ross's pumpkin bread

Canada's new Food Guide recommends consuming at least 1 orange vegetable per day. Eating pumpkin bread is a tasty way to achieve this goal!

1½ cups pumpkin purée
¾ cup packed brown sugar
½ cup canola oil
½ tsp vanilla extract
2 eggs, lightly beaten
2 cups all-purpose flour
2 tsp baking powder
1 tsp baking soda
1½ tsp ground nutmeg
1½ tsp ground ginger
1½ tsp cinnamon
¼ tsp salt
¾ cup raisins

- Preheat oven to 350°F.
- Grease and flour a loaf pan and set aside.
- Mix together pumpkin purée, brown sugar, canola oil, vanilla and eggs and set aside.
- In a separate bowl, sift together the dry ingredients.
- Mix dry ingredients into wet ingredients and stir in raisins.
- Pour into prepared loaf pan and bake for approximately 1 hour or until a toothpick inserted into the centre of the loaf comes out clean.
- Cool on wire rack for 10 minutes. Turn loaf out of pan and let cool completely on rack.

 Yield: 1 loaf

summer popsicles

Popsicles made with your child's favourite juice are a healthy alternative to the sugar-loaded store-bought varieties. Popsicles can be made with fresh or frozen fruit. If adding sugar or honey, stir in just enough to sweeten the fruit. For the following recipes, you need plastic Popsicle moulds, which you can find at a dollar store or your local grocery store. If you are unable to find them, use Dixie cups with Popsicle sticks inserted once the mixture is semi-frozen. And if you don't have time to make homemade Popsicles, try freezing a yogurt tube.

raspberry creamsicles

1 lb fresh or frozen
   raspberries
½ cup Balkan-style plain
   yogurt (above 3% MF)
½ cup milk
2 tbsp liquid honey
   (approximately)

• If using frozen raspberries, defrost them.
• Place raspberries in a food processor and purée.
• Strain raspberries with a fine-mesh sieve to remove seeds. This should produce approximately 1¼ cups raspberry purée.
• Place raspberry purée back in food processor and blend with yogurt and milk.
• Add just enough honey to sweeten the fruit and blend well.
• Pour into Popsicle moulds and freeze.

Yield: 2 cups Popsicle mix (approximately 12 Popsicles)

strawberry popsicles

1 lb fresh or frozen
  strawberries
¾ cup orange juice
1 tsp liquid honey
  (approximately)

• If using frozen strawberries, defrost them.
• Place strawberries in food processor, add orange juice and purée until smooth.

• Add just enough honey (if using) to sweeten the fruit.
• Pour into Popsicle moulds and freeze.

Yield: 2 cups Popsicle mix (approximately 12 Popsicles)

peachy popsicles

3 peaches, washed
⅓ cup boiling water
1 tsp lemon juice, freshly
  squeezed
1 rounded tbsp sugar
  (approximately)

• Plunge peaches into boiling water for 2 minutes. With a slotted spoon, remove peaches and allow to cool.
• Slit skin with a knife and peel.

Cut peaches into quarters and remove pits.
• Place peaches in food processor. Add boiling water, lemon juice and sugar to taste. Purée.
• Pour into Popsicle moulds and freeze.

Yield: 2 cups Popsicle mix (approximately 12 Popsicles)

dinner

Many families find themselves juggling gruelling work schedules and a multitude of after-school activities. So it's not surprising that the family meal is falling by the wayside. Yet family meals are crucial to the mental and physical well-being of children. They strengthen family bonds and provide an opportunity to keep track of children's daily lives. We all need to serve, eat and enjoy family meals more often.

Children who eat regular meals with their family tend to consume more fruit, vegetables and dairy products. As a result, they generally have a higher intake of calcium, fibre and vitamins. These nutrients are essential for healthy growth and development. Furthermore, studies suggest teens who eat regular family meals tend to have lower use of tobacco, alcohol and marijuana. They generally have higher grade point averages and fewer depressive symptoms.[1]

Family dinners provide a daily opportunity to model healthy eating habits and teach table manners. Young children can set and clear the table. Older children can help with cooking and washing dishes.

Encourage your children to become involved in meal preparation. Children are more likely to enjoy a meal when they are involved in preparing it. Young children can wash vegetables, mash potatoes, make salads and even mix cookies, muffins or breads.

Family meals should be enjoyable for everyone. Make an effort to create a pleasant atmosphere and remember to focus on your children, not on what they are eating. Keep in mind that parents or caregivers are responsible for what children eat, but it is up to the children to decide how much they eat. Serve small portions, with the option for seconds, and resist the temptation to harp on unfinished food. Instead, eat a healthy dinner yourself and be reassured that this is one of the most effective ways to instill lifelong healthy eating habits.

Dinners do not need to be elaborate to be nutritious. Where kids are concerned, simple is often better. Many of the following recipes are easy to prepare, and those that take a little longer can be made in bulk and frozen to provide convenient meals when needed. Other recipes can be doubled: one half for the evening's meal and the other for the freezer. To make the most of the time you have with your children, plan your meals in advance.

dinner

whole wheat thin-crust italian pizza

All kids love pizza. Making it yourself with a whole wheat crust and serving it with healthy toppings is a great way to guarantee this family favourite is a nutritional hit. A pizza stone is a worthwhile investment as it's the best way to ensure a crisp crust. The dough can be made by hand, with a food processor or with a heavy-duty electric mixer using the dough hook.

pizza

2 pkg (8 g) or 4½ tsp yeast

1 tbsp liquid honey

1¼ cups lukewarm water (not too hot or it will kill the yeast)

1½ cups whole wheat flour

1½ to 2 cups all-purpose flour

3 tbsp olive oil

2 tsp salt

Cornmeal

Pizza Sauce (page 124)

- In small bowl, proof yeast with honey and ¼ cup warm water. Let stand for 5 minutes. If active, the yeast will foam.
- In food processor, combine yeast, whole wheat flour, 1½ cups all-purpose flour, olive oil and salt.
- Pulse slowly, adding remaining warm water.
- Mix until dough comes together and pulls away from the side of the food processor, approximately 5 minutes.
- Knead dough by hand for 10 to 12 minutes, slowly incorporating the last ½ cup of flour as needed until dough is smooth and elastic.
- Oil a bowl. Place dough in bowl and turn over several times to ensure it is lightly covered with oil.
- Cover the bowl with a clean cloth and place in warm area away from drafts. Allow the dough to rise for 30 minutes.
- After 30 minutes, divide the dough into 6 equal parts and roll each segment into a ball.

- Sprinkle baking sheet with cornmeal and place balls on the sheet. Cover with a damp cloth and allow the dough to rise for another 10 minutes.
- At this point, the dough is ready to be made into pizza rounds, or it can be refrigerated for a maximum of 4 hours.
- If the dough has been in the refrigerator, remove 30 minutes before stretching into pizza rounds.
- Preheat oven to 525°F. (If your oven only goes up to 500°F, that will be fine.)
- Place stone in oven 1 hour before baking.
- Stretch dough into 8-inch rounds. Rounds should be thin with slightly thicker edges.
- Scatter baking sheet with cornmeal and place 2 rounds on sheet.
- Evenly spread 2 tbsp Pizza Sauce on each round.
- Top pizza with your favourite toppings (see page 125 for ideas).
- Place baking sheet on pizza stone (if using) and bake for 10 to 15 minutes or until cheese is bubbling and pizza is beginning to brown around the edges and the edges of the crust are firm to touch. Remove from oven and cut into slices.

Yield: Enough dough for six 8-inch pizzas

pizza sauce

This recipe makes a fairly large quantity of pizza sauce. Extra sauce can be frozen and used at a later date. It can also be tossed over pasta and served with freshly grated Parmesan cheese. Alternatively, Basil Pesto (page 199) makes a great pizza sauce served either on its own or with a little tomato sauce as well.

1 tbsp canola oil
2 shallots, finely diced, or ¼ onion, finely diced
1 can (28 oz) crushed tomatoes
¼ cup tomato paste
⅓ cup chopped fresh basil

- Sauté shallots in oil over medium heat until translucent, approximately 5 minutes.
- Add crushed tomatoes and tomato paste and mix thoroughly.
- Bring to a boil. Turn down heat and simmer for 20 minutes.
- Remove from heat, add basil and stir.
- Allow to cool.

Yield: 6 cups

toppings

Kids can have a great time creating their own pizzas, and knowing that they are choosing from a variety of healthy toppings will bring a smile to Mom's face. Having a pizza party is a fun way to entertain another family or a group of children. All you need to do is make the dough ahead of time, put out a variety of delicious toppings and let everyone choose their own. Be creative and have fun!

►sauces

- Pizza Sauce (page 124)
- Basil Pesto (page 199)

►cheeses

- Mixing equal parts shredded mozzarella and shredded white Cheddar makes a great topping that combines the stretchiness of the one with the flavour of the other. This mixture is also delicious mixed with some of these cheeses:

- fresh buffalo mozzarella
- crumbled feta
- goat cheese
- Brie

►meats

- prosciutto
- chicken
- ham
- smoked salmon
- anchovies
- canned tuna
- shrimp

►veggies and fruit

- cherry or plum tomatoes, sliced
- red, yellow and green peppers, sliced thinly
- sun dried tomatoes, sliced thinly
- artichoke hearts, sliced

- mushrooms, thinly sliced
- caramelized onions
- pineapple, cut into chunks
- baby leaf spinach
- arugula
- basil, coarsely chopped

- red onions, thinly sliced
- olives

Serving Suggestion: Serve with green salad with White Balsamic Vinaigrette (page 203).

if at first you don't succeed, try, try again!

It may take as many as 10 to 20 exposures before a young child accepts a new food. The reason Japanese children like fish and Indian children like spicy food is that, from an early age, they are repeatedly exposed to those foods. Don't decide your child doesn't like broccoli because it has been rejected once or even a few times. Instead, continue to offer a small amount without pressure. It should be okay for your child to say "No, thank you." When not pressured, children are more likely to be adventurous. Like us, children like to feel a sense of control. If they believe it is their decision to try a food, they are more likely to enjoy it. Remember, most finicky eaters grow into food-loving adults.

chicken fajitas

The following is a quick and easy family dinner. The marinade for the chicken is not terribly spicy; however, if you're making it for very young children, you may choose to either keep some chicken out of the marinade or not slice the chicken breast before marinating it to decrease the surface area that is exposed. Once you've made fajitas a few times, then you can introduce the spicier version.

2 tbsp freshly squeezed
   lime juice
2 tbsp canola oil
½ tsp chili powder
½ tsp ground cumin
2 cloves garlic, crushed
3 boneless, skinless
   chicken breasts, cut
   against the grain into
   strips
1 tbsp canola oil
½ red onion, thinly sliced
1 sweet red pepper, thinly
   sliced
1 sweet yellow pepper,
   thinly sliced
6 to 8 large soft whole
   wheat flour tortillas

toppings

1 avocado, diced
2 tomatoes, diced
10 leaves romaine lettuce,
   shredded
1½ cups shredded
   Cheddar cheese
Light sour cream or plain
   yogurt
Homemade Salsa
   (page 111) or mild store-
   bought salsa

- In a small bowl, mix together lime juice, canola oil, chili powder, cumin and garlic.
- Add chicken and toss until thoroughly coated.
- Cover with plastic wrap and allow to marinate in the fridge while preparing the rest of the meal, approximately 20 minutes or for up to 1 hour.
- While chicken is marinating, sauté onion and pepper in 1 tbsp canola oil over medium heat until peppers are tender, approximately 10 minutes.
- Transfer to a plate and cover.
- In the same pan, sauté chicken until cooked through and no longer pink inside, approximately 10 to 12 minutes.
- Warm tortillas in microwave.
- Spoon peppers and onions along middle of each tortilla and top with chicken.
- Place toppings on the table and encourage your children to help themselves.

Yield: Serves 4

Serving Suggestion: Serve with Middle Eastern Salad (page 211).

coping with the happy meal

Today, many families are eating out on a regular basis. This means more children than ever before are frequenting fast food restaurants and choosing from children's menus. Often these meals are high in salt, fat and calories. Experts believe this trend is contributing to our obesity epidemic.

Eating out does not have to mean dining on a high-calorie feast. Following a few simple guidelines can ensure your family's experience is a healthier one.

- Opt for fruit or salad instead of fries.
- Avoid chicken nuggets. They are highly caloric and generally made with low-quality, deep-fried meat.
- Instead of fried foods, choose those that have been baked, grilled, boiled, broiled or steamed.
- Avoid cream sauces.
- Start the meal with a salad. It is high in fibre and will fill children up.
- Choose from the adult menu, as it's often healthier, and ask if portions can be halved. If not, order the full meal and ask to have half packed to go.
- Choose milk or water instead of soft drinks.
- Skip or share desserts.
- Choose wrap and sandwich shops instead of burger-oriented fast food restaurants.
- Don't "supersize" your child's meal.
- The occasional trip to a fast food restaurant can be part of a healthy diet. Take the food to the park and have a picnic. After eating, play a game of tag, which will help burn off excess calories.

chicken souvlaki dinner

Souvlaki is a favourite with Cheryl's daughters. Although the portions are designed for a family of 4, using less chicken would make this meal an easy-to-prepare children's dinner for nights when you are out. Finicky eaters delight in creating their own souvlaki by adding the tzatziki and toppings themselves. And toddlers can enjoy this meal by dipping pieces of chicken, pita bread and tomato in the tzatziki. The following should be enough for a family of 4. If you have big eaters on your hands, you may want to cook another half or whole chicken breast.

3 skinless, boneless
  chicken breasts
1 tbsp olive oil
½ tsp dried oregano
1 squeeze fresh lemon
  juice
4 to 6 whole wheat pitas
1 cup Tzatziki (page 109)
10 leaves romaine lettuce,
  shredded
3 tomatoes, diced
1 sweet green or red
  pepper, diced
¼ cup diced red onion
  (optional)

• Preheat oven to 350°F.
• In a small bowl, whisk together olive oil, oregano and lemon juice.
• Cut chicken into ¾-inch cubes and toss with marinade.

• Line a cookie sheet with foil and place chicken on foil. Bake until chicken is cooked through, 15 to 20 minutes. (Wrapping cookie sheet in foil facilitates easy cleanup.)
• Warm pitas in oven or microwave until softened.
• Place 3 to 4 pieces of chicken on each pita and top with tzatziki, lettuce, tomatoes, peppers, and onion (if using).
• Roll souvlaki. Wrapping the souvlaki in a napkin or foil will make it easier for little hands to grasp.

Yield: Serves 4

Serving Suggestion: Serve with Greek Salad (page 210) and whole grain rice.

dinner

meatball souvlaki dinner

Assuming you have extra meatballs left over from last night's dinner (Spaghetti and Meatballs, page 187), the following recipe can be made in less than 10 minutes. (Toddlers can enjoy this meal by dipping meatballs, pita bread and tomatoes in the tzatziki.)

25 Meatballs (page 186)
4 to 6 whole wheat pitas
1 cup Tzatziki (page 109)
3 tomatoes, diced
10 leaves romaine lettuce, shredded
¼ red onion, diced (optional)

- Place 3 to 4 meatballs in the middle of each pita.
- Microwave pitas and meatballs until meatballs are warmed through and pitas are soft.
- Top each with 2 tbsp tzatziki, tomatoes, lettuce, and onion (if using).
- Roll up souvlaki. Wrap in a napkin or foil to make it easier for little hands to grasp.

Yield: Serves 4

is it just baby fat?

Many parents are reluctant to admit their child has a weight problem. There is a tendency to minimize the problem, attributing the excess weight to baby fat, even when the child is no longer an infant. Frequently, the problem is not addressed until adolescence, at which time behavioural habits are harder to reverse. Obese teenagers almost always become obese adults. However, children under the age of 8 have a better chance than older children of outgrowing their weight problem—especially if their parents are of normal weight.[2] If you suspect your child may be overweight, see your doctor.

chelsea's barbecued flank steak with ginger barbecue sauce

Kept in an airtight container, this sauce can be stored in the fridge for a week. It's delicious on beef burgers, too. Making your own barbecue sauce is a great way to eliminate the unnecessary additives found in most commercial ones.

ginger barbecue sauce

½ cup tomato paste

½ cup light soy sauce

⅓ cup boiling water

⅓ cup liquid honey

2 tbsp red wine vinegar

10 cloves garlic, crushed

¼ cup grated fresh ginger

1½ tsp freshly ground pepper

• Combine all of the ingredients and mix thoroughly.

Yield: 2 cups

barbecued flank steak

This is a favourite of Cheryl's daughter Chelsea. The longer the steak marinates, the better. If you have time, let it marinate overnight.

1 flank steak (approximately 1½ lb)

½ cup Ginger Barbecue Sauce

• With either a knife or a pastry brush, thickly spread barbecue sauce over both sides of flank steak and allow to marinate in the fridge for a minimum of 30 minutes.

• Remove from fridge ½ hour before cooking.

• Turn barbecue to high and sear one side of the steak for 2 minutes.

• Reduce heat to medium, turn steak over and cook for another 7 to 8 minutes.

• Remove from barbecue, tent with foil and allow to rest for 5 minutes. Cut steak thinly across the grain to serve.

• If serving to young children, cut into tiny pieces since they often find steak difficult to eat.

dinner

Yield: Serves 5 to 6

Serving Suggestion: Serve with Cath's Potato Yam Mash (page 219), Garlic Roasted Broccolini (page 217) and Kids' Caesar Salad (page 208).

iron deficiency

Iron is an essential component of hemoglobin and is necessary to carry oxygen from the lungs to all parts of the body. It helps build red blood cells, helps the body's cells do their jobs and contributes to brain development.

Iron deficiency is a condition characterized by a low level of iron in the body tissues. In an otherwise healthy child, iron deficiency occurs when the intake of iron-rich foods does not meet the needs of the individual. This is often the case when children consume excessive amounts of low-iron food or drink (such as juice and milk) at the expense of higher-iron foods. Children, particularly rapidly growing infants and toddlers, as well as menstruating teens, are at an especially high risk for iron deficiency.

Symptoms of iron deficiency may include lack of appetite, poor weight gain, recurrent illness, exhaustion, gastrointestinal problems, irritability and poor concentration. The problem has a tendency to compound itself. An iron-deficient child will lose his appetite and be less likely to eat iron-rich foods. If the problem persists, it is possible that cognitive development could become impaired.

If you suspect iron deficiency, see your doctor, who may perform a simple blood test to confirm diagnosis.

provençal chicken and bean casserole

Loaded with beans, the following recipe is an excellent source of cholesterol-lowering fibre. This dish can also be made in a slow cooker.

2⅓ cups dried small white
  beans
1 tbsp canola oil
6 bone-in chicken thighs,
  skin removed
1 onion, diced
4 carrots, peeled and
  diced (approximately
  1 cup)
4 stalks celery, diced
  (approximately 1 cup)
2 tbsp minced fresh
  ginger
4 cloves garlic, crushed
1 small can (14 oz) diced
  tomatoes
¼ cup tomato paste
4 cups low-sodium
  chicken stock
½ cup chopped cilantro
Salt and pepper

• Soak beans overnight.
• Preheat oven to 300°F.
• In a large ovenproof Dutch oven, heat oil over medium heat. Brown chicken (approximately 5 minutes) and set aside.

• In the same pot, sauté onion, carrots, celery and ginger until softened, approximately 10 minutes.
• Drain beans.
• Add garlic, tomatoes, tomato paste, chicken stock and beans to the pot and stir.
• Bring to a boil.
• Remove from heat and press chicken into beans.
• Bake, covered, until beans are tender, approximately 2½ hours.
• Remove from oven and place chicken on serving platter.
• Add cilantro to bean mixture and stir.
• Add salt and pepper to taste and serve beans with chicken.

 Yield: Serves 6

Warmed and packed in a Thermos, leftover beans make convenient school lunches.

rosemary pork tenderloin

Pork tenderloin makes a fabulous family meal—it is both inexpensive and lean. When cooking for young children, coat the adults' portion with the rub and leave the children's plain. Encourage your children to try your pork by giving them a small piece to taste. If they like it, the next time you can cover the entire tenderloin with the rub. If you don't have fresh rosemary, substitute either fresh or dried thyme, but don't use dried rosemary, as it is sticky in consistency.

1 pork tenderloin	¼ rounded tsp finely
1 tbsp canola oil	chopped fresh rosemary
1 tbsp Dijon mustard	¼ tsp salt
1 clove garlic, crushed	Freshly ground pepper

- Preheat oven to 400°F.
- In a large frying pan, sear tenderloin in oil over medium heat until meat is browned on all sides, approximately 4 minutes. This step locks in the juices.
- To make rub, mix together mustard, garlic, rosemary, salt, and pepper to taste.
- Remove tenderloin from pan and thinly coat with mustard rub. (If serving to young children, leave their portion of the meat plain.)
- Place tenderloin in oven and roast for 15 to 18 minutes. A meat thermometer inserted into the middle of tenderloin should read 160°F.
- Remove from oven, tent with foil and allow to stand for 5 minutes. This allows the meat to reabsorb the juices. When done, tenderloin should be slightly pink in the middle.
- Slice into ¾-inch medallions and serve.

Yield: Serves 4

Serving Suggestion: Serve with Wilted Garlic Spinach (page 216) and Cath's Potato Yam Mash (page 219).

how can iron deficiency be avoided?

The best way to avoid iron deficiency is to serve your children a variety of iron-rich foods. There are two types of iron: heme iron and non-heme iron. Heme iron is more easily absorbed by the body. It is found in meats, chicken and fish. The darker the meat, the more heme iron it contains. For instance, red meat contains more iron than pork or chicken. Dark chicken or turkey meat contains more than light meat.

Non-heme iron is not as easily absorbed as heme iron. It is found in the following foods: cereals that have been fortified with iron, lentils, beans, peas, dark leafy greens and eggs, as well as breads and pastas (both whole grain and enriched). The absorption of all dietary iron can be improved by pairing iron-rich foods with foods that are high in vitamin C. Such foods include fruit juices, citrus fruits and brightly coloured fruit and vegetables.

homemade turkey tacos

The following is designed to appeal to children, so the meat mixture is not very spicy. If making for adults, add ½ rounded tsp crushed red pepper flakes to the mixture. Alternatively, you could sprinkle some crushed red pepper flakes onto the adults' portion after the children have been served. Leftovers make a delicious pasta sauce or can be served over shredded lettuce with diced tomatoes and shredded Cheddar cheese to make a yummy taco salad. In fact, grown-ups can eat it as a taco salad while the kids enjoy Turkey Tacos.

½ onion, diced

2 stalks celery, diced

2 carrots, peeled and
  grated

2 tbsp canola oil

1 lb ground turkey

2 cloves garlic, crushed

½ cup tomato paste

1 rounded tbsp chili
  powder

½ tsp cumin

1 cup water

¼ cup chopped cilantro (optional)

Salt and pepper

12 large soft whole wheat flour tortillas (approximately 10 inches)

toppings

1 cup Homemade Salsa (page 111)

1 cup light sour cream or yogurt

10 leaves romaine lettuce, shredded

4 tomatoes, diced

⅓ cup diced red onion

1 avocado, diced and sprinkled with lemon juice so it doesn't turn brown

1 rounded cup shredded Cheddar cheese

- In a large frying pan, sauté onion, celery and carrots in oil over medium heat until vegetables are soft and onion is translucent, approximately 10 minutes.
- Crumble in ground turkey, then add garlic and continue to sauté until turkey is browned, 10 minutes.
- Stir in tomato paste, chili powder, cumin and water.
- Simmer for 10 to 15 minutes.
- Remove from heat, add cilantro (if using) and salt and pepper to taste.
- Spoon 2 tbsp of the meat mixture onto each tortilla and allow children to choose their own toppings.
- Fold tacos over and enjoy!

Yield: Serves 6 (2 tacos each)

Serving Suggestion: Serve with a green salad and corn on the cob.

super foods

Super foods pack a powerful punch. They are foods that are nutrient dense and contain relatively few calories. For example, a serving of broccoli is high in fibre and contains vitamin C, vitamin A, calcium and iron, as well as a multitude of disease-fighting antioxidants. In contrast, a serving of potato chips is high in calories and offers little nutrition. Introduce super foods early to increase the likelihood of acceptance, and serve them frequently to ensure they become familiar favourites.

- Wild salmon
- Eggs
- Fruits (especially orange ones)
- Oatmeal
- Berries
- Tofu
- Avocados
- Flaxseed
- Nuts and nut butters
- Legumes
- Spinach
- Vegetables (especially dark green and orange ones)

dinner

chicken enchiladas

Although enchiladas take a little longer to prepare than most of the meals in this book, they are certainly worth the effort, and the best part is that they freeze well! Doubling the recipe makes enough for the evening's meal plus one for the freezer. You can also freeze the enchiladas in individual packages, making convenient children's meals for when you're going out. Chicken enchiladas also make a nice change from lasagna when you're contributing a dish at a family gathering.

can what children eat or don't eat affect their cognitive development?

Yes, nutrient deficiencies, particularly iron-deficiency anemia, can have a negative impact on cognitive development. Iron-deficiency anemia is associated with poor performance on intelligence tests, difficulty with learning tasks and delayed academic development.[3] To ensure this doesn't happen to your child, serve iron-rich foods frequently. (See page 135 for a list of iron-rich foods.)

dinner

tomato sauce

1 large shallot, finely diced
1 tbsp canola oil
½ tsp salt
¼ tsp freshly ground pepper
1 small can (14 oz) crushed tomatoes
1 small can (14 oz) diced tomatoes
1 clove garlic, crushed
1½ tsp ground cumin
1½ tsp chili powder
¼ tsp paprika
¼ cup chopped cilantro

• In a saucepan, sauté shallots in oil with salt and pepper for 2 minutes over low heat.
• Add tomatoes, garlic, cumin, chili powder and paprika and bring to a boil. Turn down heat and simmer for 15 minutes.
• Add cilantro, stir, remove from heat and set aside.

enchiladas

2 tbsp canola oil
1 onion, diced
1 tbsp ground cumin
½ tsp salt
¼ tsp freshly ground pepper
3 skinless, boneless chicken breasts, cooked
1½ cups canned black beans, rinsed and drained
1½ cups frozen whole corn kernels
2 cloves garlic, crushed
1 small can (14 oz) diced tomatoes
¾ cup chopped cilantro
1 cup shredded mozzarella cheese (approximately 4 oz)
1 cup shredded old Cheddar cheese (approximately 4 oz)

6 large soft flour tortillas
  (approximately 10 inches)
Tomato Sauce (page 138)
Homemade Salsa
  (page 111) or Guaca-
  mole (page 112)
Light sour cream or plain
  yogurt

• In a large pot over medium heat, sauté onion in oil with cumin, salt, and pepper until onion is translucent, approximately 5 minutes.

• With clean hands, shred chicken breast lengthwise so that the chicken is almost stringy in texture.

• Add chicken, black beans, corn, garlic, diced tomatoes, and ½ cup of the cilantro and mix thoroughly.

• Sauté, stirring occasionally, for 15 minutes.

• In a bowl, mix together mozzarella and Cheddar cheeses.

• Place 1 cup of the chicken mixture in the centre of 1 tortilla and roll up to form an enchilada.

• Place enchilada seam down in the bottom of a 10" x 15" greased baking dish.

• Repeat to make remaining enchiladas.

• Top with tomato sauce and sprinkle with cheese.

• Place in oven preheated to 350°F. Bake until warmed through and cheese is bubbling, approximately 50 minutes.

• Sprinkle with remaining cilantro (optional) and serve with Homemade Salsa, Guacamole and light sour cream or plain yogurt.

Yield: Serves 8

Serving Suggestion: Serve with a green salad.

charlie's favourite roast chicken dinner

Stuffing the cavity with herbs is not essential—however, it does add flavour. Choose whatever herbs you can buy fresh or that you have on hand. Use the leftover carcass to make a Next Night Chicken Barley Soup (page 223) for the next night's dinner. If you don't have time to make the soup, the carcass can be frozen until a later date.

obesity and depression

The psychosocial implications of obesity are well known. Social isolation and poor self-image are common, especially in the severely overweight child. Younger children may be isolated from sports as a result of obesity, thus compounding the problem. Low self-esteem has been evident in obese children as young as 5 years old. In older children, problems of self-esteem can result in eating disorders, depression and poor school performance. These children are more likely to engage in risky behaviours such as smoking and consuming alcohol.[4] Being obese is not fun. Don't let it interfere with your child's happiness and progress.

1 chicken (4 to 4½ lb)
1 lemon, quartered
1 head garlic, top removed
Several sprigs fresh sage
Several sprigs fresh thyme
Several sprigs fresh tarragon
Several sprigs fresh rosemary
1 tbsp olive oil (approximately)
Salt and pepper

• Preheat oven to 400°F.
• Rinse chicken inside and out and pat dry with paper towel.
• Remove any excess lumps of fat from the cavity.

• Remove neck if still attached and giblets if they have not been removed, and set aside for the stock.
• Remove wing tips as they often burn in a hot oven. Save for stock.
• Stuff cavity with garlic, lemon and herbs.
• Tie legs together with string to truss chicken.
• Lightly brush the outside of the bird with oil.
• Sprinkle the outside of the bird with salt and pepper and place bird upside down in a roasting pan. This allows the juices to run into the breast of the bird and keeps the breast

meat moist. Place in middle of oven.

• Roast for 1 to 1¼ hours, or until juices run clear and joints move loosely in their sockets.

• If using a meat thermometer, insert it deep into the leg joint without touching a bone. The whole bird is cooked at 180°F. Remember, it takes a while for the true temperature to register on the thermometer, and the bird will continue to cook outside the oven. Therefore, remove bird from oven at 175°F and cover with foil.

• Allow bird to stand for 10 minutes before carving. This allows the juices to be reabsorbed.

 Yield: Serves family of 4 or 5

Extra chicken makes yummy Chicken Salad sandwiches (page 70).

homemade gravy

There are two tricks to making good gravy. First, purchase a separator. This allows you to separate the good pan drippings from the fat. Second, make a stock to add flavour to your gravy. The stock can be made while the bird is cooking.

Wing tips and whatever parts of the bird you have (giblets, neck, etc.)
4 carrots, peeled and chopped
1 stalk celery, chopped
1 tomato, quartered
1 small onion, quartered
Any fresh herbs you have
on hand (thyme, tarragon, sage or rosemary)
1 bay leaf
1 clove garlic
4 peppercorns
4 cups water
2 tbsp all-purpose flour
Salt and pepper (optional)

• To make stock, place chicken parts, carrots, celery, tomato, onion, herbs, garlic and peppercorns in a small saucepan. Cover with the water and bring to a boil.

- Turn down heat and simmer for 1 hour.
- Strain stock, reserving broth and discarding vegetables.
- Pour stock back into saucepan and simmer over low heat until ready to make gravy. Then transfer stock into glass measuring cup and set aside.
- Pour drippings into separator and allow fat to separate.
- Pour 2 tbsp of the drippings into same saucepan.
- Add flour and whisk over medium heat for 1 minute.
- Slowly add 1 cup of broth and whisk until gravy thickens and lumps disappear.
- Slowly add remainder of drippings and cook until gravy thickens.
- If you need more gravy, you may want to add a little extra stock until desired quantity is reached.
- Add salt and pepper (if using) to taste.

Yield: Approximately 1½ cups

Serving Suggestions: Serve with Cath's Potato Yam Mash (page 219) and Blanched Carrots and Broccoli (page 213).

portion distortion

Portion sizes have increased dramatically over the years. In the 1950s, a typical package of popcorn sold at the movies was 3 cups and 174 calories. Today, it is possible to purchase a 21-cup bag of buttered popcorn containing 1,700 calories. In 1916, a 6.5 fluid ounce bottle of Coca-Cola was 79 calories. Today, the 16 fluid ounce bottle is becoming the norm; it contains 194 calories.[5] This escalation in portion sizes parallels the rise in childhood obesity. Many of the foods being "supersized" are low-nutrient, high-calorie snack foods. As an alternative, offer nutritious fruits and vegetables for snacks, and when eating out, resist the temptation to supersize.

turkey chili

Don't be daunted by the large number of ingredients. This nutritious chili is designed to be made in bulk and frozen, providing convenient family meals. However, if serving young children, you may want to start slowly when it comes to introducing spices; eliminate the turmeric and start with only 3 tbsp chili powder. You can always add more chili powder later. If your child still finds the chili a little too flavourful, try mixing it with some light sour cream or plain yogurt. Alternatively, the chili can also be served over a baked potato or with mashed potatoes. If you prefer a spicier version, add more chili powder or a few crushed red pepper flakes to the adults' portion prior to serving.

1 onion, diced

¼ cup firmly packed grated fresh ginger

2 stalks celery, sliced (approximately 4 oz)

¼ cup canola oil

1 sweet red pepper, diced

1 sweet yellow pepper, diced

2 cloves garlic, crushed

1 cup chopped cilantro

1½ lb ground turkey

3 tbsp ground cumin

⅓ cup chili powder

1 tsp ground turmeric (optional)

½ head broccoli, chopped

½ head cauliflower, chopped

2 large carrots, peeled and sliced

1 can (19 oz) white kidney beans, drained and rinsed

1 can (19 oz) chickpeas, drained and rinsed

1 can (19 oz) black beans, drained and rinsed

1 can (19 oz) red kidney beans, drained and rinsed

1 can (14 oz) corn, drained and rinsed

2½ cans (28 oz each) diced tomatoes

1 small can (5.5 oz) tomato paste

toppings

1 cup shredded Cheddar cheese

1 bunch green onions, sliced

1 cup low-fat sour cream or plain yogurt

- In a stockpot, sauté onion, ginger and celery in oil until onion is translucent, approximately 5 minutes.
- Add peppers, garlic and cilantro and continue to sauté for another 10 minutes.
- Crumble in ground turkey and mix thoroughly. Add cumin, chili powder and turmeric and sauté for another 10 minutes.
- Add remaining ingredients, mix thoroughly and bring to a boil.
- Turn down heat and simmer with lid partially covering for 30 minutes.
- Serve sprinkled with cheese, onions and either low-fat sour cream or plain yogurt.

 Yield: Serves 10 to 12

Serving Suggestion: Serve with whole grain bread (or crusty brown rolls) and a tossed salad.

Leftovers pack well in a Thermos.

dinner

don't become a short-order cook!

Your kitchen is not a restaurant. Who has the time or energy to make separate meals every night? Involving your children in meal planning and cooking is a great way to help them feel a part of the family meal. Be aware of your children's favourite meals and try to serve them regularly.

The only way your children will learn to appreciate new foods is by exposure. When introducing a new food or one that has previously been rejected, serve a small amount with something you know your children will like. On occasion, this could mean they fill up on whole grain bread and follow up with fruit and yogurt for dessert. Be reassured that healthy children do not starve themselves, and remember that it takes multiple exposures before a new food is accepted.

tarragon turkey burgers with tzatziki

Children love hamburgers. Turkey burgers are a leaner alternative to regular ground beef patties. Extra patties can be stored in the freezer to facilitate last-minute children's meals. For little ones, you can always make mini burgers, which are a big hit at our houses. To make a mini bun, press a cookie round into a hamburger bun. Tarragon has a fairly strong flavour, so if introducing it to little ones you may want to start with ¼ tsp. If they enjoy it, try ½ tsp the next time.

⅓ cup finely diced red onion
1 stalk celery, diced
1 clove garlic, crushed
2 tsp canola oil
1½ lb ground turkey or chicken
½ cup Whole Wheat Bread Crumbs (page 146)
1 egg

½ tsp salt
½ tsp freshly ground pepper
¼ or ½ tsp finely chopped tarragon (optional)
1½ cups Tzatziki (page 109)
Whole wheat hamburger buns

• In a small frying pan, sauté onion, celery and garlic in oil over medium heat for 5 minutes.
• In a large bowl, combine onion mixture, turkey, bread crumbs, egg, salt, pepper, and tarragon (if using).
• Form into patties.
• To cook burgers on a barbecue, sear each side on high heat for 1 minute. Reduce heat to medium and cook with lid closed until burgers are cooked through and no longer pink inside, approximately 10 minutes. Burgers can also be cooked in an oven preheated to 375°F for 20 minutes or until cooked through. Flip burgers after 10 minutes.
• Serve patties on whole wheat buns topped with tzatziki and your favourite burger toppings.

 Yield: Serves 6

Serving Suggestion: Serve with Roasted Potato and Yam Chips (page 218) and steamed broccoli.

Serve either on their own or on a toasted bun with the regular burger fixings.

whole wheat bread crumbs

4 slices whole wheat bread

- Lightly toast bread.
- Remove from toaster and allow to stand for 5 minutes until bread is dry.
- Pulse in food processor until crumbs are a fine consistency.

Yield: Approximately 1 cup

lamb burgers with tzatziki

With only ¼ tsp crushed red pepper flakes, the chili flavour is very mild. If you would prefer a stronger chili flavour, double the quantity. Extra burgers freeze well to facilitate last-minute children's meals.

1½ lb ground lamb
⅓ cup diced onion
¼ cup Whole Wheat Bread Crumbs (above)
1 clove garlic, crushed
¼ tsp salt
½ tsp freshly ground pepper
1 tbsp finely chopped fresh mint
¼ tsp crushed red pepper flakes (optional)
1 egg
1 cup Tzatziki (page 109)

- In a large bowl, mix together all of the ingredients except the tzatziki.
- Form into patties.
- To cook burgers on a barbecue, sear each side on high heat for 1 minute. Reduce heat to medium and cook with lid closed until burgers are cooked through and no longer pink inside, approximately 10 minutes. Burgers can also be cooked in an oven preheated to 375°F for 20 minutes or until cooked through. Flip burgers after 10 minutes.
- Serve patties on whole wheat buns topped with tzatziki and your favourite toppings.

Yield: Serves 6

Serving Suggestions: Serve with Roasted Home Fries (page 219) or Roasted Potato and Yam Chips (page 218) and Kids' Caesar Salad (page 208).

ashley's chicken dijonnaise

As it's economical to buy chicken breasts in bulk, we usually triple or quadruple this recipe. This facilitates the freezing of a number of dinners for rushed weekday nights. To do so, package 4 bone-in chicken breasts with a portion of marinade in a freezer bag. Being frozen in its marinade allows the chicken to absorb the flavours. To serve, defrost chicken in the refrigerator and cook according to the instructions. If you do not have any fresh thyme, dried thyme can be substituted. Avoid dried rosemary—it is not very flavourful and rather sticky in consistency. Pork tenderloin also works well frozen in the same marinade.

3 tbsp canola oil
1½ tbsp Dijon mustard
1 tsp chopped fresh rosemary
1 tsp chopped fresh thyme

2 cloves garlic, crushed
¼ tsp salt
Freshly ground pepper
4 bone-in skinless chicken breasts

don't give in to panhandling

Avoid giving handouts after meals, especially when children come begging 10 minutes after an unfinished meal. The next scheduled snack should not be too far away, and children need to learn that mealtimes are for eating.

- In a small bowl, combine oil, mustard, rosemary, thyme, garlic, salt, and pepper to taste and mix thoroughly.
- Place chicken and mustard marinade in a plastic bag. Massage until marinade evenly coats the chicken and place in the refrigerator for a minimum of 20 minutes.
- Cook either on the barbecue over medium heat for 6 minutes per side or in an oven preheated to 400°F until meat is cooked through, approximately 20 minutes. When cooked, juices should run clear and a meat thermometer inserted into the middle of the breast will read 170°F.

Yield: Serves 4 to 6, depending on appetite

Serving Suggestion: Serve with whole grain rice, steamed broccoli and a green salad.

thai chicken curry with mango salsa

Packed with lots of veggies and served on whole grain rice, Thai Chicken Curry is a nutritious family meal. The combined sweetness of the coconut milk and the mango salsa helps to balance the heat of the curry, making it more appealing to children. Fish sauce, coconut milk, red Thai curry paste, bamboo shoots and lemon grass should be available in the Asian section of your local grocery store. If you cannot find red Thai curry paste, green Thai curry paste can be substituted. It is difficult to give an exact quantity for the curry paste as the hotness will vary depending on the variety used. When adding the curry paste, start slowly, adding 1 tsp at a time. Keep in mind that children will likely prefer a fairly mild curry; if the adults prefer a spicier version, crushed red pepper flakes can always be added to their portions prior to serving.

½ onion, diced

1 rounded tbsp grated fresh ginger

¼ cup lemon grass, roughly chopped (optional)

3 tbsp canola oil

½ eggplant, chopped into cubes (approximately ½ lb)

2 cans (14 oz each) light coconut milk, shaken before opening

½ cup water

2 tbsp red Thai curry paste (approximately)

1 tbsp fish sauce or soy sauce

1 can (10 oz) sliced bamboo shoots

2 skinless, boneless chicken breasts, cut into cubes (approximately 1 lb)

4 carrots, peeled and cut into matchsticks

6 oz fresh green beans, trimmed and sliced into 1-inch sticks

1 sweet red pepper, sliced

½ cup chopped cilantro

Cooked whole grain rice

Mango Salsa (recipe follows)

• Sauté onion, ginger and lemon grass (if using) in 2 tbsp of the canola oil for 5 minutes.

• Add eggplant and remaining canola oil and sauté until soft, approximately 15 minutes.

• Add coconut milk, water, red Thai curry paste to taste and fish sauce.

• Add bamboo shoots and chicken and bring to a boil. Turn down heat and simmer for 10 minutes.

• Add carrots, beans, red pepper and cilantro and simmer until vegetables are tender and chicken is cooked through, approximately 10 minutes.

• Serve over whole grain rice and top with mango salsa.

Yield: Serves 4 to 5

mango salsa

This salsa is delicious served with any grilled white fish.

1 cup diced mango
⅓ cup diced red onion
⅓ cup chopped cilantro
1 tbsp freshly squeezed
   lime juice

• Combine all of the ingredients and stir.

• Refrigerate for at least half an hour before serving.

Yield: Serves 4 to 5

avoiding food poisoning

Every year, an estimated 11 to 13 million Canadians get sick as a result of foodborne illness.[6] Most often, symptoms of food poisoning are similar to the flu and include fever, stomach cramps, diarrhea, nausea and vomiting. However, the results can be more serious, including paralysis, kidney failure and even death. Those most at risk are young children, the elderly and individuals with weak immune systems. The following safety tips will help keep your family healthy.

• Serve only pasteurized milk and juice. If they are not pasteurized, it will say so on the label.
• Cook all food thoroughly, especially red meat, poultry, fish and eggs.
• Rinse and scrub all fresh produce under running water.
• Keep cold foods cold (at or below 40°F/4°C) and hot foods hot (at or above 140°F/60°C).
• Prevent cross-contamination by using separate cutting boards for raw meat and produce.
• Wash hands and surfaces often with hot soapy water.
• Don't eat raw eggs or fish.
• Wash kitchen cloths daily.
• Do not eat foods from any can that is swollen or dented.
• Be mindful of expiration dates.

dinner

shepherd's pie

The following recipe makes two 8" x 8" shepherd's pies. One becomes the evening's meal and the other goes into the freezer for a later date.

1 onion, diced

4 stalks celery, diced

3 large carrots, diced

1 tbsp dried oregano

2 tbsp canola oil

4 cloves garlic, crushed

2½ lb extra-lean ground beef

1 can (14 oz) corn kernels

1 small can (5.5 oz) tomato paste

1 can (28 oz) diced tomatoes

1 tsp crushed red pepper flakes (optional)

⅓ cup chopped fresh parsley (optional)

for mashed potato topping:

5 large potatoes (approximately 3½ lb)

⅓ cup milk

¼ cup non-hydrogenated margarine

1 clove garlic, crushed

- In a large deep frying pan or stockpot, sauté onion, celery, carrots and oregano in oil until onion is translucent, approximately 5 minutes.
- Add garlic and slowly crumble in ground beef. Sauté until beef is browned, approximately 5 minutes.
- Drain off excess fat.
- Add corn, tomato paste, diced tomatoes, and crushed red pepper flakes (if using). Mix thoroughly and bring to a boil.
- Turn down heat and simmer for 20 minutes.
- Preheat oven to 375°F.
- Remove beef and vegetable mixture from heat, add parsley and mix thoroughly.
- Meanwhile, cook potatoes in boiling water until tender.
- Mash potatoes with milk, margarine and garlic.
- Evenly divide meat mixture into two 8" x 8" pans and top with mashed potatoes. Freeze one of the pies for another meal.

• To serve, bake pie in oven until warmed through and bubbling around the edges, approximately 40 minutes.

 Yield: Each pie serves 4 to 5

Serving Suggestion: Serve with a green salad or steamed peas. Leftovers can be packed in a Thermos for lunch.

what about e. coli?

E. coli 0157:H7 is a leading cause of foodborne illness.[7] It has been found in the intestines of healthy cattle, deer, goats and sheep. The organism is present on most cattle farms and can be transferred to the surface of the meat during butchering. Because grinding beef can spread the bacteria throughout the meat, improper handling of raw ground beef and eating undercooked hamburgers are the most common ways to come into contact with the bacteria. Make sure all ground meats are thoroughly cooked, and if you're ever served a pink hamburger, send it back.

Outbreaks have also been linked to unpasteurized milk and juice, as well as to contaminated water, sprouts, lettuce, spinach and petting zoos. Family members and those who work with children not yet toilet trained are also at risk because bacteria in the stool of an infected person can be passed from person to person. Vigorous hand washing is the best way to avoid contamination.

Symptoms of an E. coli infection can include stomach cramps, bloody diarrhea and sometimes a mild fever. In most cases, the illness will subside within 5 to 10 days. However, in some instances, particularly in children under 5 and the elderly, the illness can become more severe, causing kidney failure and even death. If you see bloody diarrhea or suspect E. coli, seek medical attention immediately.

dinner

barbecued asian leg of lamb

This is a good choice for weekend family barbecues. For best results, make the marinade in the morning and allow the lamb to sit in it for the day.

1 butterflied leg of lamb (4 to 5 lb)	½ tsp crushed red pepper flakes
1 cup freshly squeezed lime juice (approximately 6 limes)	3 tbsp crushed garlic (approximately 1 small head)
¼ cup fish sauce	1½ cups chopped cilantro
¼ cup sesame oil	⅓ cup grated fresh ginger
¼ cup hoisin sauce	Handful parsley or cilantro for garnish
¼ cup liquid honey	
2 tbsp low-sodium soy sauce	

- Cut excess fat off the lamb and set aside.
- In a small bowl, mix together all of the remaining ingredients (except garnish) and pour over lamb.
- Allow to marinate in the refrigerator for a minimum of 5 hours.
- Remove lamb from marinade and save juices.
- Pour marinade into a small saucepan and bring to a rapid boil. Turn down heat and simmer for 10 minutes. Strain.
- Place lamb on barbecue on high heat and sear on one side for 3 minutes. Turn down heat and cook for 10 minutes with lid closed. Turn again and cook for another 10 to 12 minutes, covered. (If you do not have a cover on your barbecue, it will take a little longer.) When done, the meat should be pink in the middle and an instant-read thermometer should read 145°F.
- Remove from grill, cover with foil and allow lamb to stand for 10 minutes. This allows the meat to reabsorb the juices.
- Slice lamb across the grain into half-inch slices and arrange on a platter. Drizzle lightly with sauce and garnish with either parsley or

cilantro. Do not pour too much of the sauce over the meat as the flavour can be overpowering.

• Extra sauce can be served on the side.

Yield: Serves 6 to 8, depending on the size of the leg

Serving Suggestion: Serve with Garlic Roasted Broccolini (page 217) and Bulgur Salad (page 167).

home-style chicken pie

The mashed potato topping puts a new twist on old-fashioned chicken pot pie. The recipe makes two 8" x 8" pies, one for the evening's meal and one for the freezer.

6 skinless, boneless chicken breasts (approximately 2 lb)

4 cups cold water

4 large carrots, peeled and cut into ¼-inch pieces

1 large fennel bulb, diced

3 stalks celery, cut into ¼-inch pieces

25 white fresh or frozen pearl onions, peeled and cut in half

4 cloves garlic, crushed

2 tsp chopped fresh or dried thyme

1 tbsp canola oil

2 tbsp non-hydrogenated margarine

3 tbsp all-purpose flour

1 cup milk

2 bay leaves

1 cup fresh or frozen green peas

2 tbsp chopped fresh parsley

Salt and pepper

for mashed potato topping:

5 large potatoes (approximately 3½ lb)

⅓ cup milk

¼ cup non-hydrogenated margarine

1 clove garlic, crushed

- Cut chicken into 1-inch cubes.
- Pour water into a large frying pan. Bring to a boil. Add chicken and cook, uncovered, for 5 minutes. With a slotted spoon, remove meat and set aside. Reserve the broth.
- Cook potatoes for topping in boiling water until tender.
- While potatoes are cooking, sauté carrots, fennel, celery, onions, garlic and thyme in oil in a large frying pan over medium heat for 5 minutes. Add ⅓ cup reserved cooking broth and cook for another 5 minutes. Set vegetables aside.
- Using the same frying pan, melt margarine over medium heat. Whisk in flour to form paste and cook for 1 minute over medium heat.
- Slowly add milk, whisking until sauce is smooth and lumps disappear.
- Add 2 cups of reserved broth and bay leaves and continue to simmer, whisking, until sauce thickens, 5 to 7 minutes.
- Preheat oven to 375°F.
- With a wooden spoon, slowly fold in chicken, sautéed vegetables and peas and continue to simmer for 5 minutes.
- Add parsley, and salt and pepper to taste, and mix until all ingredients are incorporated.
- Once potatoes are cooked, mash with remaining milk, margarine and garlic. Set aside.
- Evenly divide chicken mixture between 2 baking pans and remove bay leaves. Top each with potato mixture. Freeze one of the pies for another meal.
- Bake remaining in preheated oven for approximately 40 minutes or until warmed through and bubbling around the edges.

 Yield: 2 pies (each pie serves 4 to 5)

Serving Suggestion: Serve with green salad with White Balsamic Vinaigrette (page 203). Leftovers can be packed in a Thermos for lunch.

chicken tenders

The following makes a healthy alternative to store-bought chicken fingers. Instead of serving with sugary ketchup, try either Tzatziki (page 109) or Pizza Sauce (page 124).

2 skinless, boneless chicken breasts, cut into strips across the grain
1 cup plain yogurt
½ cup freshly grated Parmesan cheese
½ tsp salt (optional)
½ tbsp freshly ground pepper (optional)
½ cup cornmeal
1½ cups Whole Wheat Bread Crumbs (see page 146)
3 tbsp canola oil

- Preheat oven to 375°F.
- With a mallet, pound chicken to ¼-inch thickness.
- In a small bowl, mix together yogurt, cheese, and salt and pepper (if using).
- In a resealable plastic bag, combine cornmeal and bread crumbs and shake until well mixed.
- With tongs, dip chicken fingers in yogurt mixture, and shake to remove excess. Then dip in bread crumbs, and shake until coated.
- Evenly spread oil on cookie sheet.
- Place tenders on cookie sheet and bake for approximately 35 minutes, turning halfway through baking, or until golden brown and crispy on the outside.

Yield: 12 tenders

Serving Suggestion: Serve with vegetable sticks and a glass of milk.

beans and grains

Traditionally, meat has been the focus of the typical North American dinner. However, times are changing. Canada's new Food Guide recommends Canadians eat alternatives to meat, such as beans, peas and lentils, more often. Today, a balanced meal includes more alternatives to meat, smaller portions of meat and a greater emphasis on whole grains, vegetables and fruit.[8] Beans and grains are a healthy alternative to meat. Instead of teaching your children to expect meat at every meal, introduce them to a wide variety of whole grains, lentils, beans and peas. Plant-based proteins are high in fibre and a rich source of vitamins, minerals and antioxidants. They also have the added benefit of lowering blood cholesterol levels, as well as being inexpensive and versatile. Served with whole grain bread and a green salad, many of the following recipes make a delicious vegetarian dinner. Transported in a Thermos, beans are a nutritious addition to any packed lunch.

vegetarian chili

Chili freezes well, and this recipe is designed to be made in bulk and frozen to provide convenient family meals. If serving to young children, you may want to start slowly when it comes to introducing the spices: eliminate turmeric and start with only 3 tbsp chili powder. You can always add more chili powder later. If your child still finds the chili too flavourful, try mixing it with a little light sour cream or plain yogurt. The chili can also be served over a baked potato or with mashed potatoes. If you prefer a spicier version, add a few crushed red pepper flakes to the adult portions prior to serving.

1 onion, diced

2 stalks celery, sliced

2 cloves garlic, crushed

¼ cup grated fresh
   ginger

¼ cup canola oil

1 sweet red pepper, diced

1 sweet yellow pepper,
   diced

2 zucchinis, cut in half and
   sliced

12 mushrooms, sliced

157

½ eggplant, cut into 1-inch chunks

1 cup cilantro, chopped

1 can (19 oz) white kidney beans, drained and rinsed

1 can (19 oz) chickpeas, drained and rinsed

1 can (19 oz) black beans, drained and rinsed

1 russet potato, peeled and cut into chunks

2½ cans (28 oz each) diced tomatoes

1 small can (5.5 oz) tomato paste

½ head broccoli, cut into florets

½ head cauliflower, cut into florets

4 carrots, peeled and cut into bite-size pieces

⅓ cup chili powder

3 tbsp cumin

1 tsp turmeric powder (optional)

1 bag (70 g) fresh spinach (optional)

toppings

Shredded Cheddar cheese

Green onions, sliced

1 cup plain yogurt or low-fat sour cream

dinner

• In a stockpot, sauté onion, celery, garlic and ginger in 2 tbsp of the oil over medium heat until onion is translucent, approximately 5 minutes.

• Add the rest of the oil, along with the peppers, zucchini, mushrooms, eggplant and cilantro and continue to sauté, stirring occasionally, until mushrooms and eggplant are cooked and soft, approximately 15 minutes.

• Add the remaining ingredients with the exception of spinach and toppings. Mix thoroughly and bring to a boil.

• Turn down heat and simmer for 30 minutes, stirring occasionally.

• Remove from heat, add spinach (if using) and stir.

• Serve sprinkled with cheese, onions and either low-fat sour cream or plain yogurt.

 Yield: Serves 10 to 12

Serving Suggestion: Serve with green salad and whole wheat bread.

are vegetarian diets safe for children?

Properly managed vegetarian diets are safe and may reduce the risk of childhood obesity and other nutrition-related illnesses. There are 3 types of vegetarian diets: vegan, ovo-vegetarian and lacto-ovo vegetarian. Vegans eat only non-animal foods, ovo-vegetarians eat non-animal foods and eggs, and lacto-ovo vegetarians eat non-animal foods plus eggs and dairy. Children on extremely restricted vegetarian diets might not get enough energy, protein, calcium, iron, zinc, vitamin D and vitamin B12 if proper care is not taken in meal planning. It is possible for malnutrition to set in. As a result, the Canadian Paediatric Society recommends the less restrictive lacto-ovo vegetarian diet be promoted for vegetarian children.[9] Strict vegan diets are not considered safe for children under 2 years of age. It is important that caregivers of vegetarian children be familiar with the minimal nutritional requirements for children. Consultation with a pediatric dietitian could be beneficial.

traditional baked beans

Salt pork is available in most grocery stores, but if you cannot find it, it is possible to substitute 4 strips of bacon. Making this dish with great northern beans is preferable as they are slightly larger; however, navy beans can be substituted with similar results.

1 pkg (500 g) dried great northern beans or navy beans
1 tbsp olive oil
1 onion, diced
½ lb package cured salt pork
2 tbsp dry mustard
2 cloves garlic, crushed

159

3 tbsp molasses

1 small can (14 oz) chopped tomatoes

⅓ cup tomato paste

1 tbsp Worcestershire sauce (optional)

Pepper

- Rinse beans under cold water and soak in 6 cups of water overnight. Drain.
- Preheat oven to 300°F.
- Place beans in a large saucepan, cover with twice their volume of water and bring to a boil. Turn down heat and simmer for 30 minutes.
- Drain and reserve 2 cups of the cooking liquid.
- In a Dutch oven or ovenproof baking dish, sauté onion and pork in oil over low heat until onion is translucent, approximately 5 minutes.
- Remove pork from pot and set aside.
- Add 2 cups of reserved liquid, mustard, garlic, molasses, tomatoes, tomato paste, and Worcestershire sauce (if using) and mix thoroughly.
- Add beans, mix thoroughly and place pork on top of beans.
- Cover and bake in oven for 3 hours, checking and stirring occasionally during cooking time. If beans have absorbed too much liquid and are looking a little dry, add some boiling water.
- Once cooked, remove salt pork and discard. Add pepper to taste and serve.

 Yield: Serves 4 to 5

Serving Suggestion: Serve with a green salad and whole wheat bread.

lemon garlic chickpeas

These beans are quick to prepare and are delicious sprinkled on your dinner salad.

1 can (19 oz) chickpeas
⅓ cup olive oil
1 small clove garlic,
   crushed
½ lemon, juiced
2 tbsp chopped fresh
   parsley (optional)

½ tsp salt
Freshly ground pepper

• Combine chickpeas, oil, garlic, lemon juice, parsley, salt, and pepper to taste. Mix thoroughly.

Yield: 2 cups

my daughter is a vegetarian—what now?

If your teen suddenly announces she's a vegetarian, don't panic. Instead, embrace your daughter's decision and help her eat properly. Together, consult a dietitian and start meal planning.

It is important your daughter eat a variety of foods to avoid developing deficiencies. To replace the iron found in meat, she should eat broccoli, spinach, dried fruit, seeds and legumes, as well as iron-fortified cereals and grains. Eating iron-rich foods along with foods high in vitamin C, such as tomatoes, potatoes and fruits, will increase iron absorption. As well, she should eat a variety of protein-rich foods, such as tofu, beans, lentils, dairy products and eggs. If your daughter is not eating dairy, make sure she has an alternative source of calcium, such as tofu, broccoli, leafy greens, chickpeas, baked beans, nuts and canned salmon (with bones), as well as vitamin D–fortified soy beverage. If she is not eating any animal products, there is a risk of vitamin B12 deficiency; supplementation may be required.

Support your daughter by making the healthy choice to go veggie as a family more often. Stock your freezer with a number of vegetarian meals for the nights when the rest of the family is eating meat. You should be able to find healthy veggie burgers, burritos and even lasagna in the freezer section of your grocery store. Remember to read labels carefully when buying packaged foods, as many are high in salt, fats and other unwanted additives.

The Good Food Book for Families has a number of healthy vegetarian dinner ideas. For more ideas, see Beans and Grains (page 157) and Pasta (page 184).

asparagus, pea and mint risotto

Children tend to love fresh peas because they are naturally sweet in flavour. Try making this dish in spring or early summer, when fresh peas are readily available. If peas are not in season, you can substitute frozen peas.

16 stalks asparagus, trimmed and cut into 1½-inch
  segments
1 cup freshly shelled peas (or frozen peas)
2 tbsp canola oil
1 onion, diced
1 fennel bulb, diced
1 cup Arborio rice
⅓ cup white wine (optional)
3 cups low-sodium chicken stock (approximately; no
  more than 4 cups)
1 tbsp lemon zest
1 tbsp finely chopped fresh mint
1 cup packed freshly grated Parmesan cheese
Salt and freshly ground pepper

dinner

• Steam asparagus over boiling water until bright green and just tender, 3 to 4 minutes. Rinse under cool water to stop the cooking process and set aside.

• If using fresh peas, steam until tender, approximately 3 minutes. Rinse under cool water and set aside. If using frozen, there is no need to precook them.

• Meanwhile, in a large frying pan, sauté onion and fennel in oil until softened, approximately 5 minutes.

• Add rice and stir until coated in oil.

• Add wine (if using) and stir.

• Add chicken stock ½ cup at a time, stirring frequently. As rice absorbs stock, add more, stirring frequently to prevent rice from sticking. Reserve ¼ cup of stock to add at the end. The entire cooking time for the rice should be about 25 minutes. Rice is ready when firm but cooked through.

• During the last 5 minutes of cooking time, add vegetables, lemon zest and mint and stir gently.

• Remove from heat and add the last bit of stock, cheese, and salt and pepper to taste. Stir until cheese melts.

 Yield: Serves 4

chickpea ratatouille

Adding protein-rich chickpeas to this classic French dish elevates it from a side to a meal.

½ cup olive oil
1 eggplant, cut into
    ½-inch squares (approximately 1 lb)
2 zucchinis, cut into
    ½-inch squares (approximately 1 lb)

2 sweet red peppers, cut
    into ½-inch squares
    (approximately 1 lb)
2 sweet green peppers,
    cut into ½-inch
    squares (approximately
    1 lb)

dinner

1 large onion, cut into
½-inch squares
1 bulb garlic, crushed
1 small can (5.5 oz)
tomato paste
4 ripe tomatoes, cored
and cut into cubes
(approximately 1¼ lb)
1 small can (14 oz) diced
tomatoes
1 cup chopped fresh basil
2 tbsp finely chopped
fresh rosemary
(optional)
1 tbsp finely chopped
fresh thyme
2 cans (19 oz each) chickpeas, rinsed and
drained
Salt and pepper
Crushed red pepper flakes
(optional)
Shredded Cheddar cheese
or freshly grated
Parmesan cheese for
garnish (optional)

• In a stockpot, heat oil over medium heat.

• Add eggplant, zucchini, peppers, onion and garlic.

• Sauté for 10 minutes, stirring occasionally.

• Add tomato paste, tomatoes (canned and fresh), basil, rosemary (if using), thyme and chickpeas and bring to a boil.

• Turn down heat and simmer with lid partially on for 1 hour.

• Stir occasionally.

• Add salt and pepper to taste and crushed red pepper flakes to the adults' portions (if desired).

• Sprinkle with cheese (if using) and serve.

 Yield: Serves 6 to 8

Serving Suggestion: Serve with crusty whole grain bread and a green salad.

tofu vegetable stir fry

Although the recipe calls for egg noodles, it's also good with rice noodles or served on brown rice.

¼ cup low-sodium chicken or vegetable stock
2 tbsp sodium-reduced soy sauce
2 tbsp oyster sauce
2 tbsp rice wine vinegar
1 tbsp liquid honey
½ tsp cornstarch
¼ tsp sesame oil
½ pkg (250 g) firm tofu, cut into ½-inch cubes
½ lb Asian-style egg noodles
2 tbsp canola oil
4 carrots, peeled and cut into matchsticks
½ head broccoli, cut into florets
1 tbsp freshly grated ginger
2 cloves garlic, crushed
1 sweet red pepper, cut into strips
½ lb snap peas, trimmed and strings removed
2 green onions, trimmed
⅓ cup chopped cilantro
1 tbsp red pepper flakes (optional)

dinner

• In a small bowl, stir together stock, soy sauce, oyster sauce, rice wine vinegar, honey, cornstarch and sesame oil until smooth and set aside.
• Drizzle 2 tbsp of the mixture over tofu and let marinate while preparing the rest of the meal.
• Cook noodles until just tender. Rinse under cold water to prevent sticking and set aside.
• Heat a wok over high heat until hot.
• Add canola oil, carrots, broccoli and ginger and stir-fry for 3 minutes.
• Turn heat to medium. Add garlic, peppers and snap peas and stir-fry for 2 minutes or until carrots are crisp.

- Add broth mixture, tofu and noodles and stir for 1 minute to coat evenly.
- Add green onions and cilantro (if using) and stir to combine.
- Serve immediately and add red pepper flakes to adults' portions if a spicier stir fry is preferred.

Yield: Serves 4

vegetable barley risotto

The following recipe is a very popular one from *The Baby's Table.* It seems barley risotto is not just for babies!

1 cup pot barley
2 tbsp olive oil
1 onion, diced
1 stalk celery, chopped
2 large carrots, peeled and
  diced
1 fennel bulb, finely diced
1 clove garlic, mashed
3½ cups low-sodium or
  salt-free chicken stock
1 tbsp chopped fresh
  parsley
Salt and pepper

- Rinse barley and set aside to drain.
- In a frying pan, heat oil and sauté onions, celery, carrots, fennel and garlic until tender, approximately 10 minutes.
- Add barley and continue to stir. Add enough stock to cover

barley; bring to a boil. Reduce heat and simmer, stirring occasionally and adding stock as needed to keep barley covered, for 30 to 40 minutes or until tender but firm.

- Add parsley and stir.
- Add salt and pepper to taste.

 Yield: Serves 4

Serving Suggestion: Serve with whole grain bread, sliced Cheddar cheese and a green salad.

bulgur salad

1 cup bulgur

1 cup boiling water

20 cherry tomatoes, cut in
half (approximately 1 lb)

1 English cucumber,
trimmed, seeds
removed, and diced

5 green onions, sliced

1 bunch fresh flat-leaf
parsley, chopped
(approximately 1 cup)

dressing

Juice of 1 lemon (approximately ¼ cup)

¼ cup olive oil

2 cloves garlic, crushed

Pinch paprika (optional)

Salt and pepper

• In a large bowl, pour boiling
water over bulgur.

• Place foil directly on surface of bulgur and let stand for 30 minutes.

• Fluff bulgur with fork and drain if necessary.

• In a large salad bowl, mix together bulgur, tomatoes, cucumber, onions and parsley.

• In a small bowl, whisk together lemon juice, olive oil, garlic, paprika (if using), and salt and pepper to taste.

• Pour dressing over bulgur and mix thoroughly.

• Serve at room temperature or store in the refrigerator for up to 2 days.

 Yield: Serves 6 to 8

This salad packs well and can be made the night before.

cheryl's quinoa salad

Although considered a whole grain, quinoa is actually a small seed. It is a complete protein, containing all 9 essential amino acids. It is also a good source of iron, vitamin E, zinc, potassium and riboflavin.

1 cup quinoa

6 green onions, trimmed and sliced

1 sweet red pepper, seeded and diced

1 rounded cup frozen corn kernels

20 snap peas, trimmed and cut into ½-inch slices

½ English cucumber, seeded and diced

½ cup chopped cilantro

dressing

2 tbsp freshly squeezed lime juice

2 cloves garlic, crushed

1 tbsp sesame oil

1 tbsp olive oil

1 tsp soy sauce

½ tsp ground cumin

½ tsp granulated sugar

Salt and pepper

- Place quinoa in a sieve and rinse under running water.
- Add quinoa to a large pot of boiling water and cook for 8 to 10 minutes or until tender yet slightly crunchy.
- Strain through a fine sieve and spread on a cookie sheet to dry.
- When cooled, transfer quinoa to a large bowl.
- Add onions, red pepper, corn, snap peas, cucumber and cilantro and mix thoroughly.
- To make dressing, combine lime juice, garlic, sesame oil, olive oil, soy sauce, cumin and sugar in a small bowl.
- Toss together dressing and salad until evenly coated.
- Add salt and pepper to taste.
- Serve at room temperature or store in the refrigerator for up to 2 days.

 Yield: Serves 6 to 8

This salad packs well and can be made the night before.

fish

It is a common misconception that many children do not like fish. The truth is, many children love fish. In some cultures, fish is the primary source of protein and is regularly given to children from infancy onward. Introduce fish early to increase the likelihood of its acceptance. It is an excellent choice for babies and can be introduced as early as 8 months of age (unless you have a family history of fish allergy).

If your kids don't like fish, don't despair. *The Good Food Book for Families* has a number of recipes designed to make fish more appealing. Remember, it may take as many as 10 to 20 exposures before a new food is accepted. Because fish tends to be low in fat and is an excellent source of heart-healthy omega-3 fatty acids, your perseverance will pay off. Health Canada's new Food Guide recommends eating at least 2 servings (each serving is 75 grams or ½ cup) of fish per week.[10]

Giving exact cooking times for fish is difficult because it depends on the thickness of each piece. Fish is best when cooked quickly and at a high temperature—the general rule is 10 minutes per inch of thickness. However, it is important that it not be overcooked or else it will become dry and lose flavour. When cooked, fish flakes easily with a fork and is moist inside. When buying fish, choose either fresh or frozen, but always buy good-quality fish.

fish tacos

Even children who do not like fish are likely to enjoy these tacos. If serving to young children, omit the onion and serve the salsa on the side. Children under 5 and those with smaller appetites are likely to eat only half a taco.

1 lb white fish, cooked, skin and bones removed

6 large soft whole wheat flour tortillas (approximately 10 inches)

2 tomatoes, diced

dinner

¼ cup chopped red
   onion (optional)
¼ cup chopped cilantro
   (optional)
1 rounded cup shredded
   Cheddar cheese
1½ cups mild salsa
1 avocado, diced
½ cup light sour cream
   or plain yogurt

• Divide fish evenly among tortillas.
• Top with tomatoes, onion (if using) and cilantro (if using).

• Evenly scatter 2 rounded tbsp cheese onto each tortilla and top with 2 tbsp mild salsa.
• Broil in oven until cheese melts and edges of tortillas begin to brown.
• Remove from oven, top with avocado and fold in half. Cut each taco in half.
• Serve with remaining salsa and low-fat sour cream or plain yogurt on the side.

Yield: Serves 4 to 6

benefits of omega-3 fatty acids

Omega-3 fatty acids are long-chain polyunsaturated fatty acids. They are important for brain development, good vision and a healthy cardiovascular system. Research has revealed that omega-3 fatty acids are highly concentrated in the brain and appear to be particularly important for cognitive and behavioural function.[11] Omega-3 fatty acids are present in significant quantities in human breast milk, and this is thought to be one of the reasons breastfed babies have a cognitive advantage over formula-fed infants.

Omega-3 fatty acids are also known to reduce the risk of cardiovascular disease. Regular consumption of omega-3 fatty acids helps prevent blood clots, protects against irregular heartbeat, and lowers blood pressure, especially in people with hypertension and atherosclerosis.[12] This is thought to be the reason why populations like the Japanese and the

dinner

Greenland Inuit, who consume large quantities of fish, have lower rates of heart disease.

Furthermore, omega-3 fatty acids are also thought to have a protective effect against some cancers, depression and various inflammatory diseases, including rheumatoid arthritis, colitis, Crohn's disease and asthma.[11] In addition, a recent study suggests that intake of omega-3 polyunsaturated fatty acids is associated with a lower risk of type 1 diabetes in high-risk children.[13]

Fish is the best source of omega-3 fatty acids, especially the cold-water, higher-fat fishes like char, salmon, herring, mackerel, sardines and rainbow trout. Start your children on fish early and serve it regularly so they learn to love it.

salmon with fresh dill

Served with Lemon Dill Aïoli (page 175), this simple combination is always a hit.

1½ lb salmon, bones removed
¼ onion, thinly sliced
¼ cup finely chopped fresh dill
1 lemon, quartered

- Preheat oven to 400°F.
- Evenly spread onion over fish and sprinkle with dill.
- Squeeze lemon over fish.
- Bake in oven for 15 to 20 minutes or until fish is moist, opaque throughout and flakes easily with a fork.

Yield: Serves 4

Serving Suggestion: Serve with Bulgur Salad (page 167) and Garlic Roasted Broccolini (page 217).

lemon sole with basil and mashed potatoes

This recipe is another good way to introduce fish to young children. Sole has a mild flavour and, when mixed with mashed potatoes, little ones usually gobble it up. When introducing to very young children, mix the fish with the potato. Instead of serving the adults' fish over mashed potatoes, try it over a green salad. A little White Balsamic Vinaigrette (page 203) drizzled overtop is delicious.

1½ lb sole, skin and
   bones removed
1 lemon
¼ cup finely diced red
   onion
2 tbsp chopped fresh basil

mashed potatoes

3 large potatoes, peeled
   and cut into chunks
   (approximately 3 lb)
¼ cup milk
3 tbsp non-hydrogenated
   margarine
1 clove garlic, crushed
Salt and pepper

- Preheat oven to 400°F.
- Line a cookie sheet with foil.
- Place fish on sheet.
- Evenly squeeze lemon over fish and sprinkle with red onion.
- Cover with another sheet of foil and close at the edges to encase the fish. This enables the fish to poach in its own juices.
- Bake until cooked through and flakes easily, 7 to 10 minutes.
- Remove from oven and sprinkle with basil.
- Meanwhile, cook potatoes in boiling salted water until tender. Drain well and mash with milk, margarine, garlic, and salt and pepper to taste.
- Serve fish over mashed potatoes. For young children, mix the fish with the potatoes.

Yield: Serves 4 to 5

Serving Suggestion: Serve with a tossed green salad and steamed peas.

adhd and diet

Many parents believe that certain foods and food additives cause hyperactivity. As it turns out, there may be some truth to this. For years, doctors have been telling parents that diet doesn't influence hyperactivity. However, a recent study on children aged 3 years and 8–9 years found that they showed more hyperactive behaviour when they were given a drink with food additives (sodium benzoate and artificial food dyes).[14] What does this mean for your child? While diet alone doesn't cause ADHD, food additives seem to have an effect on behaviour in some children. Your best approach is to offer whole foods and avoid additives whenever possible, especially if your child is prone to hyperactivity or inattentiveness.

There is also some evidence to suggest that children with developmental coordination disorder who are given fish oil supplements do better with reading, spelling and behaviour.[15] Strong evidence is not yet there for children with ADHD. The bottom line: eat your fish!

halibut with fresh herbs

The following is delicious barbecued or baked. Our families often eat this in the summer, when halibut is in season and fresh mint is abundant. The minty flavour of this dish usually appeals to children. However, when offering it for the first time, it may be wise to keep a little of the halibut out of the marinade, just in case.

Juice of 1 lime (approximately 2 tbsp)
¼ cup finely chopped fresh mint
¼ cup finely chopped cilantro
2 tbsp olive oil
3 cloves fresh garlic, crushed
1½ lb halibut fillets, bones removed

dinner

- Preheat oven to 400°F.
- In a blender, purée lime juice, cilantro, mint, olive oil and garlic.
- Place fish in ovenproof baking dish.
- Pour marinade over fish, place in refrigerator and allow to marinate for a minimum of 20 minutes to a maximum of 6 hours.
- Bake in oven for 15 to 20 minutes or until moist, opaque throughout and flakes easily with a fork.

Yield: Serves 4

herb-stuffed trout with lemon dill aïoli

This is likely to appeal to young children, as the flavours are fairly mild.

4 good-quality trout, cleaned, heads and tails removed
1 lemon
¼ onion, thinly sliced
8 sprigs fresh thyme
Lemon Dill Aïoli (recipe follows)

- Preheat oven to 400°F.
- Cut lemon into quarters and thinly slice one of the quarters.
- Squeeze remaining lemon into the fish cavities.
- Stuff equal amounts of onion and thyme into fish.
- Arrange lemon slices in each fish.
- Wrap fish in foil and bake in oven for 20 to 25 minutes or until moist, opaque throughout and flakes easily with a fork.
- Serve with Lemon Dill Aïoli.

dinner

lemon dill aïoli

The following is also delicious served with salmon.

½ cup mayonnaise
2 tbsp freshly squeezed lemon juice
½ tsp finely chopped fresh dill
1 clove garlic, crushed

• In a small bowl, combine all of the ingredients and mix thoroughly.

Yield: Serves 4

Serving Suggestion: Serve with Cheryl's Quinoa Salad (page 167) and steamed veggies.

help! my child won't eat fish. how can i ensure she is getting enough omega-3?

If your children won't eat fish, follow these tips to increase their intake of brain-boosting omega-3 fatty acids.
• Try omega-3-enriched eggs.
• Ground flaxseed can be sprinkled on cereal, mixed into oatmeal and added to baked goods. Choose a whole grain bread containing flaxseed or make Cranberry Flaxseed Cookies (page 102).
• Cook with canola oil and look for omega-3-fortified milk, yogurt and orange juice at your local supermarket.
• As fish is the best source of omega-3 fatty acids, continue to serve it as part of your regular meal plan. Over time it will likely be accepted.

salmon patties

This recipe is inspired by our friend Becca. She says her kids can't get enough of these irresistible patties. We eat the patties over a green salad with White Balsamic Vinaigrette (page 203), while the kids enjoy theirs served on a whole wheat bun with the regular burger fixings. Canned salmon is a healthy choice, as it's generally the wild variety. Mash the bones with a fork and mix them into salmon—they are a good source of calcium.

2 tbsp canola oil

½ cup diced onion

½ stalk celery, diced

1 clove garlic, crushed (optional)

2 cans (213 g each) salmon, drained and skin removed

½ cup whole wheat bread crumbs (page 146)

2 large eggs, beaten

¼ tsp lemon zest (optional)

½ tsp freshly ground pepper

1 squeeze fresh lemon juice

• Sauté onion and celery in 1 tbsp of the oil over medium heat for 10 minutes.

• Add garlic (if using) and sauté for 2 minutes, being careful not to burn garlic.

• In a medium bowl, combine onion mixture with remaining ingredients and mix thoroughly.

• Scoop out ⅓ cup of the salmon mixture and flatten into patty. Repeat with remaining mixture.

• Heat remaining oil in frying pan and cook patties for 4 to 6 minutes per side or until warmed through, golden brown and have a slightly crispy coating.

 Yield: Serves 6

Serving Suggestion: Serve with Roasted Potato and Yam Chips (page 218), steamed peas and a green salad.

Salmon patties on toasted whole grain buns with a little mayonnaise and lettuce make a yummy lunch your kids are sure to gobble up.

baked halibut with basil pesto sauce

This easy-to-make dinner can be prepared with any white fish. If you don't have homemade pesto, you should be able to find a prepared version at your local grocery store. The combination of fish and salad is delicious, so try it served on a green salad, while the children enjoy their fish with steamed veggies and whole grain bread.

1½ lb halibut fillets, bones removed
2 tbsp Basil Pesto (page 199)

- Preheat oven to 400°F.
- Evenly spread pesto over fish and bake for 15 to 20 minutes or until moist, opaque throughout and flakes easily with a fork.

Yield: Serves 4

fish and mercury

Mercury is a naturally occurring element found in the earth's crust and also released into the atmosphere by industrial pollutants. Mercury can build up in living things. When it reaches toxic levels in humans, it can cause damage to the central nervous system and even death. This occurred in Japan when 111 people died or became ill after eating contaminated fish coming from waters that were seriously polluted by local industrial discharge.[16] Nearly all fish have trace levels of mercury that are harmless to humans. Because mercury accumulates in the food chain, larger predatory fish have higher mercury levels.

Young children and unborn fetuses are the most susceptible to toxicity. Therefore, pregnant and breastfeeding women, women who may become pregnant and parents of young children should be aware of which types of fish are good choices and which to eat less often. The best way to protect your family is to eat a variety of kinds. Species with low mercury levels include shrimp, salmon, canned light tuna, pollock and catfish. Health Canada advises Canadians to limit their consumption of fish with higher mercury levels, such as fresh and frozen tuna, shark, swordfish, escolar, marlin and orange roughy.[17]

Despite concerns about mercury, fish and shellfish remain an important part of a healthy diet. Fish is low in saturated fat and provides good-quality protein and omega-3 fatty acids. The benefits of eating fish far outweigh the risks.

tuna melts

With this new twist on an old favourite, tuna melts are not just for lunch anymore. Served with a green salad or veggies and dip, they make an easy last-minute dinner.

dinner

1 can (170 g) flaked light
   tuna
1 tbsp chopped cilantro or
   dill (optional)
1 rounded tbsp finely
   chopped red onion
¼ cup celery, diced
2 tbsp mayonnaise
1 squeeze fresh lemon
   juice
Freshly ground pepper
2 slices whole wheat
   bread, lightly toasted
¼ cup shredded Cheddar
   cheese

• In a small bowl, mix together tuna, cilantro or dill (if using), onion, celery, mayonnaise, lemon juice, and pepper to taste.
• Evenly divide tuna mixture between bread and top with cheese.
• Broil on high heat until cheese melts.

Yield: Serves 2

Serving Suggestion: Serve with green salad or veggies and dip.

what about canned tuna?

Health Canada recently revised its position on canned albacore tuna. Mercury levels of canned albacore tuna are higher than levels in other types of canned tuna, but are generally below the 0.5 parts per million standard. As a precaution, Health Canada recommends that women who are or may become pregnant and those who are breastfeeding can eat up to 4 Food Guide servings of canned albacore tuna (1 serving = ½ cup or 75 g / 2½ oz) per week. Children between 1 and 4 years old may eat up to 1 serving of albacore tuna per week, and children between 5 and 11 can safely eat up to 2 servings per week.[18] These recommendations do not pertain to canned light tuna; it is made from species of tuna that have relatively lower mercury levels. As children are more susceptible to toxicity, opt for canned light tuna when possible.

baked red snapper with tomato basil linguine

Mixing the fish with the tomato sauce and serving it over pasta gives this dish extra kid appeal. Instead of having the fish with pasta, the adults may enjoy it served on top of a green salad with a drizzle of White Balsamic Vinaigrette (page 203) and a drizzle of Tuscan Tomato Sauce (page 184).

1½ lb red snapper, skin and bones removed
½ lemon
¼ lb dried linguine
2 cups Tuscan Tomato Sauce (page 184)
½ cup freshly grated Parmesan cheese

- Preheat oven to 400°F.

- Line a cookie sheet with foil.
- Place fish on foil and squeeze lemon evenly over fish.
- Bake for 10 to 12 minutes or until moist, opaque throughout and flakes easily with a fork.
- Meanwhile, cook pasta until al dente and warm the tomato sauce.
- Drain and rinse pasta.
- Toss pasta with 1½ cups of the tomato sauce.

• Place a small portion of pasta on each plate and top with fish. Drizzle remaining sauce over fish.
• For younger children, mix fish into sauce and serve over pasta.
• Top with Parmesan cheese.

Yield: Serves 4 to 5

Serving Suggestion: Serve with a green salad.

roasted halibut with mango salsa

The following can be made with any white fish, but halibut is a favourite—its nice meaty texture goes well with the fruit salsa. Make the salsa before you cook the fish so the flavours combine and mellow.

mango avocado salsa
1 cup mango, diced
1 avocado, diced
⅓ cup finely diced red onion
¼ cup finely chopped cilantro
Pinch granulated sugar
Pinch salt
1 to 3 tbsp freshly squeezed lime juice

• In bowl, combine mango, avocado, onion, cilantro, sugar and salt.
• Add lime juice to taste and stir.

Yield: 2 cups salsa

roasted halibut
1½ lb halibut fillets, skin and bones removed

Juice of ½ lime
1 tbsp canola oil

• Preheat oven to 400°F.
• Squeeze lime over halibut.
• In a small frying pan, sear halibut in oil over medium heat, 1 minute per side.
• Transfer fish to baking dish and bake in oven for approximately 10 minutes or until moist, opaque throughout and flakes easily with a fork.
• Remove from oven and cut into 4 pieces.
• Top with Mango Salsa to serve.

Yield: Serves 4

Serving Suggestion: Serve with Cheryl's Quinoa Salad (page 167) and steamed asparagus.

pcbs in farmed salmon

Polychlorinated Biphenyls (PCBs) are a group of chemicals first manufactured in 1929. The term refers to any one or any combination of 209 specific chemicals. PCBs are difficult to break down and are stored in the body fat of animals. In the 1970s, concern over their impact on the environment led to a ban on manufacturing and importing PCBs. Today, the level of PCBs in our food supply is actually lower than it was several years ago.

When ingested by humans, PCBs can accumulate in the body, but we know little about their long-term effects. The number of chemicals involved complicates ongoing research. Some studies dealing with long-term, low-level exposure to PCBs suggest subtle effects on reproduction and on the development of newborns and young children.[19]

Concern over PCBs in the food supply revolves primarily around salmon. Despite concerns, salmon continues to be part of a healthy diet, and the benefits of eating salmon outweigh the risks. Salmon is low in mercury, and is an excellent source of omega-3 fatty acids, which are vital for the cognitive development of infants and young children. Although the levels of PCBs and other contaminants are slightly higher in farmed salmon than in wild species, Health Canada has determined that the levels of PCBs are well below the legal limit of 2 parts per billion. Because infants and children are more susceptible to toxicity, opt for wild salmon whenever possible. Canned salmon is an economical and healthy choice because most canned salmon is made with wild species. To further reduce your risk, remove excess fat and skin before cooking. When cooking salmon, bake, broil or grill the fish. Avoid frying, as this method retains the fat.

panko-crusted halibut fish sticks

Panko crumbs, or Japanese bread crumbs, make a deliciously light topping. You should be able to buy them in most Asian markets or even your local supermarket. If you can't find panko, substitute 1½ cups whole wheat bread crumbs mixed with ½ cup cornmeal. The following can be made with any white fish.

1¼ lb halibut
1 cup plain yogurt
1 clove garlic, crushed
¼ tsp salt
Freshly ground pepper (optional)
2 cups panko crumbs
2 tbsp canola oil

- Preheat oven to 375°F.
- Cut fish into sticks.
- In a small bowl, mix together yogurt, garlic, salt, and pepper to taste (if using).
- With tongs, dip fish into yogurt mixture and shake to remove excess.
- Place panko crumbs in a resealable plastic bag.
- Add fish and shake until evenly coated with panko crumbs.
- Evenly spread oil over baking sheet and place fish sticks on sheet.
- Bake for approximately 30 minutes, turning after 20 minutes, or until golden and coating is crispy.

Yield: Serves 4–5

Serving Suggestion: Serve with whole grain rice and steamed peas and Amanda's Ginger Yam Mash (page 216).

vitamin d

Vitamin D is made in the body when skin is exposed to sunlight. It plays a crucial role in maintaining cellular health and preventing diseases such as multiple sclerosis (MS), rickets, osteoporosis and certain types of cancers.[20] Recent evidence regarding vitamin D's role in cancer prevention indicates that current Health Canada guidelines, last published in 1997, may fall well short of the levels needed to prevent certain types of cancer, including prostate, gastrointestinal, breast and endometrial (uterine).[21]

Because of our northern location, Canadians are among the people most likely to be deficient in vitamin D. Add to this our increasingly indoor lifestyle and aversion to exposing our skin to direct sunlight and you have an equation for vitamin D deficiency. To avoid this, make an effort to serve your family foods that are a good source of vitamin D. Such foods include eggs, fatty fish, soft non-hydrogenated margarine, fortified soy beverages and milk.

So how much is enough? At a minimum, follow Canada's Food Guide recommendations of supplementing breastfed infants and anyone over 50. For the rest of us, drink 2 cups of milk per day and stay tuned as more is sure to come.

dinner

steamed asian salmon

Mirin, an essential ingredient in Japanese cooking, is often referred to as rice wine. It is sweet in flavour, very low in alcohol and now available in most grocery stores.

1 tbsp low-sodium soy sauce
1 clove garlic, crushed
1 tbsp minced fresh ginger
1 tbsp mirin
4 salmon steaks (approximately ½ lb each)

- Preheat oven to 400°F.
- Combine soy sauce, garlic, ginger and mirin.
- Pour over salmon and marinate in the refrigerator for at least 20 minutes and a maximum of 2 hours.
- Wrap in foil and bake until cooked through, 15 to 20 minutes.

Yield: Serves 4

Serving Suggestion: Serve with Cheryl's Quinoa Salad (page 167) and Garlic Roasted Broccolini (page 217).

pasta

Pasta is an inexpensive family meal, and kids love it! Mixing new foods into pasta sauces is a great way to get children to try different flavours. Pasta is rich in B vitamins, as well as complex carbohydrates, which provide the fuel growing children need. Pasta sauces freeze well, and many of the following sauces are designed to be made in bulk and frozen in meal-size containers to facilitate quick and convenient family meals.

When choosing pasta, opt for whole grain or enriched products. The enrichment process replaces some of the minerals and vitamins that were lost during the refining process. Not all products made with white flour are enriched, especially some types of pasta. To find out if the products you are buying are enriched, look for the following ingredients on the nutrients list: iron, folic acid, riboflavin, niacin and thiamin.

tuscan tomato sauce

Children love spaghetti and tomato sauce, and the best part is that it's good for them, too! Not only are tomatoes a good source of vitamin C, but they also contain lycopene, a potent antioxidant that gives tomatoes and other foods like ruby grapefruits and watermelons their red colour. Research suggests that consumption of lycopene lowers the risk of heart disease.[22] Lycopene is more available when tomatoes are cooked, making tomato sauce a healthy choice for all.

If preparing this for young children, you may choose to omit the ginger—it gives the sauce a slightly spicier taste.

1 large onion, diced

¼ cup grated fresh ginger (optional)

2 tbsp canola oil

6 cloves garlic, crushed

2½ cans (28 oz each) diced tomatoes

1 small can (5.5 oz) tomato paste

1 cup chopped fresh basil

Salt and pepper

• In large pot or frying pan, sauté onion and ginger (if using) in oil until onion is translucent, approximately 5 minutes. Add garlic and stir.

• Add diced tomatoes and tomatoes paste. Mix thoroughly.

• Turn up heat and bring to a boil.

• Reduce heat and simmer, stirring occasionally, for 20 minutes.

• With a hand blender, purée sauce. Although this step is not necessary, you may find that children prefer a puréed sauce.

• Remove from heat, add basil and stir.

• Add salt and pepper to taste.

• Extra sauce can be cooled then frozen.

 Yield: Approximately 8 cups

Serving Suggestion: Serve with freshly grated Parmesan cheese and Kids' Caesar Salad (page 208).

dinner

meatballs

Inspired by Yaya, these tasty morsels are a perfect size for little hands to grasp. Served with steamed veggies, meatballs make an easy and nutritious children's meal. Alternatively, use this recipe in Spaghetti and Meatballs (page 187) or Meatball Souvlaki Dinner (page 130). The meatballs also freeze well.

1 large onion, finely diced (approximately 2 cups)
1 large stalk celery, finely diced
1 tbsp dried oregano
1 tbsp canola oil
6 cloves garlic, crushed
1 large egg, beaten
¾ cup freshly grated Parmesan cheese
1½ lb extra-lean ground beef
⅓ cup tomato paste
½ cup finely chopped fresh flat-leaf or curly parsley

- Preheat oven to 350°F.
- In a frying pan, sauté onion, celery and oregano in oil over medium heat until onion is translucent, approximately 5 minutes.
- Add garlic and stir. Remove from heat and set aside.

- In a large bowl, combine egg, Parmesan cheese, ground beef, tomato paste and parsley.
- Add onion mixture and mix until all ingredients are thoroughly incorporated.
- Scoop up meatball mixture by the tablespoonful and roll into balls.
- Place on baking sheet and bake until meatballs are evenly browned and cooked through, approximately 20 minutes.
- Extra meatballs can be frozen in airtight containers.

Yield: 50 meatballs

Meatballs packed in a Thermos make a delicious lunch, hot or cold.

dinner

what is normal eating for a teenager?

During the teenage years, parental influence declines and peer influence increases. Teenagers become increasingly independent. The same is true of their eating, and it is not abnormal for them to make poor choices. Many consume large quantities of non-nutritious snack foods, eat frequently at fast food restaurants, choose soda pop instead of milk, skip meals and go on diets.

You can't control everything your teen eats, so don't try. "Pigging out" on junk food and feeling ill as a consequence is a learning experience. With independence comes maturity, and most teens will eventually realize this isn't a great way to eat, especially if healthy habits are the norm at home.

spaghetti and meatballs

If you are a big fan of spaghetti and meatballs, this recipe can easily be doubled and the extra sauce frozen. To do so, combine all 50 meatballs with the entire recipe of Tuscan Tomato Sauce (approximately 8 cups).

25 Meatballs (page 186)
4 cups Tuscan Tomato
Sauce (page 184)
Spaghetti for 4
Freshly grated Parmesan
cheese
¼ cup chopped fresh basil

• In a large pot, combine the meatballs with the sauce and bring to a boil.
• Turn down heat and simmer for 20 minutes or until the meatballs are warmed through.
• Cook spaghetti until al dente and drain well.
• Serve sauce over spaghetti with freshly grated Parmesan cheese and a sprinkle of basil.

 *Yield: Serves 4*

Serving Suggestion: Serve with a green salad.

val's quick and easy veggie pasta

Once the prep work is done, this dinner can be on the table in less than 10 minutes.

2 tbsp canola oil

1 sweet yellow pepper, seeded and diced

25 cherry tomatoes, halved

4 cups spinach, stalks removed and roughly chopped

1 tbsp crushed garlic

1 cup crumbled feta cheese

Salt and freshly ground pepper

Pasta for 4

- In a large frying pan, sauté peppers in oil over medium heat for 4 minutes.
- Place tomatoes skin down and sauté for 2 minutes.
- Add spinach and wilt.
- Add garlic, stir and remove from heat.
- Cook pasta until al dente and drain well.
- In a large bowl, toss pasta with vegetables and cheese.
- Add salt and pepper to taste.

Yield: Serves 4

sweet pepper pasta

You can serve this quick recipe either as a main course with salad or as an accompaniment to either fish or meat. It's delicious served with either Rosemary Pork Tenderloin (page 134) or Ashley's Chicken Dijonnaise (page 147).

1 onion, diced

1 tbsp freshly grated ginger

2 tbsp canola oil

1 sweet red pepper, seeded and diced

1 sweet yellow pepper, seeded and diced

1 sweet orange pepper, seeded and diced

2 cloves garlic, crushed

½ cup chopped fresh basil

½ cup chopped cilantro (optional)

Freshly grated Parmesan cheese

- In a large frying pan over medium heat, sauté onion and ginger in oil until onion is translucent, approximately 5 minutes.
- Add peppers and garlic and continue to sauté until peppers are soft, approximately 15 minutes.
- Add basil and cilantro (if using), mix thoroughly and sauté for another 5 minutes.
- Cook pasta until al dente and drain well.
- Toss with pepper mixture.
- Plate pasta and serve with freshly grated Parmesan cheese.

 Yield: Serves 4

Serving Suggestion: Serve with Rosemary Pork Tenderloin (page 134) and a green salad.

spaghetti caprese

The following is an easy last-minute dinner. For the following recipe, fresh mozzarella is chosen because children love its chewy texture. However, freshly grated Parmesan can be substituted with good results.

¾ cup diced onion
2 tbsp canola oil
2 cloves garlic, crushed
1 can (28 oz) diced tomatoes
2 tbsp tomato paste
¾ cup chopped fresh basil
Salt and freshly ground
   pepper
2 balls (approximately ½ lb)
fresh mozzarella, diced
Spaghetti for 4

- Sauté onion in oil until onion is translucent.
- Add garlic, tomatoes and tomato paste and bring to a boil.

Turn down heat and continue to simmer for another 20 minutes, stirring occasionally.
- If you wish, purée sauce with a hand blender.
- Remove from heat, add ½ cup of the basil and stir.
- Meanwhile, cook spaghetti al dente and drain well.
- Mound spaghetti on plates and top with tomato sauce. Scatter with mozzarella and remaining basil.

 Yield: Serves 4 to 5

how can i help steer my teenager in the right direction?

The best way to help your teenager develop healthy eating habits is to eat together as a family as often as possible. Resist the temptation to harp on "bad" choices, and continue to lead by example. The old adage "Do as I do, not as I say" is definitely true for parents of teens.

Many teenagers have huge appetites and are constantly snacking. Make sure healthy choices are readily available. Keep a bowl of fresh fruit on the counter, and keep the fridge stocked with washed vegetable sticks, yogurt, cheese, hummus and nut butters. Stock the cupboard with nuts, dried fruit and whole grain crackers. When buying snack foods, choose baked over deep-fried, and offer air-popped popcorn. Teens drink too much soda pop, so keep it out of the house. Better choices are milk, water or even fruit juice. The nutrients most likely to be deficient during the teenage years are calcium and iron. Be aware of the foods that are high in these minerals and serve them frequently. For more info on calcium and iron see pages 71, 132 and 135.

traditional ragout

This deliciously nutritious sauce is a staple for both of us. Serving iron-rich red meat with tomatoes, which are high in vitamin C, has the added benefit of increasing iron absorption. Although the use of red wine is optional, it gives the sauce a rich flavour, and much of the alcohol cooks off. This recipe is designed to be made in bulk and frozen.

3 tbsp canola oil

1 onion, diced

4 carrots, grated (approximately 1 rounded cup)

1 zucchini, grated
  (approximately 1 cup)
2 tbsp dried oregano
10 stalks celery, diced
3 lb extra-lean ground
  beef
½ head garlic, crushed
2 small cans (5.5 oz each)
  tomato paste
2 cans (28 oz each) diced
  tomatoes
¾ cup red wine
  (optional)
4 bay leaves
1 tsp crushed red pepper
  flakes (optional)
½ cup chopped fresh
  basil
Salt and pepper
Freshly grated Parmesan
  cheese

• In a stockpot, sauté onion, carrots, zucchini, oregano and half of the celery in oil over medium heat until onion is translucent and vegetables are soft, approximately 10 minutes.

• Slowly crumble in meat, add garlic and mix thoroughly.

• Sauté until meat is browned, approximately 10 to 15 minutes. Remove pot from stove and drain excess fat.

• Place pot back on stove, add tomato paste and stir until thoroughly coated. Add diced tomatoes, wine (if using), bay leaves, and crushed red pepper flakes (if using) and bring to a rapid boil. Turn down heat and simmer for 30 minutes.

• Add fresh basil and the remaining celery and simmer for another 5 minutes. Adding some of the celery at this stage gives the sauce a nice crunchy texture.

• Add salt and pepper to taste.

• Allow sauce to cool. Remove bay leaves. Pour into airtight containers and freeze.

• To serve, heat sauce, pour over cooked pasta and top with freshly grated Parmesan cheese.

 Yield: 12 to 14 cups

Serving Suggestion: Serve with green salad with White Balsamic Vinaigrette (page 203).

what should i do about a child with a big appetite?

Children's appetites vary as much as their body sizes and activity levels. Toddlers are notorious for being picky, while teenage boys are equally notorious for their "hollow legs." Many parents worry their children may be eating too much. If this is the case, the first thing to do is to calculate your child's body mass index (page 23). If he isn't overweight, don't worry about his appetite, but do make sure the food in your house is healthy. One of the easiest ways to do this is to stick to the outer aisles of your grocery store, where the whole foods are stocked. Avoid the inner rows, which tend to be full of high-calorie processed foods. Eating a variety of healthy, whole foods is one of the best ways to avoid future weight problems.

For the overweight child with a big appetite, the same applies. As well, keep healthy, lower-fat and higher-fibre foods in the kitchen. The high-fibre foods will fill him up sooner. Start meals with salad or a non-cream-based soup. Be sure to serve lots of vegetables, and encourage him to fill at least half his plate with them. It's important not to harp constantly on the amount your child is eating or else the dinner table could become a battlefield. Don't forget to make exercise part of the family routine. If you continue to be concerned, consult your doctor.

puttanesca sauce

This recipe is designed to be made in bulk and frozen to facilitate easy family meals.

2 tbsp olive oil

1 onion, diced

2 tbsp grated fresh ginger

4 cloves garlic, crushed

5 anchovy fillets, patted dry and finely diced

¾ cup Kalamata olives, pitted

2 tbsp capers, diced

1½ cans (28 oz each) diced tomatoes

3 tbsp tomato paste

½ cup chopped fresh parsley

• In a large frying pan or stockpot, sauté onion, ginger, garlic and anchovies in oil until onion is translucent, approximately 5 minutes.
• Add olives and capers and mix thoroughly.
• Add diced tomatoes and tomato paste.
• Bring to a boil, turn down heat and simmer for 30 minutes.
• Remove from heat, add parsley and stir.

 Yield: 5 ½ cups

Serving Suggestion: Serve with pasta cooked al dente, topped with grated Parmesan cheese.

TIP: Extra sauce can be frozen in airtight containers.

dinner

what about dioxins? is it safe to cook and freeze foods in plastic?

Dioxins are not thought to be found in plastics. However, some plastics contain a group of chemicals called phthalates. Phthalates are environmental contaminants that can exhibit hormone-like behaviour in humans and animals.[23] One study found a strong connection between allergies in children and the phthalates DEHP and BBzP.[24] Because heating a container increases the likelihood that chemicals will be leached into your food, cooking in plastics is not recommended. Instead, use microwave-safe products such as heat-resistant glass and ceramics. In contrast, freezing actually works against the release of chemicals, so it's safe to freeze foods in plastic containers as long as the food is cool before it's poured into the container.

prawn linguine

When serving to young children, take out 2 prawns, dice them and mix them with their pasta. That way the children are exposed to the flavour but are not dealing with the tails. Although the use of wine is optional, it does add a depth of flavour, and almost all of the alcohol will cook off.

20 prawns

8 tomatoes (approximately 2½ lb)

1 shallot, finely diced (approximately 2 tbsp)

1 tbsp minced fresh ginger

1 tbsp canola oil

⅓ cup white wine (optional)

¼ tsp saffron

¾ cup chopped cilantro (or parsley if you prefer)

Salt and freshly ground pepper

Linguine for 4

- Rinse prawns under cool water and remove veins and shells, keeping tails intact.
- To remove the skins of the tomatoes, plunge them in boiling water for 15 seconds. With a slotted spoon, remove tomatoes and slit skin with a knife. Once cool, peel skin. Remove and discard both core and seeds. Dice tomatoes.
- In a large frying pan, sauté shallots and ginger in oil over medium heat for 5 minutes.
- Add diced tomatoes, white wine (if using) and saffron and bring to a boil. Stir in ½ cup of the cilantro (or parsley), turn down heat and simmer, stirring occasionally, for approximately 12 minutes.
- Add prawns and simmer for 5 minutes or until their colour turns and they are just opaque throughout.
- Add salt and pepper to taste.
- Cook pasta until al dente and toss with sauce.
- Plate pasta, sprinkle with remaining cilantro (or parsley) and serve.

Yield: Serves 4

Serving Suggestion: Serve with a green salad.

weight maintenance

Remember these tips to help everyone in the family maintain a healthy weight.

- Offer food in appropriate portions. Serve smaller portions and let your children ask for more.
- Limit junk foods, fast foods and sugary drinks.
- Offer high-fibre foods, which are more filling (see Fibre Facts, page 33).
- Make no snacking in front of the TV a family rule. We all eat more when the TV is on.
- After the age of 2, offer reduced-fat dairy products.

- Limit fruit juices to no more than once a day, and serve only 100% real fruit juice.
- Offer nutritious snacks (such as fruits and vegetables) between meals to allay the extreme hunger that often leads to overeating. Save cookies and crackers for occasional treats.
- Encourage conversation at the table to slow the pace of the meal and give your family a chance to feel satisfied.
- Limit TV and computer time, and encourage an active lifestyle.
- Evaluate your own relationship with food and lead by example. If your children see you eating a healthy diet and living an active lifestyle, they are more likely to do so themselves. Conversely, if they see you fad dieting, they will think that is a normal way to live.
- Start the day with a healthy breakfast. Those who eat breakfast tend to consume fewer calories in a day.
- Put the scale away and focus on your child, not his weight.

cubes of sauce

The following sauces are designed to be frozen in ice cube trays for easy last-minute children's meals. Once frozen, cubes of sauce should then be transferred into freezer bags. Don't forget to label and date the bags. To serve, defrost the cubes, cook the pasta and toss it with the sauce over low heat until evenly coated (3 to 4 minutes). This works well for school lunches. The night before, place cubes of sauce in the fridge to defrost. In the morning, cook the pasta, toss it with the sauce over medium heat until warmed through (3 to 4 minutes) and pour it into a preheated Thermos. It takes less than 10 minutes to make your child a warm pasta lunch.

dinner

broccoli pesto aka "green pasta"

Broccoli Pesto is great to have on hand and makes a wonderful last-minute meal. If your child is not keen on broccoli, don't be discouraged. The strong cheese flavour almost disguises the broccoli, and no one is the wiser. Ellie, Brenda's daughter, calls this dish "green pasta"—everyone loves it! If you're lucky enough to have a broccoli lover on your hands, steam a little fresh broccoli while cooking the pasta and toss it in. Steamed peas are another tasty addition.

> TIP: You can brown pine nuts in the microwave. Place the nuts in a single layer on a plate and set on high power for a minute at a time, stirring after each minute. Nuts will be browned in approximately 3 minutes.

1½ heads broccoli, cut into florets (approximately 1½ lb)
1½ cups freshly grated Parmesan cheese
½ cup extra-virgin olive oil
1 clove garlic, crushed
1 tsp lemon zest
½ cup pine nuts, toasted
1 cup chicken stock

- Steam broccoli over boiling water until just tender, approximately 6 minutes.
- Place broccoli in a food processor. Add cheese, olive oil, garlic, lemon zest, pine nuts and chicken stock. Purée until smooth.
- Pour into ice cube trays, cover with plastic wrap and freeze.

> TIP: • Depending on the size of the portion, an individual portion of pasta will require 2 to 4 cubes of broccoli pesto.
> • Cook pasta until al dente and defrost broccoli pesto.
> • Over low heat, toss together pasta and pesto until pasta is thoroughly coated. For adult portions, add a little salt and pepper to taste, if desired.

Yield: Approximately 24 cubes

quick and easy mac and cheese

This macaroni and cheese is arguably easier to make than the commercial version and, even better, it does not have the unwanted additives found in many of these products. Steaming veggies to toss with this old standby serves to boost the nutritional content. Try it with broccoli and peas, or whatever vegetables your child most enjoys. Alternatively, you can serve the cheese sauce over steamed broccoli as a vegetable accompaniment. Try doubling the recipe so you always have cubes of cheese sauce in your freezer.

1½ tbsp non-hydrogenated margarine

1½ tbsp all-purpose flour

1½ cups milk

2 cups shredded old Cheddar cheese (½ lb)

1 cup freshly grated Parmesan cheese

Cooked fusilli or penne

Green veggies (broccoli and/or peas), steamed (optional)

- In a saucepan, melt margarine. Add flour and whisk together over medium heat until paste forms.
- Slowly add milk, whisking until lumps disappear.
- Slowly add Cheddar cheese and whisk until melted.
- Stir in Parmesan cheese and allow sauce to thicken over medium heat, approximately 5 to 10 minutes.
- Pour sauce over cooked pasta and toss with steamed veggies (if using).
- Pour extra sauce into ice cube trays, cover with plastic wrap and freeze.

TIP: • To serve, defrost cubes and cook pasta. (A child's portion of pasta will likely require 2 cubes of sauce.)

• Over medium heat, toss cubes of cheese sauce with cooked pasta and serve. If the sauce seems too thick, a little extra milk will thin it out.

Yield: Serves 5 (or makes 2 cups cheese sauce)

dinner

basil pesto

Pesto is delicious, very versatile and kids love it. Tossing pesto over pasta with steamed broccoli and/or cooked chicken is an easy last-minute kids' meal. Alternatively, pesto can be spread over fish and grilled or even mixed into your favourite soups. Try it with Judy's Vegetable Lentil Soup (page 225).

½ cup pine nuts, lightly toasted

1 cup freshly grated Parmesan cheese

4 cups packed fresh basil, thick stalks removed

3 to 4 cloves garlic

½ tsp salt

½ tsp pepper

1 cup olive oil

• In a food processor, combine pine nuts, Parmesan cheese, basil, garlic, salt and pepper. Purée, slowly adding oil until all ingredients are incorporated.

• To serve, toss pesto with cooked pasta. When adding pesto, start slowly, adding 1 tbsp at a time until desired flavour is reached.

 Yield: 10 to 12 cubes

Serving Suggestion: Serve with a green salad and grilled chicken breast.

TIP: Pour extra pesto into ice cube trays, cover with plastic wrap and freeze.

salads
and
vegetable
sides

Canada's new Food Guide recommends all Canadians eat at least one dark green and one orange vegetable per day. Eating a green salad with grated carrots for dinner is a good way to accomplish this goal. The benefits of eating salads are abundant. Salads are a rich source of vitamins, minerals, fibre and antioxidants. Antioxidants may provide protection against cataracts, arthritis, cancer and heart disease.

When choosing lettuce, always opt for the darker green varieties, such as romaine, arugula and spinach, because they are a good source of folate. Start to incorporate spinach into your evening salad by adding just a little and gradually increasing the amount until your salad is almost half spinach.

Although salads themselves are low in calories, too many people drench them in dressings that are high in fat and sugar. Be wary of high-fat additions like bacon bits, cheese and croutons—the calories add up quickly. When you are eating out, avoid creamy dressings and opt for oil and vinegar–based salad dressings. At home, making your own vinaigrette is a great way to keep your dressings healthy.

If your child rejects salad, do not give up. The rest of the family will reap the benefits, and be reassured that you are modelling good eating habits. If salad is being rejected, try to incorporate alternative green vegetables into your child's diet, such as broccoli, green peas, asparagus, spinach or kale.

Eating fresh vegetables with every meal is ideal. When possible, choose local produce—it tastes better, is more nutritious and is easier on the environment. Like salads, vegetables are high in vitamins, minerals, fibre and antioxidants. Since most vitamins break down when they come into contact with air and heat, less cooking means maximum nutrition. Vegetables should be cooked until their colour brightens and they are crisp but tender. Blanching, microwaving and steaming are the optimal methods for cooking most vegetables. When steaming and microwaving, use a minimal amount of water.

If you are too busy to shop for and prepare fresh vegetables every night, don't worry—fresh and frozen produce are almost identical in nutritional content. Frozen fruits and vegetables are picked at the peak of perfection and frozen within hours of being picked. If you live in a region where fresh produce has to be stored and shipped over long distances, frozen produce may actually be more nutritious, given that produce loses some of its nutrient value over time.

Most frozen vegetables have been blanched or partially cooked before freezing, so be wary of overcooking. Frozen vegetables are especially convenient for those nights when you are going out and only want to prepare a small portion of vegetables for your children.

white balsamic vinaigrette

The following is Brenda's go-to salad dressing. Toss it over a green salad, and for variety add a little crumbled feta cheese or a few chick-peas. If you cannot find white balsamic vinegar, substitute either red balsamic vinegar or regular white wine vinegar. White balsamic is less acidic than other vinegars, so if using another vinegar, measure only ⅓ cup. The following makes a fairly large quantity of vinaigrette. Extra can be stored in the fridge for up to 10 days. If the volume of dressing is too large for you, cut the recipe in half.

½ cup white balsamic
vinegar

2 tbsp Dijon mustard

1 cup extra-virgin olive oil

2 cloves garlic, crushed
(optional)

½ tsp salt

½ tsp pepper

• Whisk together vinegar and mustard until emulsified.

• Add olive oil, garlic (if using), salt and pepper and continue to whisk until all ingredients are incorporated.

Yield: 1½ cups

asian vinaigrette

4 tbsp seasoned rice wine vinegar
2½ tsp light soy sauce
1 tsp Dijon mustard
3 tbsp extra-virgin olive oil
1 tbsp sesame oil
Freshly ground pepper

- In a small bowl, whisk together seasoned rice wine vinegar, soy sauce and mustard until emulsified.
- Add olive oil, sesame oil, and pepper to taste and whisk thoroughly.

Yield: ½ cup

asian vegetable salad

1 head romaine lettuce, ribs removed and torn
Handful baby spinach
1 cup thinly sliced red cabbage
10 radishes, thinly sliced
1 small sweet red pepper, thinly sliced
¼ cup finely diced red onion
2 tbsp sesame seeds, toasted (optional)
½ cup Asian Vinaigrette (above)

- Combine all of the ingredients and toss thoroughly.

Yield: Serves 4 to 6

sides

is organic food worth the added cost?

Concerns for the environment and food safety have prompted many people to go organic. Organic food is produced according to legally regulated standards and grown without the use of synthetic pesticides, fertilizers and herbicides. Animals are reared without the use of hormones and antibiotics. However, regulatory bodies strictly research and monitor any substances used in the production of conventionally produced foods and only those considered safe at reasonable levels are used. Furthermore, organic farmers use "natural" pesticides that are not subject to such vigorous controls, and although thought to be less toxic, the relative risk of these pesticides compared with synthetic ones is unclear. Whether buying conventional or organic, always choose produce free of dirt, cuts, mould and insect holes, and wash it under running water.

Some studies suggest organic produce has slightly higher nutrient levels. However, studies comparing conventionally grown foods with organic foods are difficult to interpret because there are so many variables (soil quality, light, temperature) and the nutrient values of the same foods differ naturally anyway. In most cases, accurate comparisons cannot be made.[1] Although organic farming practices are better for the environment, to date there is no reason to believe organic foods are healthier or nutritionally superior in any meaningful way. The decision to choose organic foods is simply personal. Regardless of what you decide, the most important thing is that your children are eating lots of fruits and vegetables.

do some foods have more pesticide residue than others?

Yes, some conventionally grown foods are treated with more pesticides than others. What follows is a list of the 10 foods that have the highest levels of pesticide residue and the 10 that have the lowest. Keep this list in mind the next time you go grocery shopping.

highest pesticide load
- Peaches (worst)
- Apples
- Sweet bell peppers
- Celery
- Nectarines
- Strawberries
- Cherries
- Pears
- Grapes (imported)
- Spinach

lowest pesticide load
- Onions (best)
- Avocados
- Sweet corn (frozen)
- Pineapples
- Mangoes
- Asparagus
- Sweet peas (frozen)
- Kiwis
- Bananas
- Cabbage

Adapted from Environmental Working Group (http://www.ewg.org).

chinese chicken noodle salad

The following is delicious with or without chicken.

½ lb broccoli, cut into florets (approximately ½ head broccoli)
2 carrots, peeled and cut into matchsticks (approximately ¼ lb)

30 snap peas, strings removed and cut into ½-inch slices
½ lb Chinese egg noodles (or rice noodles), cooked
6 green onions, trimmed and sliced
½ sweet red pepper, seeded and thinly sliced
¾ cup chopped cilantro

¾ cup salted peanuts, chopped

1½ cups shredded cooked chicken

½ cup Asian Vinaigrette (page 204)

• Bring a large pot of water to a rapid boil. Blanch broccoli and carrots for 2 minutes.

• Drain vegetables and immediately plunge in an ice bath for 3 minutes. This will stop the cooking process.

• Drain vegetables well and place on clean dish towel to remove all excess water.

• Place broccoli and carrots in a large bowl. Add remaining ingredients and mix thoroughly.

 Yield: Serves 4 to 6

help! my kids won't eat veggies

If your child dislikes cooked vegetables, try serving raw veggies with dip. If this doesn't tempt your finicky eater, don't give up. Add grated veggies to pasta sauces, hamburgers, muffins and breads. Make homemade soups with puréed vegetables. Invest in a juicer. Combine fruits and vegetables to make your own yummy concoctions. Strawberry-carrot juice is a big hit at Brenda's house.

Although vegetables are an important source of fibre, vitamins, minerals and antioxidants, they are not the only source. Resist the temptation to bribe or force-feed. Instead, continue to offer a diet rich in a variety of foods from all 4 food groups. That is the best way to ensure your child receives adequate nutrition. Until vegetables are firmly established, make an effort to serve a variety of colourful fruits, which, like vegetables, are loaded with disease-fighting antioxidants. Orange fruits, such as mangoes, apricots, cantaloupe and papaya, are rich in vitamin A, which may be difficult to get if your diet lacks vegetables. Vitamin A is essential for the healthy growth and maintenance of skin, eyes, bones and teeth. Some other sources of vitamin A include watermelon, purple plums, tomatoes, eggs and milk.

sides

kids' caesar salad

Most kids like Caesar salad, and it's a great way to get them to eat their leafy greens. To boost the veggie content, add grated carrot. This salad can also be turned into a meal by adding cooked chicken, shrimp, crab or chickpeas.

½ rounded cup freshly grated Parmesan cheese

¼ cup mayonnaise

¼ cup extra-virgin olive oil

2 tbsp white wine vinegar

1 tbsp Worcestershire sauce

1 tbsp fresh lemon juice

1 tsp anchovy paste (or 1 anchovy, finely chopped)

2 cloves garlic, crushed

Salt and freshly ground pepper

1 large head romaine lettuce, roughly chopped

2 carrots, grated (optional)

• Whisk together Parmesan cheese, mayonnaise, olive oil, vinegar, Worcestershire sauce, lemon juice, anchovy paste (or anchovy), garlic, and salt and pepper to taste.

• Toss lettuce with dressing, being careful not to overdress the salad as that's the quickest way to ruin a good Caesar. Add grated carrots (if using) and serve.

Yield: 1¼ cups dressing (serves 4)

salade niçoise

The following salad is quick to whip up and makes a delicious dinner or weekend lunch. Because the veggies won't go soggy, it also packs well.

¾ lb green beans, trimmed

1¼ lb baby potatoes, quartered

½ cup Kalamata olives, pitted

20 cherry tomatoes, halved

¼ red onion, thinly sliced

2 cans (170 g each) light tuna

sides

½ cup White Balsamic Vinaigrette (page 203) or other vinaigrette

4 hard-boiled eggs, quartered

- Blanch beans in boiling water until bright green, approximately 3 minutes. Plunge into cold ice bath to stop the cooking process. Drain well.
- Cook potatoes in boiling water until just tender. Drain well and allow to cool.
- Toss together beans, potatoes, olives, tomatoes, onion and tuna fish and dress until evenly coated.
- Arrange salad on serving platter and place hard-boiled eggs around the edge.

 Yield: Serves 4 to 6

Serving Suggestion: Serve with crusty brown bread.

strive for more

Seventy per cent of children don't eat the minimum number of servings of Vegetables and Fruit.[2] Ensure your child doesn't become part of this statistic.

- Serve fruits and vegetables for snacks.
- Pack 1 serving each of fruit and veggies in your child's lunch.
- Add veggies to sandwiches.
- Always serve fruit at breakfast.
- Serve fruit smoothies made with frozen fruit for breakfast and snacks.
- Sprinkle berries or diced bananas on yogurt, ice cream and cereal.
- Serve fruit for dessert.
- Grate vegetables into pasta sauces, soups, muffins and breads.
- Add fresh, frozen or dried fruit to baked goods.
- Serve 100% real fruit and vegetable juices.

sides

greek salad

¼ cup extra-virgin olive oil

1 tbsp dried oregano

½ tsp salt

½ tsp freshly ground pepper

5 tomatoes (approximately 2 lb), cut into chunks

¾ English cucumber, cut into chunks

⅓ red onion, diced

1 cup feta cheese, crumbled

½ cup Kalamata olives, pitted

• Pour oil into a large serving bowl.
• Add oregano, salt and pepper.
• Add tomatoes, cucumber and onion and toss until coated in oil.
• Add feta cheese and olives.
• Toss just before serving.

Yield: Serves 4 to 5

what are phytochemicals?

Phytochemicals are plant-based chemical compounds that play a biological role in the body. They give fruits and vegetables colour, flavour and aroma. In the body, they can mimic hormones, suppress diseases and act as antioxidants. Antioxidants may provide protection against the development of cataracts, arthritis, cancer and heart disease. There are tens of thousands of phytochemicals, and only a few have been studied.

Many questions remain unanswered. Consumers should be cautioned against attributing a specific health benefit to a single compound. The foods we eat contain thousands of phytochemicals, as well as a variety of other nutrients. Each of these compounds may be capable of influencing some action in the body, and it is likely they work in overlapping or complementary ways that we do not yet understand. The best way to ensure your family stays healthy is to offer a varied diet rich in plant-based foods, such as whole grains, legumes, nuts, fruit and vegetables.

Eat your broccoli—it may contain as many as 10,000 different phytochemicals!

middle eastern salad

With or without feta cheese, this salad is a welcome addition to any meal. If you can't find Lebanese cucumbers, use English cucumber instead.

¼ cup extra-virgin olive oil

1 tbsp freshly squeezed lemon juice

1 clove garlic, crushed

½ tsp salt

¼ tsp freshly ground pepper

3 Lebanese cucumbers, halved and cut into bite-sized chunks (or ¾ English cucumber)

16 cherry tomatoes, halved

1 fennel bulb, diced

½ cup finely diced red onion

½ sweet red pepper, diced

¼ cup chopped fresh mint

¼ cup chopped parsley

½ cup crumbled feta cheese (optional)

• In a small bowl, whisk together oil, lemon juice, garlic, salt and pepper.
• Combine vegetables and herbs and toss with dressing.
• Add cheese (if using) and stir.

 Yield: Serves 4

Serving Suggestion: Serve with Middle Eastern Hummus (page 113) and Toasted Whole Wheat Pita Chips (page 106).

Because of the crisp vegetables, this salad packs well and can be made the night before.

sides

211

marinated vegetable salad

The crunchy vegetables make this salad an excellent choice for packed lunches. It can be made the night before and tastes even better once the vegetables have had a chance to marinate in the dressing. In the morning, pack the salad and add cherry tomatoes, if desired.

½ head broccoli, cut into florets (approximately ½ lb)
½ head cauliflower, cut into florets (approximately ½ lb)
2 carrots, peeled and thinly sliced
4 stalks celery, diced
10 radishes, trimmed and thinly sliced
1 cup thinly sliced cabbage
¼ cup diced red onion
⅓ cup White Balsamic Vinaigrette (page 203)
15 cherry tomatoes, halved (optional)

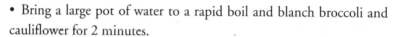

• Bring a large pot of water to a rapid boil and blanch broccoli and cauliflower for 2 minutes.
• Drain vegetables and immediately plunge into a cold ice bath to stop the cooking process. Once cool, drain vegetables well to remove excess water. You might want to drain them on a clean dish towel.
• In a large bowl, toss together broccoli, cauliflower, carrots, celery, radishes, cabbage and red onions.
• Add vinaigrette and toss until vegetables are evenly coated.
• Place salad in the refrigerator and allow the vegetables to sit in the dressing for a minimum of 30 minutes.
• Prior to serving, add cherry tomatoes (if using) and toss.

 Yield: Serves 4 to 6

ginger snap peas

½ tbsp canola oil
1 tsp grated fresh ginger
½ lb snap peas, trimmed
1 sweet red pepper,
    seeded and sliced
Dash soy sauce

• In a wok or large frying pan, sauté ginger on high heat for 20 seconds.

• Turn down heat to medium, add snap peas and peppers, and sauté, until tender but crisp, 3 to 5 minutes.
• Remove from heat, add soy sauce and stir.

Yield: Serves 4

blanched carrots and broccoli

Blanching vegetables is a French technique that preserves the flavour, colour and texture of vegetables prior to further cooking. Blanching is a great way to cook vegetables when having a dinner party, as you can prepare the vegetables hours prior to serving. This method is also frequently used in restaurants.

4 carrots, peeled and cut
    into matchsticks
½ head broccoli, cut into
    florets (approximately
    ½ lb)
1 tbsp non-hydrogenated
    margarine
½ tsp each salt and freshly
    ground pepper (optional)

• In a large pot, bring 10 cups of water to a rapid boil.
• Plunge carrots in water and cook, uncovered, for 1 minute.

• Add broccoli to the pot and cook until vegetables are brightly coloured, 2 to 3 minutes.
• Drain vegetables and immediately plunge into an ice bath for 3 minutes. This will stop the cooking process.
• Drain vegetables well and place on clean dish towel to remove all excess water.
• When ready to serve, place in ovenproof baking dish along with margarine, and salt and pepper (if using).

sides

213

- Cook in oven preheated to 400°F for 10 minutes or until warmed through.

- Remove vegetables and toss to evenly coat with margarine.

Yield: Serves 4 to 6

parmesan brussels sprouts

The following dish can be prepared ahead of time and is a yummy addition to traditional turkey dinner.

6 cups Brussels sprouts, trimmed, cored and shredded (use a knife to thinly slice them)
2 tbsp canola oil
1 large onion, diced

5 thin slices prosciutto, cut into strips
3 cloves garlic, crushed
½ cup plus 2 tbsp freshly grated Parmesan cheese
Salt and pepper

- Preheat oven to 350°F.
- In a large pot, blanch Brussels sprouts in 8 cups boiling water for 3 minutes.
- Rinse Brussels sprouts under cold water to stop the cooking process and drain well.
- In a large frying pan, sauté onion in oil over medium heat for 5 minutes.
- Add Brussels sprouts, prosciutto and garlic and sauté for another 5 minutes.
- Remove from heat, add ½ cup Parmesan cheese and mix well until cheese melts.
- Add salt and pepper to taste.
- Place mixture in a baking dish and sprinkle with the remaining Parmesan cheese.
- Bake until cheese melts and Brussels sprouts are warmed through, approximately 20 minutes.

Yield: Serves 4 to 6

sides

the mighty cruciferous family

Brussels sprouts belong to the cruciferous family. These vegetables are considered to have excellent cancer-fighting properties because they contain many phytochemicals, including isothiocyanates, which are thought to inhibit cancer cell growth. Other cruciferous vegetables include broccoli, cauliflower, cabbage, watercress, kale and radishes. Try grating cabbage on your nightly salad to boost your intake.

cauliflower and broccoli with cheese sauce

A little cheese sauce alongside some broccoli can be a strong selling point for this healthy vegetable. You can always serve the sauce in a small bowl so the kids can dip their veggies. Try it also with steamed carrots, green beans or even cherry tomatoes.

sides

½ head broccoli, cut into florets (approximately ½ lb)
½ head cauliflower, cut into florets (approximately ½ lb)
1½ to 2 cups cheese sauce (see Quick and Easy Mac and Cheese, page 198)

• Bring a pot of water to a rapid boil. Place broccoli and cauliflower in a steamer and steam until broccoli is brightly coloured and just tender, approximately 6 to 7 minutes.
• Drain vegetables and place in gratin or baking dish.
• Drizzle with cheese sauce and serve.
• If you'd like to give the cheese a golden colour, place dish in oven and broil for 2 to 3 minutes.

Yield: Serves 4 to 5

wilted garlic spinach

Spinach often gets a bad rap and, as a result, many parents don't even attempt to serve it to their kids. However, some children love spinach—you'll never know unless you try. The earlier children are exposed to new foods, the more likely it is they will develop a taste for them. Remember, when offering a new food, offer just a taste. That way the child does not feel intimidated by the large portion. If the spinach gets rejected, don't push the issue; offer an alternative green veggie you know she likes.

1 tbsp olive oil

½ lb spinach, stalks removed

1 clove garlic, crushed

Salt and freshly ground pepper

• In a large frying pan, heat oil over low heat.

• Slowly add spinach and wilt, stirring occasionally, until thoroughly cooked.

• Add garlic and salt and pepper to taste.

Yield: Serves 4

amanda's ginger yam mash

This recipe comes all the way from London, England.

2 large yams (approximately 2 lb), peeled and cut into chunks

2 tbsp non-hydrogenated margarine

1 tbsp grated fresh ginger

1 tbsp olive oil

Salt and freshly ground pepper

2 tbsp chopped cilantro (optional)

• Bring a large pot of water to a boil.
• Place yams in water and cook until tender, approximately 20 minutes.
• Drain yams and set aside.

- Using same pot, melt margarine over medium-low heat.
- Add ginger and cook until softened, 5 to 10 minutes.
- Return yams to pan, add olive oil and mash until soft.
- Mix thoroughly, add salt and pepper to taste and sprinkle with fresh cilantro (if using) to serve.

Yield: Serves 4 to 5

garlic roasted broccolini

1 bunch broccolini, trimmed
1 clove garlic, crushed
1 tbsp canola oil
¼ tsp salt
¼ tsp freshly ground pepper

- Preheat oven to 350°F.
- Toss broccolini with garlic, oil, salt and pepper.
- Place in a baking dish and cook for 20 minutes or until tender but crisp.

Yield: Serves 4

roasted winter vegetables

The following makes a delicious accompaniment to any family meal.

3 carrots, peeled and cut into ¾-inch chunks (approximately ½ lb)
3 parsnips, peeled and cut into ¾-inch chunks (approximately ½ lb)
3 beets, peeled and cut into ¾-inch chunks (approximately 1 lb)
2 tbsp canola oil
½ tsp salt
¼ tsp freshly ground pepper

- Preheat oven to 350°F.
- Toss vegetables in oil, salt and pepper.
- To facilitate an easy cleanup, place foil or parchment paper on a baking pan. Place vegetables in pan. Bake for approximately 50–60 minutes, or until cooked through and tender.

Yield: Serves 4 to 5

sides

roasted potato and yam chips

2 unpeeled yams, sliced into ¼-inch medallions

1 unpeeled russet (baking) potato, sliced into ¼-inch
medallions

2 tbsp canola oil

¼ tsp salt

¼ tsp freshly ground pepper

- Preheat oven to 375°F.
- Toss vegetables in oil, salt and pepper.
- Place vegetables in baking pan and bake for approximately 50 to 60 minutes, or until potatoes are crispy and golden on the outside and yams are tender.

Yield: Serves 4 to 5

what is acrylamide?

Acrylamide is a chemical that forms in some foods, particularly plant-based and carbohydrate-rich ones. It occurs when asparagine, an amino acid, reacts with naturally occurring sugars during cooking at high temperatures or processing.

Although found in some breads, cereals, cookies, coffee and roasted nuts, the highest levels of acrylamide are seen in french fries and potato chips. Acrylamide is not found in boiled potatoes because they aren't cooked at a high enough temperature to produce it. Although known to cause cancer in animals, acrylamide's effects on humans are still unknown, and research continues.[3] Health Canada's advice, consistent with the Food Guide, is to eat deep-fried foods less often.[4] This is just one more reason to stress the importance of whole foods and limit your trips to fast food restaurants.

cath's potato yam mash

As most children love mashed potatoes, they will likely devour Cath's Potato Yam Mash, and this dish has the added benefit of being packed full of yams, rich in vitamin A.

Don't peel the red potatoes—the skin is a good source of vitamins and fibre.

3 red potatoes, unpeeled, cut into chunks

1 large yam, peeled and cut into chunks

⅓ cup non-hydrogenated margarine

⅓ cup milk

Salt and pepper

• Bring a large pot of water to a boil. Add potatoes and yams and cook until soft, approximately 20 minutes.

• Drain well.

• Mash potatoes with margarine and milk and add salt and pepper to taste.

Yield: Serves 4 to 6

roasted home fries

These home fries are a healthy alternative to store-bought fries and perfect for little hands to grasp.

2 russet (or baking) potatoes

2 tbsp canola oil

½ tsp salt

¼ tsp freshly ground pepper

• In a bowl, toss potatoes with oil, salt and pepper. Roast in oven for 60 minutes, or until potatoes are crispy and golden.

Yield: 20 to 24 potato wedges

• Preheat oven to 375°F.
• Cut potatoes in half lengthwise. Cut each half into 5 or 6 wedges, depending on the size of the potato.

Serving Suggestion: Serve with Panko-Crusted Halibut Fish Sticks (page 182) and steamed peas.

sides

soups

Vegetable-laden soups, served with whole grain breads, make nutritious family meals. Very often, children who refuse to eat vegetables happily eat them in a soup. For those who are especially finicky, you may find puréeing the soup makes it more appealing. Soups can be puréed either in a food processor or with a hand-held emersion blender. Using a hand blender is the easiest way to purée soup and definitely worth the investment.

Canned and packaged soups are often high in salt and unwanted additives. Read nutrition labels carefully and choose soups that are lower in salt. Adding extra vegetables and/or canned beans to packaged soups is a great way to boost their nutritional content. Alternatively, Japanese miso paste, made from fermented soybeans, makes a great soup. Prepared in seconds, hot miso can be poured over steamed vegetables, diced tofu and/or noodles.

The recipes in this chapter are designed to be made in bulk and frozen in airtight containers, providing convenient family meals.

homemade salt-free chicken stock

Having a leftover chicken carcass is a great reason to make homemade salt-free chicken stock; however, it does not need to be the only reason. Chicken stock freezes beautifully, and you can buy chicken necks, carcass backs and wing tips very inexpensively from your butcher. If you do not have the time to make chicken stock, freeze the carcass to make it at a later date. Alternatively, you can buy salt-free or low-sodium stock at most grocery and specialty stores.

1 chicken carcass
Neck and giblets (if available)
Wing tips
1 onion, quartered
5 large carrots, cut into chunks
4 stalks celery, cut into chunks
1 tomato, quartered
2 bay leaves
1 sprig fresh thyme
1 sprig fresh tarragon
10 peppercorns
1 clove garlic
12 cups cold water

- Remove the stuffing and any good-quality meat from the carcass.
- Place carcass, neck and giblets (if available), wing tips, onion, carrots, celery, tomato, herbs, peppercorns and garlic in a large stockpot. Pour in water and bring to a boil.
- Turn down heat and simmer on low for about 3 hours or until there is no flavour left in any of the ingredients.
- Allow stock to cool. Drain, and discard vegetables and carcass.
- Place stock in refrigerator until fat congeals on surface.
- Remove and discard solidified fat.

Yield: Approximately 8 cups

next night chicken barley soup

This recipe calls for approximately 1 lb cooked chicken meat. If you do not have enough meat left over on your carcass, you can add an extra half or whole chicken breast. A whole chicken breast is approximately 1 lb. To cook the breast, poach or bake it. Do not cook the chicken meat in the soup; it will exude a frothy scum, which you don't want in your soup.

If you want to make this soup but haven't made the stock, don't let that stop you—just substitute commercial chicken stock. Many commercial chicken stocks are very high in salt, so look for a salt-free or low-sodium variety.

1 large onion, diced
1 tbsp canola oil
½ cup pot barley, rinsed and drained
8 cups salt-free chicken stock
1 bay leaf
5 carrots, peeled and sliced
4 stalks celery, sliced
1 lb cooked chicken, diced
¼ cup chopped fresh parsley
Salt and freshly ground pepper

soups

- In large stockpot or large pot, sauté onion in oil over medium heat until translucent.
- Add barley and stir until thoroughly coated in oil.
- Add stock and bay leaf and bring to a boil.
- Turn down heat and simmer on low for 1 hour.
- Add vegetables and chicken meat and continue to simmer until vegetables are tender, approximately 20 minutes.
- Add parsley, and salt and pepper to taste.
- Remove bay leaf.

 Yield: 10 to 12 cups

The soup packs well in a Thermos.

Serving Suggestion: Serve with whole wheat bread and a green salad.

the barley bonus

The U.S. Food and Drug Administration (FDA) recently ruled that barley products are allowed to carry the health claim that they may reduce the risk of heart disease. Barley is an excellent source of beta-glucans, a soluble fibre known to lower cholesterol levels.[1] Oats are also high in beta-glucans and can also advertise this health claim.

judy's vegetable lentil soup

2 tbsp canola oil

1 onion, diced

2 stalks celery, diced

2 cloves garlic, crushed

6 to 8 cups low-sodium or
salt-free chicken stock

1 small can (14 oz) diced
tomatoes

⅓ cup tomato paste

1 tbsp dried oregano

2 bay leaves

1 small rutabaga or
½ large one (approxi-
mately ½ lb), diced

3 carrots, diced

1 small zucchini, diced

1 parsnip, peeled and
diced

1 yam, peeled and diced

1 cup shredded kale

⅓ cup dried lentils,
rinsed and drained

Salt and freshly ground
pepper

½ cup freshly grated
Parmesan cheese

Basil Pesto (page 199)
(optional)

- In a large stockpot, sauté onion, celery and garlic in oil over medium-low heat until onion is translucent, approximately 5 minutes.

- Add 6 cups chicken stock, canned tomatoes, tomato paste, oregano, bay leaves, all of the vegetables and lentils and bring to a boil.

- Turn down heat and simmer with lid mostly on for 35 to 45 minutes or until vegetables are soft and lentils are tender.

- Depending on the size of the vegetables used, you may find your soup is a little thick. If so, add more chicken stock to desired consistency.

- Remove bay leaves.

- Add salt and pepper to taste.

- Ladle into bowls and top each serving with freshly grated Parmesan cheese and 1 tsp pesto (if using).

 Yield: Approximately 10 cups

food additives

Food additives are combined with foods during processing to make them look better, taste better and last longer. Many additives have little or no nutritional value. All additives used in Canada are subject to rigorous controls and are considered safe for the general population. However, some can cause reactions in a small number of sensitive individuals, so they must be identified on labels. Reactions can range from mild to severe. Symptoms may include cramps, diarrhea, vomiting, skin rashes, behavioral changes and even the more serious anaphylactic shock. The best way to avoid additives is to serve a diet rich in whole, unprocessed foods. When buying processed foods, read labels carefully. If you suspect an allergy or sensitivity, talk to your doctor.

quick and easy broccoli soup

Made with frozen broccoli, this soup could not be easier to prepare!

1 onion, diced
1 tbsp canola oil
1 tsp chopped fresh thyme
1 potato, peeled and cut into 1-inch cubes
1 pkg (500 g) frozen broccoli
½ pkg (150 g) frozen spinach
4 to 5 cups salt-free chicken stock
1 cup milk
Salt and freshly ground pepper
1 cup freshly grated Parmesan cheese

• In a large pot, sauté onion in oil over medium heat until onion is translucent, approximately 5 minutes.

• Add thyme, potato, broccoli, spinach and 4 cups chicken stock and bring to a boil. Turn down heat and simmer until potato is cooked through, approximately 20 minutes.

• With a hand blender, purée soup until smooth. If you do not have a hand blender, remove vegetables from pot and purée in a food processor or blender until smooth, then transfer vegetables back to stockpot.

• Add milk and simmer for another 5 minutes.

• If soup seems too thick, add extra chicken stock as needed, until desired consistancy is reached.

• Add salt and pepper to taste.

• Serve with Parmesan cheese.

 Yield: 6 cups

eating disorders

The prevalence of eating disorders has increased dramatically over the past 3 decades. They rank as the third most common chronic illness in adolescent females.[2] People with eating disorders often have low self-esteem and an excessive fear of weight gain. There are 2 major subgroups of the disease: anorexia nervosa, in which food intake is severely limited, and bulimia nervosa, in which the person will binge and then try to purge the food through vomiting, excessive exercise or the use of laxatives.

Although more common in girls, these disorders do also occur in boys. The medical complications in adolescents may not be reversible. Such complications may include growth retardation, increased risk of osteoporosis later in life and even death. If you suspect an eating disorder, see your doctor immediately. The earlier treatment is started, the better the prognosis. For more information, see Possible Signs of an Eating Disorder (page 229).

autumn roasted tomato soup

The flavour of this soup depends on the quality of the tomatoes used. If you cannot find Roma tomatoes, regular tomatoes can be substituted. For best results, make this soup when tomatoes are in season.

4 lb Roma tomatoes, quartered

¼ cup canola oil (plus an extra drizzle)

1 head garlic, top removed

1 onion, diced

4 carrots, grated

2 tbsp canola oil

7 to 8 cups salt-free or low-sodium chicken stock

Salt and freshly ground pepper

⅓ cup finely chopped fresh basil

• Preheat oven to 375°F.

• Line 2 baking sheets with foil or parchment paper. Place tomatoes on baking sheets and drizzle with ¼ cup oil.

• Drizzle a little more oil over garlic, wrap in foil and place on baking sheet.

• Bake tomatoes and garlic in oven for 45 minutes.

• In a stockpot or large pot, sauté onion and carrots in 2 tbsp oil for 10 minutes or until soft.

• Remove tomatoes from oven and unwrap garlic. Once cool, squeeze garlic onto tomatoes and discard skin.

• Add roasted tomatoes and garlic to stockpot and sauté for another 5 minutes.

• Using hand blender, purée vegetables until smooth. If you do not have a hand blender, remove vegetables from pot and purée in a food processor or blender until smooth, then transfer vegetables back to stockpot.

• Add 7 cups of stock, mix thoroughly and bring to boil. Turn down heat and simmer for 30 minutes.

• If soup seems too thick, add extra stock as needed, until desired consistency is reached.

• Add salt and pepper to taste.

• Ladle soup into bowls and sprinkle each serving with 1 tsp basil.

 Yield: 10 cups

Serving Suggestion: Serve with crusty whole grain bread.

soups

possible signs of an eating disorder

- a preoccupation with body weight, calorie counting and food
- unrealistic body image and feeling "fat" when not
- bizarre and/or ritualistic eating patterns
- obsession with exercise
- evidence of the use of laxatives or diet pills
- noticeable weight loss, more common in anorexia
- excessive binge-eating, often on high-calorie foods in the case of bulimia
- scratch marks on the back of hands from repetitive induced vomiting in the case of bulimia
- loss of periods or irregular menstruation
- low self-esteem, depression, irritability and fatigue
- feelings of guilt or shame about eating

roasted tomato and red pepper soup

If you cannot find Roma tomatoes, regular ones can be substituted.

3 lb Roma tomatoes, cored and quartered

3 sweet red peppers, seeded and halved

¼ cup canola oil (plus an extra drizzle)

1 head garlic, top removed

1 onion, diced

4 carrots, grated

2 tbsp canola oil

7 to 8 cups salt-free or low-sodium chicken stock

Salt and freshly ground pepper

- Preheat oven to 350°F.
- Line 2 baking sheets with foil or parchment paper. Lay tomatoes and peppers on baking sheets and drizzle with ¼ cup oil.
- Drizzle a little more oil over garlic, wrap in foil and place on baking sheet.

soups

- Bake tomatoes, peppers and garlic for 45 minutes.
- In a large pot or stockpot, sauté onion and carrots in 2 tbsp oil for 10 minutes or until soft.
- Remove vegetables from oven and unwrap garlic. Once cool, squeeze garlic onto vegetables and discard skin.
- The edges of the peppers will likely have blackened. If this is the case, cut these edges off and discard blackened bits.
- Add roasted vegetables to stockpot and sauté for another 5 minutes.
- Using hand blender, purée vegetables until smooth. If you do not have a hand blender, remove vegetables from pot and purée in a food processor or blender until smooth, then transfer vegetables back to stockpot.
- Add 7 cups of stock, mix thoroughly and bring to a boil, then turn down heat and simmer for 20 minutes.
- If soup seems too thick, add extra stock as needed, until desired consistency is reached.
- Add salt and pepper to taste.

 Yield: 10 cups

sulphites

Sulphites are used as a preservative and are found in a wide variety of foods, including baked goods, condiments, processed meats, as well as dried, canned and frozen fruits and vegetables. They are also used to stop the growth of microorganisms in fermented foods such as wine. Although sulphites are safe for most people, those who are sensitive report mild to severe reactions, and people who suffer from asthma appear to be most at risk for sulphite sensitivity. If you suspect your child is sensitive to sulphites, consult your doctor and read labels carefully. Sulphites can also be listed as follows: potassium bisulphate, sodium bisulphate, sulfur dioxide, sulphiting agents, metabisulphite and sulphurous acid.

butternut squash and chickpea soup

If your children are not keen on chickpeas, you can purée them so no one is the wiser. If making this for young children, you may want to start with only ½ tsp curry powder. You can always add more later. Alternatively, add a little milk to the children's soup.

2 (approximately 3 lb total) butternut squash, peeled and cut into chunks

¼ cup canola oil (plus an extra drizzle)

1 head garlic, top removed

2 tbsp canola oil

1 large onion, diced

1½ cups grated carrot (approximately 3 large carrots)

1½ tbsp ground cumin

1½ tsp curry powder

7 to 9 cups low-sodium chicken stock

1 can (19 oz) chickpeas, drained and rinsed

Salt and freshly ground pepper

⅓ cup chopped cilantro (optional)

• Preheat oven to 375°F.

• Line 1 baking sheet with foil or parchment paper. Place squash on baking sheet and drizzle with ¼ cup oil. Toss so squash is coated with oil.

• Drizzle a little more oil over garlic, wrap in foil and place on baking sheet.

• Bake squash and garlic for 45 minutes.

• Meanwhile, in a large pot or stockpot, sauté onion and carrots for 10 minutes in 2 tbsp oil until soft.

• Remove vegetables from oven and unwrap garlic. Once cool, squeeze garlic onto squash and discard skin.

• Place roasted squash in stockpot; add cumin and curry powder and sauté for 5 minutes.

- Using hand blender, purée vegetables until smooth. If you do not have a hand blender, remove vegetables from pot and purée in a food processor or blender until smooth, then transfer vegetables back to stockpot.
- In the same large stockpot, mix puréed vegetables with 7 cups stock and add chickpeas.
- Mix thoroughly and bring to a boil, then turn down heat and simmer with lid partially on for 20 minutes.
- Add salt and pepper to taste.
- If your soup seems a little thick, add extra stock as needed.
- Remove from heat, add cilantro (if using) and stir.

 Yield: 10 to 12 cups

msg

Monosodium glutamate (MSG) is a sodium salt of the amino acid glutamic acid. MSG is used to enhance flavour, and is often added to Asian foods, canned vegetables, chicken stocks, soups and processed meats. Although safe for the general population, large amounts of MSG can cause mild transitory reactions in sensitive individuals. The best way to avoid MSG is to read labels and choose an MSG-free restaurant the next time you go out for Asian food.

vegetable miso soup

Miso paste, common in traditional Japanese cooking, is made from fermented soybeans. When buying miso, choose a brand that's MSG-free. Keeping miso paste in the fridge or freezer makes this soup as quick to prepare as any packaged soup. If your child is not keen on tofu, substitute cooked rice noodles or pasta.

2½ cups water

¼ cup miso paste

¼ tsp sesame oil

1 green onion, sliced

1 carrot, cut into thin matchsticks

⅓ cup fresh or frozen peas

1 large handful spinach, stalks removed

½ pkg (175 g) semi-firm tofu, cut into bite-sized cubes

- In a small saucepan, thoroughly mix together water, miso and sesame oil.
- Add green onion and carrot and bring to a boil.
- Turn down heat, add peas, spinach and tofu and simmer for 3 minutes.
- Stir and serve.

 Yield: Serves 2

aspartame

Aspartame is a low-calorie artificial sweetener composed of two amino acids. It is also one of the most studied food additives in the world. Despite claims to the contrary, it is safe for the general population. However, it should be avoided by people suffering from phenylketonuria (PKU), a rare genetic condition, and pregnant women who suffer from hyperphenylalanine.

desserts

When it comes to dessert, moderation is the key. Too many children grow up expecting a nightly high-fat dessert, full of empty calories. Such desserts should be the exception and not the rule. When continued into adulthood, the dessert habit can be difficult to break and may lead to serious health consequences. Furthermore, children who are served high-calorie desserts may eat less of their dinner to save room for dessert. Children needing calories for growth spurts should be encouraged to eat second helpings of their main course.

In an age when childhood obesity is on the rise, it is time to rethink our approach to dessert. Delicious desserts do not need to be high in calories, and all should have some nutritional value. Dessert is the perfect opportunity to promote fruit, which is high in fibre and rich in vitamins and disease-fighting antioxidants. Research indicates that eating fruit is associated with a lower risk of cancer of the digestive system.[1]

It's important to choose well-ripened fruit, which is sweeter in flavour. When ripe, most fruit will smell fragrant. In the case of bananas that are getting too ripe, simply throw them in the freezer. When you're ready to use them, just defrost, mash and add to one of the following: Banana Bread (page 115), Banana Pecan Muffins (page 42) or Banana Cake from the Lake (page 240).

As often as possible, choose local fruit in season. It is less expensive, tastier and easier on the environment. In the summer, choose nectarines, peaches, plums, apricots, melons and berries. In the fall, go for apples and pears. During the winter, opt for citrus fruits, bananas and the more exotic pineapple, mango, kiwi and papaya. Canned fruit is fine as long as it is packed in unsweetened juice, not syrup.

Most of the desserts in this chapter contain fruit, and all of them have some nutritional value. For dinners when you don't have time to make a dessert, encourage your child to eat fruit. Fruit with yogurt makes a simple last-minute dessert. Buying plain yogurt and mixing it with either fresh fruit, fruit salad or one of the fruit sauces on the following pages is a great way to eliminate the unwanted additives, sweeteners and sugar in many flavoured yogurts. There is no reason a dessert cannot be both nutritious and delicious!

nectarine blueberry crisp

This crisp can be made with any combination of fruit; however, choose local fruit when in season. Try peaches and raspberries in the summer and apples and cinnamon in the fall. When substituting other fruits, you will need 5 to 6 cups.

5 nectarines (approximately 2 lb)
1 cup fresh blueberries
1 tbsp granulated sugar
1 tbsp all-purpose flour
½ cup rolled oats
½ cup all-purpose flour
Pinch salt
5 tbsp cold unsalted butter
5 tbsp packed brown sugar
2 tbsp granulated sugar

• Preheat oven to 375°F.
• Cut nectarines into eighths and place in 9-inch or 10-inch pie pan, cake pan or gratin dish.
• Sprinkle with blueberries.
• Mix together 1 tbsp sugar and 1 tbsp flour and sprinkle over fruit.
• In a food processor, pulse oats, flour and salt until thoroughly mixed.

• Add butter, brown sugar and 2 tbsp sugar and pulse until just mixed and crumbly.
• Evenly spread topping over fruit.
• Place crisp in middle of oven and bake for 30 to 45 minutes, checking after 30 minutes. If the topping has browned enough but the fruit is not cooked through, cover loosely with foil and turn down heat to 350°F.
• The crisp is done when the topping is golden brown and the fruit juices are bubbling around the edges.

Yield: Serves 6

desserts

roasted summer fruit

Here's another recipe that can be made with any combination of fruit. In the summer, try peaches and blueberries or plums with a little orange juice and zest.

8 fresh unblemished
  apricots (approximately
  16 oz), pitted and
  quartered
1 handful raspberries
  (approximately 4 oz)
⅓ cup granulated sugar

• Preheat oven to 350°F.
• In a shallow baking dish or gratin dish, place apricots skin side down in single layer, touching but not overlapping.
• Dot with raspberries.
• Sprinkle with sugar.

• Place fruit in middle of oven and bake for 30 to 40 minutes, checking after 30 minutes.
• When done, the fruit should have exuded its juices, leaving a delicious syrup on the bottom of the dish.

 Yield: Serves 5

TIP: Roasted fruit can be served either warm or cold over ice cream or with plain yogurt. It's also great on cereal.

238

baked bananas

This simple dessert is a staple at Brenda's house. The bananas can be eaten on their own, with plain yogurt or with French-style Homemade Vanilla Ice Cream (page 251).

3 very ripe bananas
¼ cup butter
¼ cup packed brown
   sugar
Pinch ground nutmeg
   (optional)

• Preheat oven to 325°F.
• Line baking pan with foil or parchment paper.
• Slice bananas in half and place on baking pan.

• In a saucepan, melt butter over medium heat.
• Add sugar and nutmeg (if using) and whisk until ingredients are incorporated. Simmer for 3 to 4 minutes.
• Pour syrup over bananas and bake for 20 minutes.

Yield: Serves 3 to 4

hidden sugars

Even if you limit your children's consumption of candies, cookies and cakes, they are probably consuming more sugar than you realize. Added sugars are becoming increasingly common in the foods we eat. They are used to make foods more appealing, and manufacturers are sneaky about putting sugar in many healthy-sounding products. Some of the worst culprits include breakfast cereals, granola bars, energy bars, soy milk, some peanut butters, frozen dinners, crackers, pasta sauces, breads and condiments. Sugar is even added to some canned fruits and vegetables. It is often added to low-fat products such as yogurt and salad dressings to enhance flavour.

A steady intake of sugar adds calories and is thought to be a contributing factor in our obesity epidemic. Increased consumption of sugar will also increase your child's risk of dental cavities.

To avoid these sugars, serve a diet rich in whole foods, limit processed foods and read ingredients lists carefully. Sugars can be disguised under any of the following names: fruit concentrates, dextrose, high fructose corn syrup, fructose, liquid sugar, sucrose, honey, maltose, maple syrup, glucose and fruit juice concentrates, among others. The ingredient listed first on a label is the one that represents the largest amount. Be leery of products listing several different types of sugar. Even if sugar is not listed first, it may be the main ingredient when the sugars are added up. When choosing a breakfast cereal, opt for a whole grain cereal with the smallest number of grams of sugar per serving. Four grams of sugar is equivalent to 1 tsp of sugar. Instead of adding sugar to your morning cereal, sweeten it with fresh or dried fruit instead.

banana cake from the lake

This recipe comes from Nanny Di, who lives on Lake Huron. To make a healthier version of this cake, substitute ½ cup of canola oil for the butter.

2¼ cups all-purpose flour
2 tsp baking powder
1 tsp baking soda
½ tsp salt
½ tsp ground nutmeg
½ cup unsalted butter
¾ cup granulated sugar
2 eggs, lightly beaten
1½ cups mashed ripe bananas (about 4)
¾ cup low-fat buttermilk (1.5% MF)

1 tsp vanilla extract
Cream Cheese Frosting (recipe follows)

- Preheat oven to 350°F.
- Grease and flour a 9-inch round cake pan.
- In a bowl, sift together flour, baking powder, baking soda, salt and nutmeg.
- In a separate bowl, use an electric mixer to cream together butter and sugar until creamy and colour lightens.
- Add eggs, mashed banana, buttermilk and vanilla and mix thoroughly, scraping down the sides of the bowl with a spatula to make sure all ingredients are incorporated.
- Fold dry ingredients into wet ingredients in 3 additions and mix until all ingredients are incorporated.
- Pour into cake pan and bake for 35 to 45 minutes or until cake is golden brown on the top and a toothpick inserted in the middle comes out clean.
- Place pan on cooling rack for 10 minutes.
- Run a knife around the edges of the cake to loosen it. Invert cake and place on cooling rack right side up.
- Once cool, ice with cream cheese frosting.

cream cheese frosting

4 oz cream cheese, softened
¼ cup unsalted butter, softened
2½ cups icing sugar, sifted
1 tbsp vanilla extract

- Cream together cream cheese and butter until blended.
- Slowly add icing sugar and mix until incorporated.
- Add vanilla and mix.

type 2 diabetes and children

Type 2 diabetes was originally called adult onset diabetes, as it was only known to occur in adults, but it is becoming increasingly common among children. Type 2 diabetes in adolescence represents one of the most rapidly growing forms of the disease.

Type 2 diabetes, which is characterized by a resistance to insulin, occurs either when there is not enough insulin to move glucose into the body's cells to be used as energy or when the body does not use the insulin properly. The blood glucose level becomes elevated, and over time this can lead to blindness, heart disease, kidney disease, nerve damage, limb amputations and even death.

Although a family history of the disease is typical in diagnosed cases, obesity is the hallmark. Up to 85 per cent of the children affected are obese or overweight at the time of their diagnosis.[2] For the vast majority of children, the disease can be prevented with a healthy diet and an active lifestyle.

blueberry tart

Don't let the thought of making pastry stop you from creating this nutritious dessert. Packed with over 5 cups of blueberries, it's loaded with disease-fighting antioxidants. This recipe makes extra pastry, which can always be used for the Seasonal Mini Fruit Tarts on page 244.

pastry

Extra pastry can be frozen for later use.

2 cups all-purpose flour
Pinch salt
⅓ cup granulated sugar
¾ cup cold unsalted butter, cut into cubes
1 egg, beaten
½ tsp vanilla extract
2 to 3 tbsp ice water

- Preheat oven to 375°F.
- In a bowl, sift together flour and salt. Add sugar and mix with a fork.
- Place flour mixture in food processor. Add butter and pulse 10 to 15 times. The texture should resemble coarse meal.
- Add egg, vanilla and 2 tbsp cold water and pulse again just until dough comes together as a ball. Add an extra tbsp of water if required.
- Place dough on floured work surface. Shape into a disc and wrap in plastic wrap.
- Place dough in refrigerator for 90 minutes (or at least 1 hour). If you're pressed for time, place dough in freezer for 25 minutes.
- Remove dough from freezer or refrigerator, unwrap and place on floured work surface. Roll pastry into an 11-inch round about ⅛ inch thick. Wrap dough around rolling pin and gently place in tart pan. Press dough into pan.
- Prick pastry with fork.
- Line tart shell with foil or parchment paper and fill with dried beans or rice to weigh down. This helps to prevent the bottom of the shell from puffing up and shrinking as it cooks.
- Place tart in oven and bake for 25 minutes. Remove weights and bake for another 5 to 10 minutes or until golden brown.
- Transfer tart shell to wire rack and let cool completely.

blueberry jam

3 cups fresh blueberries
½ tsp freshly squeezed
  lemon juice
¼ tsp lemon zest
2 to 3 tbsp granulated
  sugar

- In a small saucepan, combine blueberries, lemon juice, zest and 2 tbsp granulated sugar.
- Cook on low to medium heat, adjusting the heat so as not to burn the fruit, for approximately 25 minutes.
- The berries will exude their juices and cook down into a thick jam.
- Test to see if your jam is sweet enough. If not, add extra sugar and stir until sugar dissolves.
- Allow jam to cool.

to finish tart

2½ cups fresh blueberries

1 to 2 tbsp icing sugar

• Evenly spread jam over bottom of tart.

• Top with fresh berries. The tart should be nicely rounded but not overflowing.

• Sieve icing sugar over tart just prior to serving.

Yield: One 9-inch blueberry tart (serves 8)

seasonal mini fruit tarts

When making these tarts, use whatever seasonal fruit looks best. Try a combination of berries and tree fruits. In the summer, you can choose from blueberries, raspberries, strawberries, peaches, plums, nectarines and apricots. In the winter, try mangoes, papaya, kiwi and any berries you can find. Children love to choose their own fruit and assemble their tarts.

Pastry: approximately ⅓ quantity from the recipe on page 242 (or whatever is left over after making the tarts)

1 cup Balkan-style plain yogurt (above 3% MF)

2 cups fruit, cut in small bite-size pieces

1 to 2 tbsp icing sugar

• Preheat oven to 375°F.

• Roll out pastry so that it is ⅛ inch thick.

• Press a glass or large cookie round into the pastry to cut out circles.

• Line muffin tins with pastry circles and prick with a fork.

• Bake until pastry is golden brown, approximately 20 minutes.

• Remove from oven and cool on racks.

• Fill each tart with 1 tbsp of the yogurt.

• Top with fruit.

• Use a sieve to sprinkle icing sugar over tarts just prior to serving.

Yield: 6 or 7 tarts

peach melba

Served with French-Style Homemade Vanilla Ice Cream (page 251), this traditional dessert is "to die for." During the winter, substitute canned peaches for poached ones. Remember to always buy fruit packed in juice, not syrup.

poached peaches

- 1½ cups granulated sugar
- 4 cups water
- Squeeze of lemon
- 3 ripe peaches (or nectarines)
- Squeeze of lemon

• In a saucepan, combine sugar, water and lemon and bring to a boil. Reduce heat and allow syrup to simmer for 10 minutes.

• Place peaches in syrup, cover with lid and poach for 6 minutes.

• Turn off heat and allow peaches to cool in syrup for 20 minutes, covered.

• Remove peaches from syrup. Once cool, remove skin, cut in half and remove pit.

 Yield: 3 peaches

raspberry coulis

- 2½ cups fresh or frozen raspberries
- 2 tbsp granulated sugar (approximately)

• If using frozen raspberries, defrost.

• Place raspberries in a small saucepan, add sugar to taste and simmer for 5 minutes, stirring with a wooden spoon.

• Pour raspberries into a food processor and purée.

• Strain purée to remove seeds.

• Discard seeds and set coulis aside.

Yield: Approximately 1¼ cups coulis

to serve

• Place peaches on a plate and drizzle with raspberry coulis.

 Yield: Serves 3 to 6

fruit sauces

Berry season is a great opportunity to whip up a variety of summer sauces that freeze well. These sauces provide a nutritional boost when served either with plain yogurt or over vanilla ice cream.

To facilitate serving individual children's desserts, pour the sauce into ice cube trays, cover with plastic wrap and freeze. To serve, defrost 2 cubes of sauce and mix either with plain yogurt or pour over Homemade Vanilla Ice Cream (page 251). A homemade berry sauce is a healthy alternative to maple syrup when served over pancakes or French toast.

berry delicious summer sauce

1 cup fresh raspberries

1 cup fresh strawberries, hulled and sliced

1 cup fresh blueberries

1 cup fresh cherries, pitted

½ tsp freshly squeezed lemon juice

2 to 3 tbsp granulated sugar

• In a small saucepan, simmer raspberries, strawberries, blueberries, cherries and lemon juice over medium heat with 1 tbsp of the sugar until berries exude their juices, approximately 15 minutes. If sauce seems a little tart, add another 1 to 2 tbsp sugar.

Yield: Approximately 2½ cups

very cherry sauce

This delicious cherry sauce makes a yummy dessert served hot or cold on vanilla ice cream or mixed with plain yogurt. Because well-ripened cherries are so sweet, only 1 tbsp sugar is usually required. Remember, when choosing cherries, the darker the better.

1½ lb cherries, pitted
½ tsp freshly squeezed lemon juice
1 tbsp granulated sugar (approximately)

• In small saucepan, simmer cherries, lemon juice and sugar to taste over medium heat until sugar dissolves and cherries exude their juices, approximately 15 minutes.

Yield: Approximately 2½ cups

homemade blueberry sauce

The following recipe can be made with either fresh or frozen fruit.

4 cups fresh or frozen blueberries
½ tsp freshly squeezed lemon juice
2 to 3 tbsp granulated sugar

• In a saucepan, gently heat blueberries, lemon juice, and sugar to taste until the berries exude their juices (approximately 15 minutes).

Yield: Approximately 2½ cups

poached pears in blueberry sauce

4 ripe pears, peeled
4 cups water
1 cup granulated sugar
1 cinnamon stick
Juice of 1 lemon
Homemade Blueberry Sauce (page 247)

- Slice off the bottom of each pear with a knife so that it is flat and therefore able to stand upright.
- In a saucepan, combine water, sugar, cinnamon stick and lemon juice and bring to a boil. Reduce heat and simmer for 10 minutes.
- Place pears in syrup, cover with lid and poach for 6 minutes.
- Turn off heat and allow pears to cool in syrup for 20 minutes, covered.
- Remove pears from syrup.
- Place each pear on a plate and drizzle with blueberry sauce.

 Yield: Serves 4

summer yogurt

⅓ cup plain yogurt
⅓ cup Very Cherry Sauce (page 247) or Berry Delicious
   Summer Sauce (page 246)

- Thoroughly mix together yogurt and fruit sauce.

 Yield: Serves 1

chocolate dippers

Kids love chocolate dippers! When making them, choose dark chocolate—it's packed full of immune-boosting antioxidants, particularly flavonoids. Recent research suggests that flavonoids protect against the development of cardiovascular disease.[3]

Dried fruit is also good dipped in chocolate. Try dried peaches or apricots.

1 pkg (300 g) semi-sweet chocolate chips
20 strawberries
1 kiwi fruit, peeled and sliced
2 bananas, cut into 1-inch slices

- Line 2 cookie sheets with parchment paper.
- In a double boiler, melt chocolate over medium heat.
- Turn down heat to low and begin dipping fruit into the chocolate as follows:
- Hold strawberry by its stem and dip into chocolate. The chocolate should come three-quarters of the way up the strawberry. Place on cookie sheet and allow to cool. Repeat with remaining strawberries.
- Hold kiwi slice at the top and dip into chocolate. The chocolate should come halfway up the slice of fruit. Place on cookie sheet to cool. Repeat with remaining kiwi slices.
- Pierce banana slice with fork and dip into chocolate. The chocolate should completely cover the banana. Place on cookie sheet. Repeat with remaining banana slices.
- Place fruit in the refrigerator or in a cool, dry place to allow the chocolate to harden. Once the chocolate is hard, remove fruit from cookie sheet and place on a serving platter. Do not leave the fruit in refrigerator for longer than 15 minutes as condensation will form on chocolate.

Yield: Serves 10

homemade ice cream

Just about all of us scream for ice cream, kids and parents alike. Making homemade ice cream is a great way to eliminate the unwanted additives, stabilizers, and artificial colour and flavourings found in many commercial ice creams. Making ice cream with puréed fruit will also boost its nutritional value.

There are essentially 2 methods of making ice cream. The simpler method is to combine puréed fruit and whipping cream. Alternatively, traditional French ice cream is made with crème anglaise or a custard base. Milk, eggs and sometimes whipping cream are used.

easy raspberry ice cream

This is the simplest method for making ice cream and works with any of your favourite fruits. Just substitute 2 cups puréed fruit for the raspberries. As a general rule, the more flavourful fruits tend to make better ice cream. The following has a very intense raspberry flavour, and although a favourite at our houses, it may not appeal to very young children. When adding sugar, start slowly and add just enough to sweeten the ice cream. The more tart the fruit, the more sugar will be required.

2 lb fresh raspberries
½ cup granulated sugar
    (approximately)
1 cup whipping cream

• Purée raspberries in food processor, then press through a sieve to remove seeds.
• Measure 2 cups puréed raspberries and pour into a large bowl.

• Add whipping cream and ½ cup sugar or to taste depending on the sweetness of the fruit. Mix thoroughly.
• Pour into an ice cream maker and freeze according to manufacturer's instructions.

Yield: Approximately 3½ cups

french-style homemade vanilla ice cream

12 egg yolks
½ cup granulated sugar
2 vanilla beans
2 cups whipping cream
2 cups milk

- Using an electric mixer, beat egg yolks, slowly adding sugar until mixture lightens.
- Slit vanilla beans in half and run a knife along the length of the vanilla pods to scrape out the seeds. Place seeds and pods in a saucepan. Add cream and milk. Simmer over medium heat, stirring constantly until steam is rising off the milk and tiny bubbles are forming along the edge of the pan.
- Slowly add warm milk mixture to egg mixture, whisking until blended. Watch out: if milk is added too quickly, the eggs will cook.
- Return mixture to saucepan and simmer over low heat for 10 to 12 minutes, stirring constantly to ensure the eggs don't scramble. Be sure to sweep the bottom of the pan with either a heatproof silicone spatula or a wooden spoon to ensure the eggs are not cooking on the bottom of the pan.
- When ready, mixture should be the consistency of heavy cream. The cream should be thick enough to coat the back of a wooden spoon. Using a clean finger, you should be able to draw a line across the back of the wooden spoon and the cream should be thick enough to hold the line. Alternatively, an instant-read thermometer should read 160°F.
- Pour mixture through a fine sieve into a clean bowl to remove vanilla pods and bits of egg that may have solidified. Place mixture on an ice bath (a larger bowl filled with water and ice) to cool down. Continue to stir while mixture is cooling.

• When cold, pour into the canister of an ice cream maker and freeze according to manufacturer's instructions.

Yield: Approximately 6 cups

Serving Suggestion: Serve with fresh fruit or one of the homemade berry sauces (page 246–47).

ellie belly's strawberry ice cream

Named after Brenda's daughter, the following is sure to be a hit. To save the trouble of cleaning and hulling strawberries, frozen strawberries are used. If you are not keen on strawberries, try it with another fruit. Just substitute 2 cups puréed fruit for the strawberries. Remember that the more flavourful fruits make better ice creams.

4 egg yolks
½ cup granulated sugar
1 cup milk
1 cup whipping cream
1 pkg (600 g) frozen strawberries, defrosted

• Using an electric mixer, beat egg yolks, slowly adding sugar until mixture lightens.
• In a saucepan, combine milk and cream over medium heat.
• Simmer, stirring constantly, until steam is rising off the milk and tiny bubbles are forming along the edge of the pan.
• Slowly add warm milk mixture to egg mixture, whisking until blended. Be careful: if milk is added too quickly, the eggs will cook.
• Return mixture to saucepan and simmer over low heat for 10 to 12 minutes, stirring constantly to ensure the eggs don't cook. Be sure to sweep the bottom of the pan with either a heatproof silicone spatula or a wooden spoon to ensure the eggs are not cooking on the bottom of the pan.

- When ready, mixture should be the consistency of heavy cream. The cream should be thick enough to coat the back of a wooden spoon. Using a clean finger, you should be able to draw a line across the back of the wooden spoon and the cream should be thick enough to hold the line. Alternatively, an instant-read thermometer should read 160°F.

- Pour mixture into a clean bowl through a fine sieve to remove bits of egg that may have solidified. Place mixture in an ice bath (a larger bowl filled with water and ice) to cool down. Continue to stir while mixture is cooling.

- Place strawberries in food processor and purée until smooth.

- Measure 2 cups of puréed strawberries and mix with chilled custard.

- Pour into the canister of an ice cream maker and freeze according to manufacturer's instructions.

Yield: 5 cups

food processor frozen yogurt

The following is excellent served with sliced bananas on top. If the yogurt is in the freezer for longer than 3 hours, it will likely freeze solid, in which case you can soften it by removing from the freezer half an hour before serving.

2 cups Balkan-style plain yogurt (above 3% MF)
2 cups frozen raspberries (or frozen mixed berries)
2 tbsp liquid honey (or to taste)

• Place all ingredients in food processor and purée until smooth.
• Transfer the purée to an airtight container and freeze for at least 1 hour prior to serving.

Yield: 4 cups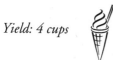

The following meal planners are designed to help you use Canada's Food Guide. A Food Guide serving is only a reference to help you understand what and how much you should be eating on a daily basis. For younger children and those with smaller appetites, a Food Guide serving can be broken up and served over several sittings. Older children and those with larger appetites will likely eat several Food Guide servings at a single sitting. For example, a young child might eat approximately ¼ cup blueberries for a snack and ¼ cup peas with dinner. That counts as 1 serving of Vegetables and Fruit. A younger child might eat a small bowl of cereal, which is approximately 1 serving of Grain Products, whereas an older child might eat a large bowl of cereal, which is 2 to 3 servings of Grain Products. A typical sandwich made with 2 slices of bread counts as 2 servings of Grain Products. A teenage boy might drink 2 cups of milk with dinner, which is equivalent to 2 servings of Milk and Alternatives.

Portion sizes are getting larger. A typical restaurant portion of meat or fish can actually be 2 to 3 servings of Meat and Alternatives. Children who are at a healthy weight but need more food, such as those who are going through growth spurts and/or those who are very active, should be encouraged to eat additional servings from the 4 food groups. The following meal planners are designed to be used as guidelines. Do not get bogged down in the details. You are not expected to measure out Food Guide servings, nor do you have the time to do so. Do not worry if your child skips a snack or picks at his meal. He will likely make up for it later. When served a wide variety of healthy foods from all 4 food groups, children tend to eat what they need to thrive.

recommended number of food guide servings for 2- to 3-year-old boys & girls

vegetables & fruit	grain products	milk & alternatives	meat & alternatives
4	3	2	1

sample 5-day meal planner for 2- to 3-year-olds

day 1

breakfast 1 small bowl **Daf's Homemade Granola** with ½ cup milk & glass water

snack 1 apricot & glass water

lunch ½ tuna sandwich on whole wheat bread, veggie sticks with dip & ½ cup milk

snack 3 strawberries & glass water

dinner 1 small bowl spaghetti with **Traditional Ragout**, ½ cup milk & **Traditional Baked Beans**

snack ½ cup milk

day 2

breakfast 1 **Whole Wheat Double Berry Pancake** & ½ cup milk

snack Cubed cantaloupe & glass water

lunch ½ **Veggie Pita Pocket** & ½ cup milk

snack ½ banana & glass water

dinner **Ashley's Chicken Dijonnaise,** whole grain rice, steamed peas & carrots & 1 cup milk

snack ¼ cup apple sauce & glass of water

- If your child is unable to drink milk, fortified soy beverage can be substituted.
- All recipes are in bold type.
- Servings are approximate.
- Children should be encouraged to drink water throughout the day to alleviate thirst.

sample 5-day meal planner
for 2- to 3-year-olds continued

day 3

breakfast	1 **Blueberry Bran Muffin** with non-hydrogenated margarine & ½ cup orange juice
snack	¼ cup blueberries & glass water
lunch	1 small bowl **Judy's Vegetable Lentil Soup**, ½ cup milk & ½ slice bread
snack	1 slice whole grain toast with 1 tbsp peanut butter & ½ cup milk
dinner	½ **Fish Taco, Kids' Caesar Salad** & 1 cup milk
snack	½ an orange & glass water

day 4

breakfast	1 small bowl whole grain cereal with ½ cup milk & glass water
snack	Papaya cubes & water
lunch	½ **Veggie Wrap**, ½ apple with ½ cup milk
snack	1 slice **Ross's Pumpkin Bread** & glass water
dinner	1 serving **Traditional Baked Beans** (or canned equivalent) with steamed broccoli, carrots & peas & 1 cup milk
snack	¼ cup fresh raspberries & glass water

day 5

breakfast	1 **Soft-Boiled Egg with Whole Wheat Toast Soldiers** & glass water
snack	**Toasted Whole Wheat Pita Chips** & **Guacamole** & glass water
lunch	½ **Fiona's Veggie Sandwich** & 1 cup milk
snack	1 homemade **Strawberry Popsicle** & glass water
dinner	1 small serving **Salmon with Fresh Dill**, steamed broccoli, **Cath's Potato Yam Mash** & ½ cup milk
snack	½ cup milk poured over small bowl fresh raspberries

recommended number of food guide servings for 4- to 8-year-old boys & girls

vegetables & fruit	grain products	milk & alternatives	meat & alternatives
5	4	2	1

sample 5-day meal planner for 4- to 8-year-olds

day 1

breakfast 1 small bowl **Daf's Homemade Granola** with ½ sliced banana & ½ cup milk & glass water

snack 1 apricot & glass water

lunch ½ **Mighty Tuna Pita Pocket**, veggie sticks with **Tzatziki** & ½ cup milk

snack **Toasted Whole Wheat Pita Chips** with **Guacamole** & glass water

dinner Spaghetti with **Traditional Ragout**, green salad & ½ cup milk

snack ½ cup raspberries with ½ cup milk poured on top

day 2

breakfast 1 small bowl whole grain cereal with ½ cup milk, small bowl mixed fruit & glass water

snack 1 slice cantaloupe & glass water

lunch ½ peanut butter and jam sandwich on whole grain bread, veggie sticks with dip & ½ cup milk

snack 2 **Oatmeal Raisin Cookies** & glass water

dinner ½ **Fish Taco** with **Kids' Caesar Salad** & ½ cup milk

snack **Baked Bananas** & ½ cup milk

- If your child is unable to drink milk, fortified soy beverage can be substituted.
- All recipes are in bold type.
- Servings are approximate.
- Children should be encouraged to drink water throughout the day to alleviate thirst.

sample 5-day meal planner
for 4- to 8-year-olds continued

day 3

breakfast	1 **Toad in a Hole** & ½ glass orange juice
snack	1 **Homemade Granola Bar** & ½ cup milk
lunch	½ **West Coast Salmon Pita Pocket**, papaya slices & ½ cup milk
snack	Red pepper strips & carrot sticks with **Middle Eastern Hummus** & glass water
dinner	**Asparagus, Pea & Mint Risotto**, green salad & 1 cup milk
snack	½ cup applesauce & glass water

day 4

breakfast	1 **Blueberry Bran Muffin** with non-hydrogenated margarine, 1 banana & ½ cup milk
snack	Veggie sticks with **Tzatziki** & glass water
lunch	**Cheese Quesadilla** with **Homemade Salsa**, 1 nectarine & 1 cup milk
snack	½ whole wheat bagel, toasted, with **Middle Eastern Hummus** & glass water
dinner	½ **Chicken Enchilada**, steamed carrots & broccoli & ½ cup milk
snack	1 **Poached Pear in Blueberry Sauce** & glass water

day 5

breakfast	1 **Whole Wheat Double Berry Pancake** with **Homemade Blueberry Sauce** & ½ cup orange juice
snack	1 **Homemade Granola Bar** & glass water
lunch	½ **Fruit-Filled Almond Butter Pita Pocket**, carrot sticks & ½ cup milk
snack	1 homemade **Peachy Popsicle** & glass water
dinner	1 small piece **Chelsea's Barbecued Flank Steak**, ¼ cup steamed green peas, **Roasted Potato and Yam Chips** & 1 cup milk
snack	1 slice **Banana Bread** & ½ cup milk

recommended number of food guide servings for 9- to 13-year-old boys & girls

vegetables & fruit	grain products	milk & alternatives	meat & alternatives
6	6	3 to 4	1 to 2

sample 5-day meal planner for 9- to 13-year-olds

day 1

breakfast 1 small bowl **Daf's Homemade Granola** with ½ cup milk & ½ cup blueberries on top & **Mixed Fruit Smoothie**

snack 1 apple, cut in quarters, & glass water

lunch 1 **Mighty Tuna Pita Pocket**, veggie sticks with dip & ½ cup milk

snack **Toasted Whole Wheat Pita Chips** with **Guacamole** & glass water

dinner **Spaghetti & Meatballs**, green salad, 1 cup milk & **Food Processor Frozen Yogurt**

snack 1 slice **Ross's Pumpkin Bread** & glass water

day 2

breakfast 1 small bowl whole grain cereal with ½ cup milk, bowl of grapes & ½ cup orange juice

snack 1 banana with glass water

lunch **Cheese Quesadilla** with **Homemade Salsa**, 1 nectarine & ½ cup milk

snack 2 **Cranberry Flaxseed Cookies** & glass water

dinner **Fish Tacos, Asian Chop Chop Salad** & 1 cup milk

snack 1 bowl of yogurt with fresh blueberries sprinkled on top

- If your child is unable to drink milk, fortified soy beverage can be substituted.
- All recipes are in bold type.
- Servings are approximate.
- Children should be encouraged to drink water throughout the day to alleviate thirst.

sample 5-day meal planner
for 9- to 13-year-olds continued

day 3

breakfast	2 **Mixed Berry Oatmeal Muffins** with non-hydrogenated margarine, 1 banana & **Strawberry Mango Smoothie**
snack	Papaya, cut in cubes, & glass water
lunch	1 **West Coast Salmon Pita Pocket**, veggie sticks with **Roasted Garlic and White Bean Hummus** & 1 cup milk
snack	1 **Homemade Granola Bar** (or whole grain equivalent) & glass water
dinner	**Vegetarian Chili**, 1 slice whole grain bread, green salad, 1 cup milk & **Peach Melba**
snack	1 bowl of yogurt & glass water

day 4

breakfast	1 bowl **Banana Nutmeg Porridge** with ½ cup milk, papaya & ½ cup orange juice
snack	Veggie sticks with **Tzatziki** & glass water
lunch	1 **Veggie Wrap**, watermelon & 1 cup milk
snack	**Toasted Whole Wheat Pita Chips** with **Middle Eastern Hummus** & glass water
dinner	**Rosemary Pork Tenderloin**, whole grain rice, assorted steamed veggies, 1 cup milk & yogurt
snack	2 **Oatmeal Raisin Cookies** with ½ glass milk

day 5

breakfast	2 **Whole Wheat Double Berry Pancakes** with **Homemade Blueberry Sauce** & ½ cup orange juice
snack	1 **Homemade Granola Bar** (or whole grain equivalent) & ½ cup milk
lunch	1 **Veggie Hummus Pita Pocket**, 1 cup milk, **Food Processor Frozen Yogurt** & glass water
snack	1 homemade **Peachy Popsicle** & glass water
dinner	**Roasted Halibut with Mango Salsa**, **Bulgur Salad**, **Garlic Roasted Broccolini** & 1 cup milk
snack	½ cup raspberries with ½ cup milk poured on top

recommended number of food guide servings for 14- to 18-year-old males

vegetables & fruit	grain products	milk & alternatives	meat & alternatives
8	7	3 to 4	3

sample 5-day meal planner for 14- to 18-year-old males

day 1

breakfast 1 large bowl **Daf's Homemade Granola** with 1 cup milk & ½ cup blueberries on top & **Mixed Fruit Smoothie**

snack 1 slice **Ross's Pumpkin Bread** & glass water

lunch 1 **Black Bean Quesadilla** with salsa, assorted veggie sticks, papaya slices & 1 cup milk

snack Carrot sticks & cucumber slices with **Roasted Garlic and White Bean Hummus** & glass water

dinner 1 large bowl spaghetti with **Traditional Ragout**, green salad, 1 cup milk & **Peach Melba**

snack 1 apple & glass water

day 2

breakfast **Danny's Scrambled Wrap**, 1 banana, ½ cup orange juice & glass water

snack 1 **Mixed Berry Oatmeal Muffin** with non-hydrogenated margarine & glass water

lunch **Cheese Quesadilla** with **Homemade Salsa, Guacamole**, cantaloupe & 1 cup milk

snack Carrots, red pepper strips with **Middle Eastern Hummus** & glass water

dinner 1 **Fish Taco**, green salad, 1 cup milk & **Baked Bananas**

snack Yogurt with cantaloupe & glass water

- If your child is unable to drink milk, fortified soy beverage can be substituted.
- All recipes are in bold type.
- Servings are approximate.
- Children should be encouraged to drink water throughout the day to alleviate thirst.

sample 5-day meal planner
for 14- to 18-year-old males continued

day 3

breakfast	2 **Carrot Zucchini Breakfast Muffins** with non-hydrogenated margarine, sliced papaya, **Strawberry Mango Smoothie**
snack	1 cup milk & **Homemade Granola Bar**
lunch	1 **West Coast Salmon Pita Pocket**, veggie sticks with **Peanut Butter Hummus**, 1 peach & 1 cup milk
snack	Red & green pepper strips with dip & glass water
dinner	1 large bowl **Vegetarian Chili**, green salad, 1 slice whole grain bread, **Blueberry Nectarine Crisp** & 1 cup milk
snack	2 **Cranberry Flaxseed Cookies** & glass water

day 4

breakfast	1 large bowl **Steel Cut Oats with Caramelized Green Apples**, cantaloupe, cut into cubes, ½ cup orange juice & glass water
snack	2 **Cranberry Flaxseed Cookies** & 1 cup milk
lunch	1 egg salad sandwich on whole wheat bread, 1 banana & 1 cup milk
snack	Carrots & red pepper strips with **Roasted Garlic and White Bean Hummus** & glass water
dinner	1 **Tarragon Turkey Burger** on whole wheat bun, **Kids' Caesar Salad, Roasted Home Fries**, 1 cup milk & yogurt with blueberries
snack	Mango & glass water

day 5

breakfast	2 **Whole Wheat Double Berry Pancakes** with **Homemade Blueberry Sauce**, 1 apricot, ½ cup orange juice & glass water
snack	1 **Homemade Granola Bar** & glass water
lunch	1 **Fruit-Filled Almond Butter Pita Pocket**, veggie sticks with **Tzatziki** & 1 cup milk
snack	**Jeff's Blueberry Blitz** & ½ whole wheat bagel with non-hydrogenated margarine
dinner	Large piece **Roasted Halibut with Mango Salsa, Bulgur Salad, Garlic Roasted Broccolini**, 1 cup milk & **Poached Pears in Blueberry Sauce**
snack	1 **Oatmeal Raisin Cookie** & ½ cup milk

recommended number of food guide servings for 14- to 18-year-old females

vegetables & fruit	grain products	milk & alternatives	meat & alternatives
7	6	3 to 4	2

sample 5-day meal planner for 14- to 18-year-old females

day 1

breakfast 1 large bowl **Daf's Homemade Granola** with 1 cup milk & ½ cup blueberries on top & 1 **Mixed Fruit Smoothie**

snack 1 apple & glass water

lunch 1 **Mighty Tuna Pita Pocket**, veggie sticks with **Tzatziki** & 1 cup milk

snack 1 homemade **Raspberry Creamsicle** & glass water

dinner 1 large bowl spaghetti with **Traditional Ragout**, green salad, **Peach Melba** & 1 cup milk

day 2

breakfast 1 large bowl whole grain cereal with 1 cup milk, ½ cup fresh raspberries, ½ glass orange juice & glass water

snack 1 **Mixed Berry Oatmeal Muffin** with non-hydrogenated margarine & glass water

lunch **Butternut Squash and Chickpea Soup**, 1 slice whole grain bread, 1 apple & 1 cup milk

snack Veggie sticks with **Roasted Garlic and White Bean Hummus** & glass water

dinner 1 **Fish Taco, Kids' Caesar Salad,** 1 cup milk, & assorted fruit & yogurt

- If your child is unable to drink milk, fortified soy beverage can be substituted.
- All recipes are in bold type.
- Servings are approximate.
- Children should be encouraged to drink water throughout the day to alleviate thirst.

sample 5-day meal planner
for 14- to 18-year-old females continued

day 3

breakfast   2 **Blueberry Bran Muffins** with non-hydrogenated margarine, yogurt with sliced banana, ½ cup orange juice & glass water

snack   1 **Homemade Granola Bar** & 1 cup milk

lunch   1 **Black Bean Quesadilla** with salsa, assorted veggie sticks & 1 cup milk

snack   Carrot & red pepper strips with **Middle Eastern Hummus** & glass water

dinner   1 large bowl **Vegetarian Chili**, 1 slice whole grain bread, green salad & 1 cup milk

day 4

breakfast   1 large bowl **Banana Nutmeg Porridge**, cantaloupe cubes & 1 **Mixed Berry Smoothie**

snack   1 **Mixed Berry Oatmeal Muffin** & glass water

lunch   **Roasted Tomato & Red Pepper Soup**, 1 slice bread, watermelon & 1 cup milk

snack   Veggie sticks with **Middle Eastern Hummus** & glass water

dinner   1 **Chicken Enchilada**, steamed carrots, green salad & 1 cup milk

day 5

breakfast   2 **Buckwheat Banana Pancakes** with **Homemade Blueberry Sauce**, ½ cup orange juice & glass water

snack   1 **Homemade Granola Bar** & ½ cup milk

lunch   1 large bowl **Marinated Vegetable Salad**, 1 slice whole grain bread & 1 cup milk

snack   Handful almonds & ½ cup milk

dinner   **Roasted Halibut with Mango Salsa**, 1 large bowl **Bulgur Salad, Garlic Roasted Broccolini**, 1 cup milk & sliced papaya

appendix II
resources

websites

AMERICAN ACADEMY OF ALLERGY ASTHMA & IMMUNOLOGY
WWW.AAAAI.ORG

AMERICAN ACADEMY OF PEDIATRICS
WWW.AAP.ORG

AMERICAN DIETETIC ASSOCIATION
WWW.EATRIGHT.ORG

ANEMIA INSTITUTE
WWW.ANEMIAINSTITUTE.ORG

BC HEALTH GUIDE
WWW.BCHEALTHGUIDE.ORG

BRITISH COLUMBIA MEDICAL ASSOCIATION
WWW.BCMA.ORG/HEALTHYKIDS

CANADA'S PHYSICAL ACTIVITY GUIDE
WWW.PHAC-ASPC.GC.CA/PAU-UAP/PAGUIDE

CANADIAN FOOD INSPECTION AGENCY
WWW.INSPECTION.GC.CA

CANADIAN FITNESS AND LIFESTYLE RESEARCH INSTITUTE
WWW.CFLRI.CA

CANADIAN PAEDIATRIC SOCIETY
WWW.CPS.CA

CENTERS FOR DISEASE CONTROL AND PREVENTION
HTTP://APPS.NCCD.CDC.GOV/DNPABMI/CALCULATOR.ASPX

CHILDHOOD OBESITY FOUNDATION
WWW.COFBC.CA

DIAL-A-DIETICIAN
WWW.DIALADIETICIAN.ORG

DIETICIANS OF CANADA
WWW.DIETICIANS.CA/EATWELL

EATING WELL WITH CANADA'S FOOD GUIDE
WWW.HC-SC.GC.CA/FN-AN/FOOD-GUIDE-ALIMENT/
INDEX_E.HTML

EATING WELL WITH CANADA'S FOOD GUIDE: FIRST NATIONS,
INUIT AND MÉTIS
WWW.HC-SC.GC.CA/FN-AN/PUBS/FNIM-PNIM/INDEX_E.HTML

GO FOR GREEN
WWW.GOFORGREEN.CA

HEALTH CANADA
WWW.HC-SC.GC.CA

LESLIEBECK.COM
WWW.LESLIEBECK.COM

NATIONAL CENTER FOR HEALTH STATISTICS: CENTER FOR
DISEASE CONTROL GROWTH CHARTS
WWW.CDC.GOV/GROWTHCHARTS/

SELF-ESTEEM AND BODY IMAGE RESOURCES FOR PARENTS
WWW.MISSIONNUTRITION.CA

books

Bradshaw, Brenda, & Laura Donaldson Bramley, (2004). *The Baby's Table.* Toronto: Random House Canada.

Laumann, Silken. (2006). *Child's Play.* Toronto: Random House Canada.

Legere, Henry Joseph (2004). *Raising Healthy Eaters.* Cambridge, MA: Da Capo Press.

Satter, Ellyn. (1987). *How to Get Your Kid to Eat . . . But Not Too Much.* Boulder: Bull Publishing.

Walker, W. Allan (2005). *Eat, Play and Be Healthy: The Harvard Medical School Guide to Healthy Eating for Kids.* New York: McGraw-Hill.

Waverman, Emma & Eshun Mott, (2007). *Whining & Dining.* Toronto: Random House Canada.

notes

Introduction

1. Health Canada, "Eating Well with Canada's Food Guide: A Resource for Educators and Communicators," 2007. http://www.hc-sc.gc.ca/ fn-an/alt_formats/hpfb-dgpsa/pdf/pubs/res-educat_e.pdf (accessed February 6, 2007).

chapter 1

1. Ellyn Satter, *How to Get Your Kid to Eat . . . But Not Too Much* (Boulder: Bull Publishing, 1987), p. 14.
2. Health Canada, "Eating Well with Canada's Food Guide: A Resource for Educators and Communicators," 2007. http://www.hc-sc.gc.ca/ fn-an/alt_formats/hpfb-dgpsa/pdf/pubs/res-educat_e.pdf (accessed February 6, 2007).
3. Health Canada, "TRANSforming the Food Supply, Report of the Trans Fat Task Force, Submitted to the Minister of Health, June 2006," 2006. http://www.hc-sc.gc.ca/fn-an/alt_formats/hpfb-dgpsa/ pdf/nutrition/tf-gt_rep-rap_e.pdf (accessed June 21, 2007).
4. Canadian Paediatric Society, "Healthy Active Living for Children and Youth," Index to Position Statements, 2002. http://www.cps.ca/english/ statements/HAL/HAL02-01.htm (accessed November 21, 2005).
5. Statistics Canada, "Canadian Community Health Survey: Overview of Canadians' Eating Habits," The Daily. http://statcan.ca/Daily/ English/060706/d060706b.htm (accessed July 9, 2006).

6. Health Canada, "Family Guide to Physical Activity for Children (6–9 years of age)," 2002. http://www.phac-aspc.gc.ca/pau-uap/paguide/child_youth/pdf/kids_family_guide_e.pdf (accessed June 21, 2007).

chapter 2

1. Canadian Living Foundation, "Breakfast for Learning," n.d. http://www.breakfastforlearning.ca/english/who_we_are/a_our_mission.html (accessed February 27, 2006).

2. Statistics Canada, "Canadian Community Health Survey: Overview of Canadians' Eating Habits," The Daily. http://statcan.ca/Daily/English/060706/d060706b.htm (accessed July 9, 2006).

3. Joanne Slavin, "Whole Grains and Human Health," *Nutritional Research Reviews* 17 (2004): p. 14.

4. Berkeley University of California, "Give Yourself a Berry Boost," Wellness Letter 22 (2006): pp. 1–8.

5. Health Canada, "Nutrition Facts Table," 2003. http://www.hc-sc.gc.ca/ahc-asc/media/nr-cp/2003/2003_01bk1_e.html (accessed April 9, 2007).

6. Health Canada, "Eating Well with Canada's Food Guide," 2007. http://www.hc-sc.gc.ca/fn-an/alt_formats/hpfb-dgpsa/pdf/food-guide-aliment/view_eatwell_vue_bienmang_e.pdf (accessed June 21, 2007).

chapter 3

1. Statistics Canada, "Canadian Community Health Survey: Overview of Canadians' Eating Habits," The Daily. http://statcan.ca/Daily/English/060706/d060706b.htm (accessed July 9, 2006).

2. J. Fisher et al., "Maternal Milk Consumption Predicts the Tradeoff Between Milk and Soft Drinks in Young Girls' Diets," *J Nutr* 131(2)(2001): pp. 246–50.

3. Health Canada, It's Your Health, "Severe Allergic Reactions," 2007. http://www.hc-sc.gc.ca/iyh-vsv/med/allerg_e.html (accessed April 17, 2007).

4. Johns Hopkins Bloomberg Public Health News Center, "Researcher Dispels Myth of Dioxins and Plastic Water Bottles," 2007. http://www.jhsph.edu/publichealthnews/articles/halden_dioxins.html (accessed January 25, 2007).

5. Health Canada, It's Your Health, "Risks Associated with Sprouts," 2007. http://www.hc-sc.gc.ca/iyh-vsv/food-aliment/sprouts-germes _e.html (accessed March 5, 2007).

chapter 4

1. G. A. Bray, S. J. Nielsen, and B. M. Popkin, "Consumption of High-Fructose Corn Syrup in Beverages May Play a Role in the Epidemic of Obesity," *Am J Clin Nutr* 79(4)(2004): pp. 537–43.

2. Eleanor Noss Whitney and Sharon Rady Rolfes, *Understanding Nutrition* (Belmont, CA: Thomson/Wadsworth, 2005), p. 466.

3. Health Canada, "Eating Well with Canada's Food Guide: A Resource for Educators and Communicators," 2007. http://www.hc-sc.gc.ca/fn-an/alt_formats/hpfb-dgpsa/pdf/pubs/res-educat_e.pdf (accessed February 6, 2007).

4. M.F. Jacobson, Center for Science in the Public Interest, "Liquid Candy, How Soft Drinks are Harming America's Health," 2005. http://www.cspinet.org/new/pdf/liquid_candy_final_w_new _supplement.pdf (accessed August 28, 2006).

chapter 5

1. M. E. Eisenberg et al., "Correlations between Family Meals and Psychosocial Well-being among Adolescents," *Arch Pediatr Adolesc Med* 158(8)(2004): pp. 792–96.

2. Childhood Obesity Foundation, "Identifying, Evaluating and Promoting Best Practices for Childhood Obesity," n.d. http://www.cofbc.ca/ (accessed August 28, 2006).

3. Dietitians of Canada, "School Food and Nutrition Recommendations for Ontario Ministry of Education Regarding Snacks and Beverages Dispensed by Vending Machines," 2004. http://www.dietitians.ca/news/downloads/DCRpt1_Eng_OntarioSchoolFood.pdf (accessed June 21, 2006).

4. R. S. Strauss, "Childhood Obesity and Self-esteem," *Pediatrics* 105(1)(2000): e15.

5. Canadian Paediatric Society, *Healthy Kids, Active Kids*, Childhood Obesity Foundation n.d. http://www.cofbc.ca/childobese.html (accessed August 28, 2006).

6. Health Canada, "Food Related Illnesses," 2006. http://www.hc-sc.gc.ca/fn-an/securit/ill-intox/index_e.html (accessed April 11, 2007).

7. Centers for Disease Control and Prevention, "Division of Bacterial and Mycotic Diseases: *Escherichia coli 0157:H7*," 2006. http://www.cdc.gov/ncidod/dbmd/diseaseinfo/escherichiacoli_g.htm (accessed January 24, 2007).

8. Health Canada, "Eating Well with Canada's Food Guide: A Resource for Educators and Communicators," 2007. http://www.hc-sc.gc.ca/fn-an/alt_formats/hpfb-dgpsa/pdf/pubs/res-educat_e.pdf (accessed February 6, 2007).

9. Canadian Paediatric Society, "Feeding Your Vegetarian Child," *Caring for Kids*, 1999. http://www.caringforkids.cps.ca/eating/vegetarian.htm (accessed April 12, 2007).

10. Health Canada, "Eating Well with Canada's Food Guide: A Resource for Educators and Communicators," 2007. http://www.hc-sc.gc.ca/fn-an/alt_formats/hpfb-dgpsa/pdf/pubs/res-educat_e.pdf (accessed February 6, 2007).

11. University of Maryland Medical Center, "Omega-3 Fatty Acids," 2006. http://www.umm.edu//altmed/articles/omega-3–000316.htm (accessed July 15, 2007).

12. Eleanor Noss Whitney and Sharon Rady Rolfes, *Understanding Nutrition* (Belmont, CA: Thomson/Wadsworth, 2005), p. 160.

13. J. M. Norris et al., "Omega-3 Polyunsaturated Fatty Acid Intake in Islet Autoimmunity in Children at Increased Risk for Type 1 Diabetes," *Jama* 298(12)(2007): pp. 1420–28.

14. Donna McCann et al., "Food Additives and Hyperactive Behaviour in 3-year-old and 8/9-year-old Children in the Community: a Randomized, Double-blinded, Placebo-controlled Trial," *The Lancet.com,* (2007). http://www.thelancet.com/journals/lancet/article/PIIS0140673607613063/abstract?isEOP=true.

15. A. J. Richardson and P. Montgomery, "The Oxford–Durham Study: A Randomized, Controlled Trial of Dietary Supplementation with Fatty Acids in Children with Developmental Coordination Disorder," *Pediatrics* 115(5)(2005): pp. 1,360–66.

16. J. E. Foulke, Food and Drug Administration, "Mercury in Fish: Cause for Concern?" 1995. http://www.fda.gov/fdac/reprints/mercury.html (accessed April 26, 2006).

17. Health Canada, "Health Canada's Revised Assessment of Mercury in Fish Enhances Protection While Reflecting Advice in Canada's Food Guide," 2007. http://www.hc-sc.gc.ca/ahc-asc/media/advisories-avis/2007/2007_31_e.html (accessed April 12, 2007).

18. Health Canada, "Health Canada Advises Specific Groups to Limit Their Consumption of Canned Albacore Tuna," 2007. http://www.hc-sc.gc.ca/ahc-asc/media/advisories-avis/2007/2007_14_e.html (accessed March 5, 2007).

19. Health Canada, It's Your Health, "PCBs," 2005. http://www.hc-sc.gc.ca/iyh-vsv/environ/pcb-bpc_e.html (accessed June 16, 2007).

20. K. L. Munger et al., "Vitamin D Intake and Incidence of Multiple Sclerosis," *Neurology* 62(1)(2004): pp. 60–65.

21. G. G. Schwartz and H. G. Skinner, "Vitamin D Status and Cancer: New Insights," *Curr Opin Clin Nutr Metab Care* 10(1)(2007): pp. 6–11.

22. H. D. Sesso et al., "Dietary Lycopene, Tomato-based Food Products and Cardiovascular Disease in Women," *J Nutr* 133(7)(2003): pp. 2,336–41.

23. Johns Hopkins Bloomberg Public Health News Center, "Researcher Dispels Myth of Dioxins and Plastic Water Bottles," 2007. http://www.jhsph.edu/publichealthnews/articles/halden_dioxins.html (accessed January 25, 2007).

24. C. G. Bornehag et al., "The Association between Asthma and Allergic Symptoms in Children and Phthalates in House Dust: A Nested Case-control Study," *Environ Health Perspect* 112(14)(2004): pp. 1,393–97.

chapter 6

1. Dietitians of Canada, Frequently Asked Questions (FAQ), "Organic Food," 1999. http://www.dietitians.ca/public/content/eat_well_live _well/english/faqs_tips_facts/faqs/index.asp?fn=view&id=3419&idstring= 3419 (accessed November 28, 2006).

2. Statistics Canada, "Canadian Community Health Survey: Overview of Canadians' Eating Habits," The Daily. http://statcan.ca/Daily/English/ 060706/d060706b.htm (accessed July 9, 2006).

3. Health Canada, "Acrylamide and Food—Questions and Answers," 2005. http://www.hc-sc.gc.ca/fn-an/securit/chem-chim/acrylamide/ acrylamide_and_food-acrylamide_et_aliment_e.html (accessed November 9, 2005).

4. Health Canada, "Statement from Health Canada about Acrylamide in Food," 2005. http://www.hc-sc.gc.ca/ahc-asc/media/nr-cp/2005/ 2005_stmt-dec_acrylamide1_e.html (accessed February 22, 2007).

chapter 7

1. Berkeley University of California, "Wellness Facts," Wellness Letter 22 (2006): pp. 1–8.

2. Canadian Paediatric Society, Index to Position Statements, "Eating Disorders in Adolescents: Principles of Diagnosis and Treatment," 1996. http://www.cps.ca/english/statements/AM/am96–04.htm (accessed November 26, 2006).

chapter 8

1. World Health Organization (WHO), "Cancer: Diet and Physical Activity's Impact," 2007. http://www.who.int/dietphysicalactivity/ publications/facts/cancer/en/ (accessed June 14, 2007).

2. Canadian Paediatric Society, Index to Position Statements, "Healthy Active Living for Children and Youth," 2002. http://www.cps.ca/ english/statements/HAL/HAL02–01.htm (accessed November 21, 2005).

3. F. M. Steinberg, M. M. Bearden, and C. L. Keen, "Cocoa and Chocolate Flavonoids: Implications for Cardiovascular Health," *J Am Diet Assoc* 103(2)(2003): pp. 215–23.

bibliography

American Dietetic Association. "Almonds: Grab a Handful for Heart Health," http://www.eatright.org/ada/files/almonds.pdf.

———. "Barley: A Healthy Heart Solution," http://www.eatright.org/ada/files/Barley.pdf.

———. "Canola Oil: Good for Every Body!" http://www.eatright.org/ada/files/Canola_Fact_Sheet_FINAL.pdf.

———. "Eating Better Together: A Family Guide for a Healthy Lifestyle," http://www.eatright.org/ada/files/0305_Factsheet_Wendys.pdf.

———. "What's a Mom to Do? Healthy Eating Tips for Families," http://www.eatright.org/ada/files/Wendys.pdf.

Bornehag, C. G., J. Sundell, C. J. Weschler, T. Sigsgaard, B. Lundgren, M. Hasselgren, and L. Hagerhed-Engman. "The Association between Asthma and Allergic Symptoms in Children and Phthalates in House Dust: a Nested Case-control Study." *Environ Health Perspect* 112 (14) (2004): pp. 1,393–97.

Bradshaw, Brenda, and Lauren Bramley. *The Baby's Table.* Toronto: Random House, 2004.

Bray, G. A., S. J. Nielsen, and B. M. Popkin. "Consumption of High-fructose Corn Syrup in Beverages May Play a Role in the Epidemic of Obesity." *Am J Clin Nutr* 79 (4) (2004): pp. 537–43.

Canadian Living Foundation. "Breakfast for Learning," http://www.breakfastforlearning.ca/english/who_we_are/a_our_mission.html.

Canadian Paediatric Society. "Eating Disorders in Adolescents: Principles of Diagnosis and Treatment," http://www.cps.ca/english/statements/AM/am96–04.htm.

———. "Feeding Your Vegetarian Child," http://www.caringforkids.cps.ca/eating/vegetarian.htm.

———. "Healthy Active Living for Children and Youth," http://www.cps.ca/english/statements/HAL/HAL02–01.htm.

———. "Nutrition Recommendations Update: Dietary Fat and Children," http://www.cps.ca/english/statements/N/n94–01.htm.

Centers for Disease Control and Prevention. "Division of Bacterial and Mycotic Diseases: *Escherichia coli 0157:H7*," http://www.cdc.gov/ncidod/dbmd/diseaseinfo/escherichiacoli_g.htm.

Childhood Obesity Foundation. "Identifying, Evaluating and Promoting Best Practices for Childhood Obesity," http://www.cofbc.ca/.

Covington, M. B. "Omega-3 fatty acids." *Am Fam Physician* 70 (1) (2004): pp. 133–40.

———. "Colour Your World with Vegetables and Fruit," http://www
.dietitians.ca/resources/resourcesearch.asp?fn=view&contentid=5766.

———. "Dietary Fat—the Good, the Bad and the Ugly,"
http://www.dietitians.ca/resources/resourcesearch.asp?fn=view&
contentid=8435.

Dietitians of Canada. "How Do I Recognize an Eating Disorder?"
http://www.dietitians.ca/public/content/eat_well_live_well/english/faqs
_tips_facts/faqs/index.asp.

———. "It's Always a Great Time for Grains," http://www.dietitians.ca/
resources/resourcesearch.asp?fn=view&contentid=5760.

———. "Making the Most of Meat and Alternatives," http://www
.dietitians.ca/resources/resourcesearch.asp?fn=view&contentid=5762.

———. "Marvelous Milk Products."

———. "Organic Food," http://www.dietitians.ca/public/content/
eat_well_live_well/english/faqs_tips_facts/faqs/index.

———. "School Food and Nutrition Recommendations for Ontario
Ministry of Education Regarding Snacks and Beverages Dispensed
by Vending Machines," http://www.dietitians.ca/news/downloads/
DCRpt1_Eng_OntarioSchoolFood.pdf.

———. "Thanks for the Great Lunch!" http://www.dietitians.ca/resources/
resourcesearch.asp?fn=view&contentid=5758.

———. "What Do I Need to Know if My Child Doesn't Drink Milk?"
http://www.dietitians.ca/public/content/eat_well_live_well/english/faqs
_tips_facts/faqs/index.

Eisenberg, M. E., R. E. Olson, D. Neumark-Sztainer, M. Story, and L. H. Bearinger. "Correlations between Family Meals and Psychosocial Well-being among Adolescents." *Arch Pediatr Adolesc Med* 158 (8) (2004): pp. 792–96.

Environmental Working Group. "Food News Shopper Guide," http://www.ewg.org.

Fisher, J., D. Mitchell, H. Smiciklas-Wright, and L. Birch. "Maternal Milk Consumption Predicts the Tradeoff between Milk and Soft Drinks in Young Girls' Diets." *J Nutr* 131 (2) (2001): pp. 246–50.

Foulke, J. E. "Mercury in Fish: Cause for Concern?" *Food and Drug Administration*, http://www.fda.gov/fdac/reprints/mercury.html.

———. "Acrylamide and Food—Questions and Answers," http://www .hc-sc.gc.ca/fn-an/securit/chem-chim/acrylamide/acrylamide_and _food-acrylamide_et_aliment_e.html.

———. "Aspartame," http://www.hc-sc.gc.ca/fn-an/securit/addit/ sweeten-edulcor/aspartame01_e.html.

———. "Canada's Food Guide: History of the Food Guide," http:// www.hc-sc.gc.ca/fn-an/food-guide-aliment/context/hist/index_e.html.

———. "Canada's Physical Activity Guide for Children," http://www .phac-aspc.gc.ca/pau-uap/paguide/child_youth/children/index.html.

———. "Eating Well with Canada's Food Guide," http://www.hc-sc.gc.ca/ fn-an/alt_formats/hpfb-dgpsa/pdf/food-guide-aliment/view_eatwell_vue _bienmang_e.pdf.

———. "Eating Well with Canada's Food Guide: A Resource for Educators and Communicators," http://www.hc-sc.gc.ca/fn-an/alt_formats/hpfb-dgpsa/ pdf/pubs/res-educat_e.pdf.

———. "Fact Sheet: Food Safety and PCBs Found in Fish," http://www.hc-sc.gc.ca/ahc-asc/media/nr-cp/2004/2004_pcb-bpc_e.html.

———. "Fact Sheet on Trans Fats," http://www.hc-sc.gc.ca/ahc-asc/media/nr-cp/2004/2004_trans_e.html.

———. "Family Guide to Physical Activity for Children (6–9 Years of Age)," http://www.phac-aspc.gc.ca/pau-uap/paguide/child_youth/pdf/kids_family_guide_e.pdf.

Health Canada. "Food Guide Facts: Background for Educators and Communicators." Ottawa: Health Canada, 1992. Microform.

———. "Food Related Illnesses," http://www.hc-sc.gc.ca/fn-an/securit/ill-intox/index_e.html.

———. "Government of Canada Assures Public that Farmed and Wild Salmon are Safe to Consume," http://www.hc-sc.gc.ca/ahc-asc/media/nr-cp/2004/2004_45_e.html.

———. "Health Canada Advises Specific Groups to Limit Their Consumption of Canned Albacore Tuna," http://www.hc-sc.gc.ca/ahc-asc/media/advisories-avis/2007/2007_14_e.html.

———. "Health Canada Reminds Canadians about the Risks in Eating Sprouts," http://www.hc-sc.gc.ca/ahc-asc/media/advisories-avis/2007/2007_08_e.html.

———. "Health Canada's Revised Assessment of Mercury in Fish Enhances Protection while Reflecting Advice in Canada's Food Guide," http://www.hc-sc.gc.ca/ahc-asc/media/advisories-avis/2007/2007_31_e.html.

———. "Nutrition Facts Table," http://www.hc-sc.gc.ca/ahc-asc/media/nr-cp/2003/2003_01bk1_e.html.

————. "PCBs," http://www.hc-sc.gc.ca/iyh-vsv/environ/pcb-bpc_e.html.

————. "Risks Associated with Sprouts," http://www.hc-sc.gc.ca/iyh-vsv/food-aliment/sprouts-germes_e.html.

————. "Severe Allergic Reactions," http://www.hc-sc.gc.ca/iyh-vsv/med/allerg_e.html.

————. "Statement from Health Canada about Acrylamide in Food," http://www.hc-sc.gc.ca/ahc-asc/media/nr-cp/2005/2005_stmt-dec_acrylamide1_e.html.

————. "Sulphites—One of the Nine Most Common Food Products Causing Severe Adverse Reactions," http://www.hc-sc.gc.ca/fn-an/securit/allerg/fs-if/allergen_sulphites-sulfites_e.html.

————. "TRANSforming the Food Supply, Report of the Trans Fat Task Force, Submitted to the Minister of Health, June 2006," http://www.hc-sc.gc.ca/fn-an/alt_formats/hpfb-dgpsa/pdf/nutrition/tf-gt_rep-rap_e.pdf.

Hendricks, Kristy M., W. Allan Walker, and Christopher Duggan. *Manual of Pediatric Nutrition.* 3rd ed. Hamilton, ON: B.C. Decker, 2000.

Hirayama, S., T. Hamazaki, and K. Terasawa. "Effect of Docosahexaenoic Acid-containing Food Administration on Symptoms of Attention-deficit/Hyperactivity Disorder—a Placebo-controlled Double-blind Study." *Eur J Clin Nutr* 58 (3) (2004): pp. 467–73.

Jacobson, M. F., Center for Science in the Public Interest. "Liquid Candy: How Soft Drinks are Harming America's Health," http://www.cspinet.org/new/pdf/liquid_candy_final_w_new_supplement.pdf.

Johns Hopkins Bloomberg Public Health News Center. "Researcher Dispels Myth of Dioxins and Plastic Water Bottles," http://www.jhsph.edu/publichealthnews/articles/halden_dioxins.html.

Legere, Henry J. *Raising Healthy Eaters: 100 Tips for Parents.* Edited by M. Cochran. Cambridge, MA: Da Capo Press, 2004.

McCann, Donna, Angelina Barrett, Alison Cooper, Debbie Crumpler, Lindy Dalen, Kate Grimshaw, Elizabeth Kitchin, Kris Lok, Lucy Porteous, Emily Prince, Edmund Sonuga-Barke, John O. Warner, and Jim Stevenson. "Food Additives and Hyperactive Behaviour in 3-year-old and 8/9-year-old Children in the Community: a Randomized, Double-blinded, Placebo-controlled Trial." *The Lancet.com* (September 6, 2007), http://www.thelancet .com/journals/lancet/article/PIIS0140673607613063/abstract?isEOP=true.

Munger, K. L., S. M. Zhang, E. O'Reilly, M. A. Hernan, M. J. Olek, W. C. Willett, and A. Ascherio. "Vitamin D Intake and Incidence of Multiple Sclerosis." *Neurology* 62 (1) (2004): pp. 60–65.

Norris, J. M., X. Yin, M. M. Lamb, K. Barriga, J. Seifert, M. Hoffman, H. D. Orton, A. E. Baron, M. Clare-Salzler, H. P. Chase, N.J. Szabo, H. Erlich, G.S. Eisenbarth, M. Rewers. "Omega-3 Polyunsaturated Fatty Acid Intake and Islet Autoimmunity in Children at Increased Risk for Type 1 Diabetes." *Jama* 298(12)(2007):pp. 1420–28.

Public Health Agency of Canada, Canadian Health Network. "Childhood Obesity: an Alarming Trend," http://www.canadian-health-network.ca/.

Richardson, A. J., and P. Montgomery. "The Oxford–Durham Study: a Randomized, Controlled Trial of Dietary Supplementation with Fatty Acids in Children with Developmental Coordination Disorder." *Pediatrics* 115 (5) (2005): pp. 1,360–66.

Satter, Ellyn. *How to Get Your Kid to Eat . . . But Not Too Much.* Boulder: Bull Publishing, 1987.

Schwartz, G. G., and H. G. Skinner. "Vitamin D Status and Cancer: New Insights." *Curr Opin Clin Nutr Metab Care* 10 (1) (2007): pp. 6–11.

Sesso, H. D., S. Liu, J. M. Gaziano, and J. E. Buring. "Dietary Lycopene, Tomato-based Food Products and Cardiovascular Disease in Women." *J Nutr* 133 (7) (2003): pp. 2,336–41.

Slavin, Joanne. "Whole Grains and Human Health." *Nutritional Research Reviews* 17 (2004).

Statistics Canada. "Canadian Community Health Survey: Overview of Canadians' Eating Habits," http://statcan.ca/Daily/English/060706/d060706b.htm.

Steinberg, F. M., M. M. Bearden, and C. L. Keen. "Cocoa and Chocolate Flavonoids: Implications for Cardiovascular Health." *J Am Diet Assoc* 103 (2) (2003): pp. 215–23.

Strauss, R. S. "Childhood Obesity and Self-esteem." *Pediatrics* 105 (1) (2000): pp. e15.

University of California, Berkeley. "Give Yourself a Berry Boost." Review of Reviewed Item. *Wellness Letter* (10) (2006), http://www.wellnessletter.com/access/password_info.php?msg=private&page=/subCorner/scWL06Archive.php.

———. "Wellness Facts." Review of Reviewed Item. *Wellness Letter* (7) (2006), http://www.wellnessletter.com/access/password_info.php?msg=private&page=/subCorner/scWL06Archive.php.

University of Maryland Medical Center. "Omega-3 Fatty Acids," http://www.umm.edu/altmed/articles/omega-3–000316.htm.

U.S. Food and Drug Administration. "Food Allergies: Rare but Risky," http://www.cfsan.fda.gov/~dms/wh-alrg1.html.

———. "What You Need to Know about Mercury in Fish and Shellfish," http://www.cfsan.fda.gov/~dms/admehg3.html.

Voigt, R. G., A. M. Llorente, C. L. Jensen, J. K. Fraley, M. C. Berretta, and W. C. Heird. "A Randomized, Double-blind, Placebo-controlled Trial of Docosahexaenoic Acid Supplementation in Children with Attention-deficit/ Hyperactivity Disorder." *J Pediatr* 139 (2) (2001): pp. 189–96.

Walker, A. W. *Eat, Play and Be Healthy: The Harvard Medical School Guide to Healthy Eating for Kids.* New York: McGraw-Hill, 2005.

Whitney, Eleanor Noss, and Sharon Rady Rolfes. *Understanding Nutrition.* 10th ed. Belmont, CA: Thomson/Wadsworth, 2005.

Wikipedia: the free encyclopedia. "Organic Food," http://en.wikipedia.org/ wiki/Organic_food.

World Health Organization (WHO). "Cancer: Diet and Physical Activity's Impact," http://www.who.int/dietphysicalactivity/publications/facts/ cancer/en/.

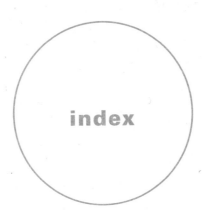

index

Health and Nutrition Information

acknowledgements

We would like to thank those who generously shared their time, expertise and knowledge with us. Our appreciation and thanks go to Shey Simpson, Jen Boyle, Dr. Richard Goldbloom, Julia Armstrong, John Sweet, Sharon Hodgins, Nancy Stairs and our editor at Random House, Pamela Murray.

In addition, we would like to thank all those who donated, inspired or tested recipes. They are as follows: Daphne Hebb, Fiona Sinclair, Dan Kalla, Jeff Petter, Val Bradshaw, Barb Petter, Stephanie Butterfield, Diane Petter, Amanda Howard, Sarah Bell, Judy Kalla, Catherine Runnals, Julia Rudd, Tyler MacDonald, Becca Coval, Trish Ross, Jacquie Trafford, Shannon Vrlak, Lorraine Meade and Shaughn Mohammed.

I would like to thank my oldest and dearest friends whose support and ideas contributed greatly to this book. Thank you, Karen Fryer, Daphne Hebb, Lauren Donaldson and Sarah Bell. To my parents, Val and Dick Bradshaw, who instilled in me a love of good food, thank you for always believing in me. A special thanks goes to my mother for patiently teaching me the finer points of baking—thanks, Mum! And last but not least, I would like to thank my husband, Jeff, and children, Charlie and Elliotte, for their love and understanding while our home was turned into a test kitchen.   —Brenda

I would like to thank Hoong Lim, medical librarian extraordinaire for his hasty replies to all my inquiries. Thanks to all my patients and their families, who provided so much of the motivation for this book. Special thanks to my husband, Dan, for all his editorial, technical and emotional support. Thanks to my two wonderful daughters, Chelsea and Ashley, for giving me the opportunity to put theory into action and for always trying "at least one bite." Thanks to my mother for being the inspiration for how to get a wholesome meal on the table by 6 p.m. every night.

—Cheryl